Sean Connery

by the same author

MICHAEL CAINE
A Class Act

Sean Connery
The Measure of a Man

Christopher Bray

faber and faber

First published in 2010
by Faber and Faber Ltd
Bloomsbury House
74–77 Great Russell Street
London WC1B 3DA

Typeset by Faber and Faber Limited
Printed in England by CPI Mackays, Chatham

A CIP record for this book
is available from the British Library

ISBN 978–0–571–23807–1

2 4 6 8 10 9 7 5 3 1

To the memory of my father

Contents

Illustrations

Introduction

Reviewing *Indiana Jones and the Last Crusade* (1989), the long-time *New Yorker* critic Pauline Kael mentioned 'a friend . . . who's in his early fifties and is eminent in his field [who] says that when he grows up he wants to be Sean Connery'.[1] Him and every other guy born in the past half-century or so. Certainly you can't be a child of the sixties, as I am, and not have given over several moments of your life to regretting the fact that you are not Sean Connery. From the moment I first set eyes on Connery, in a clip from *Diamonds Are Forever* (1971) on the BBC children's movie quiz *Screen Test*, at least part of my fate as a dreamer was sealed. Whoever this man was ('He's a has-been,' my father told me over dinner), he had showed me a vision of the man I wanted to be. In other words, he was a movie star — one of our age's secular icons. As Philip Kaufman, who directed Connery in *Rising Sun* (1993), once said, 'There's a sense in which people go to films to learn how to behave; the fact is people are very attracted by the way Sean behaves. They have an empathy with him — or they would like to have empathy. They would like to feel that they have his qualities, his grace under pressure.'[2]

I have, I should stress, no wish to know Sean Connery. I have no fantasies about our being best buddies. I find all varieties of nationalism offensive and stupid; golf and football — Connery's favourite sports — bore me; and beyond his own career he has never exhibited much interest in film history. Besides, all the reports suggest that he is a combative soul who grows prickly at the idea of being the object of even distanced veneration. He has never really understood the mania he is still, turning 80, capable of inducing. Partly, I suspect, this is because Connery himself didn't grow up venerating anyone. Though as a child he occasionally went to the cinema, he has never to my knowledge admitted to being fond of any particular star. Unlike, say, Michael Caine, who grew up wanting to imitate the derring-do of Errol Flynn and the insolent jabber of Humphrey Bogart, Connery nursed no fantasies of being Edinburgh's Clark Gable (as he might so easily have done). Indeed, the movies, the theatre, narrative itself, didn't really impact on him until he was well into his twenties. So the realisation, in his thirties, that there were people out there whose lives were lived through vicarious reveries came as a huge shock to him. His own feet planted firmly on the ground, he couldn't begin to conceive why so many men had their heads in the clouds.

There's no denying, of course, that part of the wish to be Connery is a wish to be what Kael called 'the smooth operator James Bond'.[3] A few months back the cover of the *Radio Times* was given over to a picture of the TV star Rupert Penry-Jones, suitably attired in black tie and tuxedo, atop the words 'I want to be Bond'. Granted, Penry-Jones is an actor and thus has as much of a professional as a personal interest in the fantasy so many men share. But what of the man who is our new prime minister? For in the same week of that *Radio Times* cover, the Conservative leader David Cameron used an interview in the *Guardian* to assure us that, while he is a Bond obsessive (at school he had a complete collection of the original novels lined up chronologically on his shelves), the rumours of his wanting to be Bond were untrue. 'I am not Bond,' he rather unnervingly assured us. 'I just love the films, I'm afraid. The escapism . . . The books are very good, but I just love the films.'[4]

That clunking sound you hear is of a man hedging his bets. For Cameron, like Bond's first begetter Ian Fleming, is an Old Etonian. Unlike Fleming, though, Cameron is keen to play down his patrician roots. Whereas Fleming was an unreconstructed stuffed shirt appalled at the casting of what he called 'that fucking truck driver' in Harry Saltzman and Albert Broccoli's movie version of *Dr No* (1962), Cameron is a populist wise to the idea that most of us prefer the democratised snobbery of the Bond films to the elitist snobbery of the books. Which is a way of saying that while Fleming might have kick-started this fantasy, it was Sean Connery who actually got it on the road and motored it round the world. If part of wanting to be Connery is wanting to be Bond, that is, the whole of wanting to be Bond is wanting to be Connery. Nobody ever fancied themselves the next Roger Moore.

You can call these starry identification fantasies childish, and doubtless they are. But childishness exists, and it may be more childish to believe adults can divorce themselves entirely from it than to admit that they occasionally go with its flow. Which is a way of saying that this is a book about the movies and what they have done to us. Read it and you will, I believe, get a pretty accurate account of what we know of Sean Connery's eight decades on the planet. But Connery has not cooperated on the book – just as he has not helped any previous biographer – and for the purposes of research I have had recourse to the same few interviews he has granted a handful of journalists over the years. Nor were many people who know or have worked with Connery willing to talk to me about him. What we know of Connery's private life, then, amounts to very little – little more, in fact, than that he does not suffer fools gladly and is quite handy with a golf club.

We know even less about the private life of Leonardo da Vinci, of course, and the sources on him are finite in a way they are not yet on Connery, though that doesn't stop critics and historians and biographers writing about him. The same goes for Michelangelo and Shakespeare. And no, I am not surreptitiously lining Connery up in exalted company – merely making the point that biographies get written about people not because of who they are but because of what they have done. Without the *Mona Lisa* and those prototype

3

helicopters and artillery, those pencil studies of horses and fluvia, what possible interest could Leonardo have for us? Who would Shakespeare be had he not written those plays and poems? The same goes for Sean Connery. Without his work in the movies, what hold could he have over anyone but his friends and family? It may be that when he is dead all number of people come crawling out of the woodwork to bitch and moan about the real-life Connery they knew. Some of what they want to tell us may even be verifiably true. But so what? We can all of us be bitched and moaned about. Not many of us have managed to sustain a career of international movie stardom for nigh on half a century.

Which means that what holds our attention about Connery is something more – and something less – than a man. The character you and I refer to when we talk about Sean Connery is just that: a character, a construct, a fiction – and a fiction composed of sundry other fictions at that. Back in the sixties, as his movies broke box-office record after box-office record, it was commonplace to refer to Connery as a phenomenon. But in the Kantian scheme of things the term is more generally applicable. All we know about Connery is what Kant would have called the phenomenon – his weight, his height, his colouring, his sensorily apprehensible presence in the world. As to the Connery noumenon – what he is really like beneath that crust of apprehensions – well, that is another matter. All we can meaningfully talk about is his work in the movies.

Is it, though, sensible or fair to talk about *Sean Connery*'s work in the movies? Isn't he just an actor at the service of directors and producers and screenwriters? The answer is both a qualified yes and a qualified no. Certainly in his early days, Connery – like all struggling actors – was absolutely at the behest of those above him in the cinematic pecking order. But since the Bond series sent him soaring into fame's empyrean he has pretty much run things the way he wants. If he wants to change a character here, a line of dialogue there, a plot twist at the end of the second act, he can and does. True, he has never written a script (though he has helped out on the rewrites of many of the movies he has appeared in). True, he has never directed a film (though he has directed a few stage productions, and in later years has been executive producer of several pictures). On the other hand, movies have been made simply because of his existence. Connery doesn't just appear in movies. Movies appear around him, around the idea of his very presence. Back in the early 1950s, Terence Young, who would go on to direct three of the first four Bond pictures, was feted by a number of French auteurist critics, yet which of us has ever said, 'Let's go see the new Terence Young movie'? Countless, though, are they who have raced to see 'the new Sean Connery movie'.

I am one of those people. I like watching Sean Connery. I like watching him move through a room. I like watching him sit down and cross his legs. I especially like watching him open and close doors. I like the way he curls his lips as he changes down a gear. I like the idea of a big, big man being so light on his feet. Part of the reason I like the idea is because I wish the same could be said about me – average height, clumsy and heavy-footed. This need to be in the company of another being – a need, in a way, to *be* that other being – is, I think, not that different from love.

Except that love is almost universally celebrated as a positive force in the world, and I am not at all sure that the increasingly second-hand lives so many of us have led since the invention of the movies are any good to anybody. At school and at university I was taught that the novel and the drama find their moral worth in taking people out of themselves so that they can see the world through the eyes of others. Reading, that is, makes good little liberals of us. Well, maybe, though as the critics George Steiner and Stanley Fish have pointed out, there is a lot of evidence to countermand the belief. But whatever, I don't believe such a claim could ever have been reasonably made about the movies. Novels and plays just might one day be found to have been good for us. The movies, which like so many other developments of free market capitalism might have been invented to make us less happy, are never going to be able to stake a similar claim.

For the movies, it is becoming clear, have ruined us. They have made Jay Gatsbys of all who have fallen under their spell. They have encouraged us in directionless dreaming, they have indulged us in our fondness for surfaces and sentiment, they have made us measure ourselves against improbable standards of beauty and grace under pressure, they have helped us to forget our need for truths that cannot be trapped in light, they have made it far too easy to fall in — and therefore out of — love, they have made fantasising ironists of us all. There is nothing more manipulable than desire, and movies and their stars are a way of making sure both that we do not want what we have and cannot have what we want. So we would be better off without them — which does not mean that I shall ever stop being grateful for having been around while Sean Connery was doing his stuff . . .

1

On the Road

He travels light, Sean Connery. A small grip with 'a clean shirt, spare trousers' is enough for him. 'If I'm in a place more than a day or two I just send it to the laundry.'[1] And though he has properties in New York, in California, in the Bahamas and sundry other places around the world, he has never found 'anywhere that I want to live permanently'.[2] Instead, he says, 'Home is where you're working.'[3] And Connery has worked pretty much everywhere. That last remark was made in 1994, not long after the wrap on his fifty-sixth movie, a picture whose shoot had taken him deep into the wilds of South Africa. Much of the previous year had been spent filming in Los Angeles, while in 1992 Connery had endured a long, less than comfortable shoot in the jungles of Mexico. Seen through rose-tinted spectacles, the life of the big-shot movie star can seem as wondrous and wandering as that of the globe-trotting secret agent. Seen *au naturel*, it can look an awful lot like the lifestyle of what used to be called the itinerant class – the class to which generations of Connery's antecedents had belonged.

Hence what Holden Caulfield called 'all that David Copperfield kind of crap'[4] is sketchy about Connery's background. When Thomas (later Sean) Connery was born, in Edinburgh in 1930, his father's forebears had been in Scotland for less than fifty years. Before fetching up in Glasgow, the Connerys – Irish Catholics – had plied their travelling tinker's trade over the water in County Wexford.[5]

Given that nomadic background, the Connerys are unlikely to

have abandoned the mother country because of the rent-raising strictures of Gladstone's second Irish Land Act of 1881. What we do know is that James Connery, who had been born in 1839, was 42 years old (well into middle age back then) when he made the move. And that Elizabeth McPhillips, the woman we must assume was James's wife, was some fifteen years his junior. They had met back in 1865, when Elizabeth was just eleven. A year later, she gave birth to their first child, another James; in 1870 to their second, another Elizabeth; and in 1879, shortly before their departure for the city on the Clyde, to their last-born – Sean Connery's grandfather, Thomas.*

Like his father before him, Thomas Connery preferred his girls young. As the nineteenth century gave way to the twentieth, the then 22-year-old Thomas set up home in Garscube with 13-year-old Jeanie McNab. (Barely an expression on a map, Garscube was an area of Glasgow so poor they gave allotments to the unemployed there.) A year later, in 1902, she bore Thomas an illegitimate son whom they called Joseph. (The couple were not actually married until 1938, a couple of years before Jeanie died of cancer, aged 52.) In 1905, with the family now resident in the no less impoverished – though rather more central – area of Cowcaddens, a second son, James, was born.

Poverty is never pleasant but we should be wary of overplaying how tough the Connery family found Glasgow life a century ago.

---

* They ordered things differently back then, of course, though quite how differently might be thought moot. In 1989, aged 59, Sean Connery was voted the world's sexiest man. In 1999, aged 69, he was voted the sexiest man of the century. And only five years ago, in 2005, the then 75-year-old Connery was voted Britain's sexiest pensioner. Read about on paper, a movie like *Entrapment* (1999) is risible. What is this caper, after all, but the sadly not-at-all Buñuelian tale of an old, old man and a beautiful young girl? Seen on the screen, though, we believe in this not-quite romance because we have been told over and over again – and not just by surveys, but by wives and girlfriends – that pretty much every woman in the world, the bulk of whom must by definition be many years younger than Sean Connery, would happily bed the octogenarian star.

Rough and ready as the districts they lived in were (and Sean Connery has said Thomas was never happier than when he was bare-knuckle fighting[6]), the city itself – the *soi-disant* 'second city of empire' – was doing very well indeed, thank you. Given its then rock-solid economic bases of engineering and shipbuilding, there were far worse places for a skilled man to ply his trade. Or even an unskilled one. For though Thomas Connery had no skills to speak of, much less to write home about – like so many men of his class he was illiterate – the horse and cart he had made his living from since his early teens served him well in the city's thriving scrap-metal trade. Nonetheless, come the outbreak of the First World War, Thomas decided to try his luck in the country's capital city, Edinburgh.

If there was any logic behind this move then, the better part of a century on, it is hard to discern what it might have been. During the war, Glasgow and the Clyde Basin would, predictably enough, grow into Britain's most vital centre of munitions manufacture. The pickings for a scrap-metal trader can have only become richer there. To be sure, Edinburgh did well enough too. But as Edwin Muir was to note on his *Scottish Journey* (a trip made when Sean Connery was just three or four years old), 'the most historical part of Edinburgh . . . is a slum intersected by ancient houses that have been segregated and turned into museums and training colleges'.[7] More, the city that calls itself the Athens of the North was and is an altogether more cerebral town than Glasgow. The print trade was one of its backbones – and print calls for literacy. All things considered, life for the Connerys can hardly have been any easier in their new city than it had been in their old. Except, one surmises, that to Thomas the fact of Edinburgh's 'newness' was all that mattered. The nomadic bug still bit this family deep.

It went on doing so. Until well into his twenties Sean Connery had no idea of where he was going, or of what he was doing. And looking at his career as he went into his thirties – that ungainly slalom between the series of films that made his name and the more ambitious dramas he hoped would sustain it – it can be difficult to abstract a line of attack. Sure, Bond was artless, mindless, so by all means work with the likes of Alfred Hitchcock or Harry Andrews while out of the 007 armour. But with Basil Dearden? With Edward Dmytryk? With Richard Harris? By the mid-sixties, Connery was one of the highest-paid actors in the world, but he was never happy being tied down to what most people – and certainly most actors – would have considered a nice big earner. He was forever beefing about this, bemoaning that. The family models he had to work from, the examples of peddlers and chancers and men who couldn't settle, had stayed with him.

Certainly, Sean Connery's early life was as unsettled, as unfocussed, as unpredictable as any young man's has ever been. He was born Thomas Sean Connery in Edinburgh's Royal Maternity Hospital on 25 August 1930, a big, big baby boy, weighing in at around ten and a half pounds. His size was much commented on, because the Connery men had never been particularly hefty. Joe Connery, the boy's father, was built as solidly as any skill-free workman, but he topped out at a less than imposing five feet eight inches. But they say that you get your height from your mother, and while the photographic evidence doesn't quite endorse Diane Cilento's claim that Joe's wife Euphemia (*née* Maclean) stood 'a good head taller' than he did,[8] nonetheless she was tall for a woman and stood head-to-head with her husband.

They had married at Tynecastle Parish Church, a couple of years before Thomas's birth, on 28 December 1928, when Joe was 26 and Effie (as Euphemia was always known) was 20, and there are reasons other than her long legs to believe the labourer had done well for himself. Euphemia was a favourite name for Protestant girls of the time, which means that Joe was moving away from those lowly Catholic roots so frowned upon by many Scots. 'I understand,' John Buchan rued in a speech to the House of Commons not long after Thomas Connery had come into the world, 'that every fifth child

born now in Scotland is an Irish Roman Catholic.'[9] Despite his
Hibernian middle name, the new Connery wasn't going to be one
of them.

Unlike Joe's parents, Effie's parents were married. By the time
Thomas was old enough to know them they had left Edinburgh and
retired to Lassodie, a coalmining village north of Dunfermline, 30
or 40 miles as the crow flies across the Firth of Forth. Retirement
presupposes an earlier period of work, and Neil Maclean had
indeed held down a job all his life. He had started out as a plasterer,
a skilled trade from which he worked his way up the ladder to
the titled job of Public Works Foreman. Something of an achiever
then, especially when his achievements are set next to those of the
Connery tinkers. Little wonder, perhaps, that the two families were
uneasy around one another. His parents' wedding celebrations,
Connery has told us, were cut short because a fight was about to
break out between his two grandfathers.[10]

At the time Thomas Connery was born, Joe was being paid £2
a week as a labourer in the North British Rubber Company's mill.
This last was not far from the Fountainbridge area of Edinburgh,
in one of whose run-down, two-room tenement apartments the
Connerys had set up home. Ablutions were carried out in cold
water at the kitchen sink, more private matters in the shared
toilet on the tenement's back stairwell. Tam, as baby Thomas was
immediately nicknamed, slept in a drawer at the foot of the family
wardrobe. 'My background,' he would tell a reporter years later,
'was harsh.'[11] So, of course, was that of everyone with whom he
came into contact. As he remembered, 'the attitude at home was
the prevalent one in Scotland – you make your own bed and so you
have to lie in it'.[12]

It sounds like a hard and harsh life, but the childhood photographs
we have of Connery rather belie the image. They show a very well-
cared for young fellow. There is a picture of him at five or six at
Edinburgh's Tollcross Primary School in which he is turned out
with so much more pride – that jacket! that tie! that parting in his

hair! – than the other boys around him. And in *Being a Scot*, his idiosyncratic history of his home country, Connery prints another picture of his young self, surrounded by what he calls 'the Stewart Terrace school gang'. Here he is, a beaming-faced and hearty-looking angel, surrounded by what one can only call the junior great unwashed. As Connery himself asks of the picture, 'Why am I the only one who is wearing a tie?'[13] Who can say? But it is perhaps worthy of note that, his most famous movie role aside, the mature Connery has almost never been seen in his best bib and tucker.

Indeed, stories told by his brother Neil (born eight years after Thomas) give us an altogether rougher Connery than the one those photographs prepare us for – a Connery who is in and out of hospital after twists and tumbles and head-first dives into trees from sledges. Neil has described an incident in which Tommy cut his hand very nastily – by gripping the glass knob on the door to his parents' bedroom so tightly that it shattered. 'Sean was the quiet one of the family,' Neil remembered, 'and inclined to be an over-sensitive child.'[14] 'When I met him,' his second wife Micheline Roquebrune said of the Connery she has known since his early forties, 'I very quickly wanted to protect him. He needs protection.'[15]

Connery's first wife, Diane Cilento, has latterly claimed her erstwhile husband was a troubled and troublesome youngster. Many children go shoplifting, for instance, but she says that when Connery did, he did so *with his mother in tow*. Did so, moreover, using baby Neil's pram as the cover for his ill-gotten comics and chocolates. One day, writes Cilento, Mrs Connery 'flipped back the blanket and uncovered the stolen goodies. After a public belting in the street, Effie dragged him back to the shop by his ear, forcing him to apologise to the shopkeeper and replace the lot.'[16]

And yet, one suspects Tam was his mother's rather than his father's son. Likely the fact that he was the first Connery we have come across who learned to read was down to Effie's influence. More, he liked the printed word – if only in the form of those comic books.

Still, enough of it rubbed off on him for a teacher at Bruntsfield Primary School to praise one of his early compositions.* Yet for all his love of words (and his speed at mental arithmetic, a trait perhaps inherited from his bookie's runner grandfather), when the time came for him to move on to secondary school he opted for a place not at Boroughmuir – a fee-paying school, though one open to scholarship boys, where they taught subjects like economics and modern languages – but at the rather more practically minded Darroch.

His reasoning was simple enough. Though he had passed the requisite exams, attending Boroughmuir would have meant having to play the dreaded English public-school game of rugby. At Darroch he was able to play the soccer he loved and loves. Fair enough. The trouble was, he seems to have done little else while there. 'I never remembered anybody making school sufficiently stimulating or interesting to make me want to stay,' he would say, close on half a century after leaving Darroch.[17] Well, maybe. One of his teachers, a Mrs Hardy, saw things rather differently though. 'He wasn't a fool,' she remembered. 'He wasn't stupid, but just bare average.'[18] Like other bare average kids of the day, he did just two years at secondary school, leaving in July 1944, a month before his fourteenth birthday.

Not that anyone could have called him lazy. During those years at Darroch Connery was spending much of his waking life hard at work. Accounts vary as to the age he was when he began earning the money to pay his own way, but we know for sure that within days of leaving school he was working for St Cuthbert's Dairy for a guinea a week as a barrow boy.[19] And we know that within a few weeks of that start-date, he was promoted to transport duties – driving a horse and cart around the city delivering milk.

Though the bulk of the money he earned was handed over to

---

* Bruntsfield was a rather more selective institution than Tollcross; Connery was offered and took up a place there in 1937.

Effie to help out with the rent, Connery was spending less and less time at home. Even when not working, he was out of the house, taking care of his new best friend, Tich – the horse that pulled his milk-cart. 'He was horse daft,' Effie would tell a reporter years later. 'Always taking my dusters to rub down the milk horse.'[20] You can call such behaviour soft-headed, even sentimental, though it may be that what Connery found in tending to his charge was a way of being alone – and artists need to find ways of being alone.

Then again, maybe he just wanted out of an increasingly fraught home life. According to Neil, there were tensions between his father and his elder brother, tensions he believes explicable by the latter's 'developing too fast. He was too big for his age, too bold, the bread-earner too early.'[21] The real problem, one suspects, was that around the time Thomas commenced earning a wage, his father stopped doing so. One weekend he returned home from Glasgow, where he had been labouring at the Rolls-Royce factory, having broken his nose and wrist in what he called an accident. For the next eighteen months the money Thomas earned, together with what Effie managed to bring in from her work as a part-time charlady, were the mainstays of the family income.

Years later, with his son become an international movie star, Joe Connery would characterise himself as 'not the sort that would like to sit around and let a son take care of him'.[22] And yet Diane Cilento has claimed that when she first met Joe for a drink, some time in the late fifties, she saw Connery surreptitiously slip his father some money under the table. Later, when the man who was then her boyfriend had gone to the bar, Joe turned to Cilento and asked her, 'How long have you known Tommy?' Told they had met a year or so before, Joe feigned amazement at the relationship's longevity: 'But ye've never met . . . his wee brother, Neil. Well, he's no' so wee the noo. He's in the army. He's the *one*, ye know . . . once you've met Neil, you'll never look at Tommy again . . . and he's nine [*sic*] years younger than Tommy, too. Have you noticed he's going thin on top?'[23] You don't have to be a strict Freudian to conceive that there might have been something Oedipal going on here.*

Consider the curious incident of Thomas's sixteenth birthday spending spree. Effie, it turned out, had not had to use all the money he had been handing over to her from his weekly wages. She had managed to salt away some of it in a Post Office savings account. Come the day he turned 16, young Connery was surprised to learn that he had somewhere north of £75 put by. Horse-lover or not, he told the family that he had decided to treat himself to a motorbike.

Now remember, this was 1946 – only a year since the end of the war. British youth culture was hardly a force to be reckoned with. Over in America they were inventing the teenager, but in Britain – and perhaps even more so in Scotland – there was no such thing. There were children and there were adults, and the children did what the adults told them to do. And the adult of the Connery household told the eldest child that, no, he would not be buying a motorbike. By then, of course, the boy everyone called Big Tam towered over his father. But Marlon Brando and Nicholas Ray were not yet making movies and he had no example of youthful insurrection to follow.† And so, while he did indeed storm out of the family home to kick and cool his heels on the streets, he did not buy himself that motorbike.

He bought himself a piano. It cost him £56 10s[24] – and neither he nor any other member of the Connery household could play a note on it. So remember, too, that that household lived in extremely cramped quarters. And that even the smallest piano is a bulky item, swallowing wall and floor space. As any pianist knows,

---

* To be fair to Joe, he might once have had a point. The young Neil Connery was altogether smoother and finer featured than his elder brother. But we are talking of the late fifties, when the times they were a-changing – and Sean's rough edges were destined to become cutting edges in the next decade.

† As a youngster Connery was a regular picturegoer. He was a big fan of westerns, and has said that he 'always used to think about being an Indian'. Ben Fong-Torres, 'Connery, Sean Connery', *American Film*, May 1989.

territorial rights are forever being fought over their instrument. Hardly surprising, then, that Joe wanted rid of it. Or that Big Tam refused – insistent that he was going to take lessons, the first sign of the sensitive, creative side of his personality that would come to the fore over the next few years. Except that he never did learn to play the piano. Still, the instrument stayed put, and a small battle was won. This was a boy who more than paid his own way around the home. He had a right to keep his things in it.

So Joe Connery was doubtless mighty relieved the day the boy came home and announced that he had signed up with the Royal Navy. Certainly he wished him well on his adventure. Effie was rather less happy, says Neil Connery – and not just because she counted on the money Tam brought home every week. The boy was only just seventeen, after all, and his decision to leave home and family had come out of the blue.

Alas, though he signed up for twelve years' service – seven as a sailor, five in the Naval Reserve – Connery no more enjoyed his time as a cadet than he did his years at school. Homesickness was partly to blame. Connery might have thought he wanted out of Fountainbridge, but Portsmouth, where he fetched up after basic training at Bultaw Camp near Lochinver, was the first place he had been to outside Scotland, and he found little there to make him happy. Among the things he did on his first days off was to have two tattoos emblazoned on his right arm. One read 'Scotland Forever', the other 'Mum and Dad'.[*]

If that last tattoo sounds like sentimentality, consider that young Connery was now having to deal with men who thought rather less of him than his father ever had. Bluntly, the Royal Navy was a disciplined outfit and Connery turned out to be no good at taking orders. 'I was a boy seaman,' he would recall years later, 'and there was an ordinary seaman above me, and if you reached his status there was a naval seaman and beyond that a leading seaman, and

---

[*] Badly covered in panstick, the tattoos are visible in more than one Bond movie.

then a petty officer and a chief petty officer – and I was aware that I had not done enough to make this kind of progress.'[25]

Asked about his time in the navy by another reporter, he warmed to his theme: 'I don't like anyone telling me what to do.' But haven't you got to be able to take orders before you can give them? 'Put it another way. I don't so much mind being told what to do provided I have respect for the person who is telling me, but there is nothing more boring, more annoying, more maddening than being told to do something by someone who is incompetent.'[26] Perhaps not, though it is hard to believe that every superior Connery came up against during his time in the Royal Navy was incompetent. What really goaded him, one suspects, was the perhaps unforeseen class structure of His Majesty's Armed Forces (as they then were). Whether they could take orders or not, largely uneducated commoners without received-pronunciation accents were never going to get anywhere in the Senior Service. 'It's ridiculous to say there are no class barriers in this country,' Connery would fume in the mid-sixties. 'I try to ignore class now. But there were times when people wouldn't let me.'[27]

By then, of course, Connery's instinct for insurrection was being put to good use in the creation of his most famous role. 'Discipline, 007, discipline,' Connery's James Bond chastises himself as he realises he really mustn't waste time chasing another pretty girl in *Goldfinger* (1964). Unlike Ian Fleming's original, Connery's Bond had no time at all for what he saw as the uptight stuffiness of his superiors. Such roguish rebellion was as much a product of the changing times as it was a reflection of Connery's own urges. Still, it goes some way to explaining Connery's being cast in a role nobody believed he was seriously up for. Indeed, as we shall see, it seems to have been Connery's chippiness that played a big part in getting him cast in the first place.

Given all that bellyaching, Thomas Connery didn't last long in the Navy. By July 1949, a mere seventeen months after quitting the firm, he was back at St Cuthbert's Dairy – having been invalided out of the forces with a real bellyache in the form of a duodenal ulcer. These days such a troubled adolescent would likely have been given a course of antibiotics and told to get on with it. But it is only recently that the majority of stomach ulcers have been proven to be bacterial in origin. Sixty years ago they were thought to be the product of stress – just the kind of thing a boy seaman needs to be able to handle. If he couldn't, it was time to ship out.

Back home in Edinburgh, opinions differed among Connery's friends as to the state of his health. There were those who thought their rebellious pal had pulled the wool over the eyes of the military medicos. And there were those who said yes, but don't ulcers run in the male side of his family? And doesn't he look like he's in pain? And perhaps he did, though this needn't have been entirely down to his stomach problems. The fact was that, the headstrong purchase of that piano aside, joining the Navy had been the only real decision Tam Connery had made for himself. And it had not worked out. A couple of years after signing on, he was back on his parents' couch with nothing to show for his adventure but a 6s 8d (33p) a week pension. And what 18-year-old wants to be known as an invalid?

Could that have been why he suddenly took up weightlifting? Difficult for us, who have known Sean Connery for almost half a century as one of the movies' biggest men, to conceive that he might at one time have been less than strapping. But there are pictures from his Navy days in which he is, for all his height, less than imposing. Back at home, meanwhile, there was talk of Tam's skinniness, of the fact that he weighed too little for his 6ft 2in frame. And so, for a 15s (75p) membership fee and 1s 6d a week subscription, he joined the Dunedin Amateur Weight-Lifting Club and began pumping iron there every Monday, Wednesday and Friday. He wanted, he would later say, to look good for the girls.

On the evidence of the paintings and sketches made of Connery at an Edinburgh College of Art life-class a few years later, he got his wish. Though contact between painters and models was strictly forbidden, Connery could have seen and heard that the girl students were much taken with what one of them would later call his 'jet black hair and dark eyebrows' and his 'spectacular' body.[28] Though he was paid a mere 15s an hour for his modelling efforts, it was in those classes that he began to see that his physique might turn out to be his fortune.

Hence, perhaps, his quitting the dairy again, a mere six months after his return. It was 7 January 1950 – the first Saturday of the year – when he handed in his notice for the second time there. Was it, one wonders, some kind of New Year's resolution in this, his twentieth year? If so, it was a peculiarly unfocussed one. For the next three years Connery drifted through a succession of menial manual-labouring jobs – three weeks delivering coal here, a few more weeks working on the roads there, a couple of months at a steelyard in between times. Of resolve about any of these labours there is no sign.

And then, in early 1951, the military, through the offices of the British Legion, came to his aid. Thanks to his being a disabled ex-servicemen, Connery was eligible for them to pay his fees for a scholarship that would enable him to learn a trade. He chose, of all things, French polishing – a rewarding but repetitive task highly unsuited, one would have thought, to a man who had signally failed to settle to anything. And indeed, though he mastered the basic skills on a crash course, and was soon back home polishing coffins for Vinestock's in the east of Edinburgh, he was with them no later than the spring of 1952. As he would recall a decade or so later, 'I usually left a job as soon as I got fed up or had £50 in the bank.'[29]

Still, that time at Vinestock's was not entirely wasted. In Peter Moran, a fellow apprentice, Connery had met someone who would turn out to have a huge impact on his future life. For Moran had family in London – and he had been invited down to take a look at the Festival of Britain Exhibition on the South Bank. Would Connery care to come, too? So it was that one summer weekend in 1951, a fast-coming-of-age Connery had his eyes opened to another

world. Not just to the Festival's much-feted Dome of Discovery
and the Skylon, but to the Dick Whittington promise of London
itself. Hitherto, Connery had flailed and fluttered his way through
life. But as with so many young people before and since, something
awakened in him during that visit to the capital – the realisation
that one's background need not be one's backdrop. Asked, more
than thirty years later, about his peripatetic adolescence and youth,
Connery would say, 'I was obviously looking for something and
not finding it.'[30] Or, as he confided to his notebook that year:

> The lyres of time sang softly,
> I cared not how I fared,
> For free with the strength of ignorance,
> How could I have been impaired?
> My armour bright and virile
> Entombed a passionate heart,
> That nurtured dreams of fire,
> But to where, to where to start.[31]

To where indeed?

First of all, back to 'Edinburgh, where the past is so strong, and the
memory of Scottish history is perpetually reminding you, if you are
a Scotsman, that this was once a capital, the half-meaninglessness
of Scottish life overwhelms you more strongly than anywhere
else'.[32] Certainly, all the way through Connery's youth Scottish
nationalism had been on the rise. In 1934, when Connery was
just four years old, the Scottish National Party was born, but it
would be another eleven years before the SNP won a parliamentary
seat in the Motherwell by-election – and that seat was lost three
months later in the Labour landslide of July 1945. The movement
gained little traction on the body politic largely because it was,
and is, a victim without a villain. Nobody could convincingly
have called the Scotland of the twentieth century the victim of
oppression. Depression is another thing, though. As with so many

areas of England outside the south-east hub today, the Scotland of the thirties and forties was half-alive to the notion that it had ceased to have any useful economic function. To live in Edinburgh as any kind of sentient being was to have what would today be called issues.

For the moment, though, Connery's issues took him no further than Edinburgh's outdoor swimming baths – the Portobello – there to be a lifeguard. It wasn't quite as aimless a move as it sounds. All day long, naked save for a pair of shorts, he got to strut his pumped and preened body around the poolside – the man in charge, the man ready for action. It is not too fanciful, I think, to see these days and weeks at the pool as Connery's first public performances. Certainly, there are pictures of him at the Portobello surrounded by giggling young women, a wide, dumb grin on his face – pictures of a man beginning to waken to the fact of his physical beauty.

Outdoor poolwork is strictly seasonal, of course, and by the end of the year Connery was back inside – cleaning the printing presses of the *Edinburgh Evening News*. Uninspiring and unpleasant work, as I can testify, but one night Connery spied an ad in the paper telling readers that Dame Anna Neagle was on the lookout for six-foot-plus male extras for her pre-London tour of the historical musical *The Glorious Days* (filmed as *Lilacs in the Spring* in 1954).* No sooner had he finished his shift than Connery was straight down to the stage door of the Empire Theatre to request an audition. Dame Anna's people snapped him up and for a five-week Christmas run he took his first steps on the stage, dressed as a guards officer.

There is no evidence, it should be said, that the job meant much more to him than an extra bit of cash for the party season. Nor is there any reason to doubt the logic of his claim that 'I only got the job because they wanted someone tall'.[33] But what we can say is that for his thespian debut Connery was cast not in order to

---

* See imdb.com for rumours that Connery is to be seen in silhouette during one of the movie's dance sequences. I for one am not going to check.

be someone else but to be himself. Which is a way of saying that this was less like an audition for the theatre, where shape-changing character construction is the order of the day, than for the movies, where commanding the camera with the presence of the self is called for.

Certainly, that brief stint on stage boosted his confidence a little more. By March the next year, a photograph of one Tom Connery, 'Well-muscled member of the Dunedin Weightlifting Club, Edinburgh', was to be seen inside the front cover of *Health and Strength* magazine.[34] And when, a few weeks later, Archie Brennan (a onetime Mr Scotland who had taken it upon himself to be Connery's personal trainer) suggested the two of them enter the London heats of the 1953 Mr Universe contest, Connery had no doubt that it was a good idea. For one thing, he would be out on stage and under the lights again. For another, this stage and these lights would be down in London. For all he knew, he might even win a passage through to the next round . . .

In the event, he took bronze in the tall men's class. Years later he would admit to having been shocked at the size of the opposition. As well he might have been. There is a photo of Connery posing on the stage of London's now demolished Scala Theatre as the results for the Mr Universe heats are read out. At 6ft 2in he stands half a head higher than even his tallest opponent, but there is no denying that he is carrying nothing like the weight these other guys are. But so what? asks the cultural historian. These days, when every bit-part actor over the age of thirteen has his packs and pecs and his 24/7 personal trainer, we are apt to forget that half a century ago a muscle-bound actor was a rarity. Nor does that age's definition of muscularity chime with our own. Burt Lancaster once said that the problem with weightlifting was that it made your muscles tight. Gymnastics and acrobatics, on the other hand, lengthened them. Whatever training regime he had been putting himself through, the net effect of Connery's had been to lengthen rather than tighten his physique. Bluntly, he looked more like Burt

Lancaster than the 'brown condom full of walnuts' Clive James famously described Arnold Schwarzenegger as resembling.[35] And had Connery looked like that he would probably not have been in line for what was coming up.

For Stan Howlett and Vic Harmon, two fellow competitors in the Mr Universe contest, told Connery that while he might not have taken first prize at the Scala there was still work to be had for men of his stature. For the past few months they had been making a living in the back row of the musical *South Pacific*. Now the show, twenty months or so into its two-year run at the Drury Lane Theatre, was going on tour – *sans* Harmon, who was emigrating to Canada – and auditions were to be held for his part in the chorus. Connery jumped at the chance. He couldn't sing and his dance moves were limited to ballroom shimmying, but after those walk-ons at the Edinburgh Empire he had fallen for the stage. He loved the feeling of control it gave him, the way it allowed him to be admired from a distance.

Still, the auditions didn't go well. A fellow Mr Universe entrant was rejected out of hand, and Connery, nervous in mid-speech, fumbled and dropped the pages of his script. From somewhere out in the dark of the auditorium he caught the director, an Orson Welles lookalike by the name of Joshua Logan, giving him a mumbled bad-mouthing. He sighed and turned and started to walk. 'Are those shoulders all your own?' barked the voice from the dark. (The question was not a fatuous one since the fifties fashion for padded drape coats could make the reediest weakling look like Robert Mitchum.) Connery replied that yes, they were. In that case, said Logan, the part was his too.

There was method in Logan's madness. His new chorus boy might not have chorused at all convincingly, and his dance steps might have been near to disastrous, but he had in spades what the producer knew this show – any show – needed. 'Feel it in your crotch!' Logan barked at his boys as they worked at the moves for 'There Is Nothing Like A Dame'.[36] And his new boy, though no

Fred Astaire, moved pretty well for a big guy. Whether or not this young man was feeling it in his crotch, Logan was in no doubt that his audience would.

For the next two years, Connery mimed and *sotto voced* his way through Rodgers and Hammerstein's numbers nigh on a thousand times. To begin with, he was paid £12 a week, a sum Joe Connery – though disdainful of what he saw as his son's ne'er-do-well strolling-player ways – found highly impressive. As well he might have done. Few skilled tradesmen grossed £600 a year in the early fifties, and Sean Connery – for that was the name of the actor listed as playing Sergeant Waters in the *South Pacific* programme – was being paid the sum for a few hours' work a night.

Quite what he considered himself to be doing moving into the theatrical game, though, is unclear. True, Connery had always had that sensitive, romantic side – the piano, the poetry, the wanderlust. And it is also true that there are many photographs of him as a young man in which he clowns for the camera. (Such clowning will recur throughout his career. There is a charming picture of Connery being photographed by Tippi Hedren on the set of *Marnie*, in which he jokingly removes his jacket from his shoulder, like a striptease artist. And many of the documentaries on the latest Bond DVD releases boast footage of Connery gurning and comically flexing his muscles for Ken Adam's home movies of the productions.) Still, while Connery stuck with Rodgers and Hammerstein's show for as long as he had ever stuck at anything, in the years to come he would tell more than one reporter that he conceived of his stage debut as little more than 'a giggle'.[37] 'The whole idea of travelling around the country . . . was what appealed to me.'[38] 'It was an adventure,' he told another journalist, 'but there was no future in it for me.'[39] On the other hand, he found out during *South Pacific's* long, long tour that he liked what he was doing, would like to do more of it, would like to improve at it.

None of which might have come to pass had Connery not palled up with Robert Henderson, the touring version of *South Pacific's*

Captain Brackett, and an actor with more than a passing interest in the history of his craft and the theatrical tradition sustaining it. As 1953 became 1954, Connery and Henderson shared lodgings during the show's nine-week stint at the Manchester Opera House and the older man (born in Michigan in 1904, Henderson was a couple of years senior to Joe Connery) took the younger man under his wing.

The tutelage began when the two men were walking home one night and Henderson casually mentioned Ibsen. Who's Ibsen? asked Connery. Henderson explained saying that, if he were interested, Connery should read *Hedda Gabler* or *The Wild Duck* or even *When We Dead Awaken*. 'I was so impressed by actors and how articulate they were,' Connery later recalled. 'How much they seemed to know about everything. I was impressed by most people I met. I was impressed by people that could express themselves. I had no confidence in terms of intellect at all because I'd had absolutely no exposure to it.'[40] And so, the next morning he took himself off to the local library and started working his way through Henderson's reading list. When he had finished, he returned to his mentor for more suggestions.

Henderson was taken aback: 'Most young men are keen to be stars,' he would say years later, 'but they're also dead lazy.'[41] Not this young man Connery, though, who took Henderson's next batch of suggestions – among them works by Proust, Stendhal and Tolstoy – and earnestly worked his way through them, too. Also in that second list of required reading was a work of non-fiction – Constantin Stanislavsky's *My Life in Art*.

Now this is not one of Stanislavsky's works of high theory. For the most part it is a memoir of a young man growing up in pre-revolutionary Russia. But the book, first published in 1924, was hot once more because of something that had been going on in the American theatre and cinema. Marlon Brando's work – particularly his work as Stanley Kowalski in Elia Kazan's movie version of Tennessee Williams's *A Streetcar Named Desire* (1951) – had made

Stanislavsky's acting technique (the Method, Stanislavsky's preferred term – or the System –) famous all around the world. More than that – it had made famous the notion that a leading actor need not look like the mid-twentieth century's stereotype of a leading actor. And Connery, argued Henderson, could very well trade on this aesthetic about-turn. 'You have to be a bit of a contradiction to what you are,' Connery recalls being counselled.[42] Henderson, for his part, says he told Connery that he looked 'like a truck-driver [but] if you could acquire a background, in other words if you could look like a truck-driver and talk like Dostoevsky, I think you could make a success in films'.[43]

Prescience long after the fact, of course, though there is no denying that with his coffee-dark skin, his Neanderthal mono-brow, his fondness for check shirts and faded jeans, the young Connery did have something of the truck-driver about him. But the hidebound British film industry of the mid-fifties could find no use for actors who looked like truckers – other than in pictures about truckers. Three years later, indeed, Connery was to appear in just such a film, *Hell Drivers* (1957). A couple of years earlier, meanwhile, a *Sunday Times* journalist called Ian Fleming had published his first novel – a glamorously fantastic tale of international intrigue entitled *Casino Royale*. Its hero was a public-school-educated former naval officer turned gourmand secret agent called James Bond. Anyone less like a truck-driver – or, indeed, like any character from Dostoevsky – it would be hard to imagine.

Certainly Fleming's Bond would have had little time for football. But Connery, who had been a regular with the Fet-Lor amateurs back home in Edinburgh, still played a useful game and was a regular on the *South Pacific* team. One of the games he played in took place during the show's stay in Manchester, where Connery had been spending much time on his programme of earnest self-improvement. 'He had made his decision,' Robert Henderson would later say, 'to really go for it.'[44] But had he? For the football match happened to be seen by a talent scout working for Manchester United's then manager Matt Busby. 'This guy,' the scout told Busby, 'is just what you're looking for.' Days later, Connery was offered a trial at Old Trafford.

So this was it! Rootless and routeless, Connery was being offered a way through the woods. To be sure, football was not then the big earner that it can be now. But the acting game offered no guarantee of riches, either. Connery might not have been at it long, but he had been at it long enough to have seen that a lot of people who had been at it for rather longer had little to show for their efforts. Robert Henderson, for instance. He might have known his way round the classics as well as he knew his way round the stage, but he was hardly living the high life. Henderson, though, was adamant. The chances were, he argued, that the chance Manchester United was offering Connery would come to not very much. And whatever it might come to, it wouldn't last long. Connery would turn 24 in a few months' time, and no matter how good a footballer he was, no matter how much Busby and his men could help him build on his talent, he wasn't going to be playing the game much beyond another five years. Sure, he'd have fun, but by the time he was 30 he would be back where he was, scrabbling round for work, uncertain of what would happen next.

It should be said that Jerome White, the producer on *South Pacific*, saw things rather differently. Although by the time the show arrived in Liverpool in November 1953 he had promoted Connery to the role of Sergeant Kenneth Johnston, he held out no great hopes for the young man. 'In this business,' he told Henderson, a nobody like that beefcake chorus boy would 'probably sink like a stone'.[45] On the strength of Connery's achievements thus far, you'd have needed 20–20 foresight to not side with White.

Connery, though, sided with Henderson and turned down Manchester United. The *South Pacific* tour continued, as did Connery's studies. Late at night, when the show was over and he was back in his lodgings, he would carry on working his way through the classical repertoire. The mornings he gave over to self-administered elocution lessons, reading aloud into a tape recorder and listening to the results with a disgusted grimace. Movie critics might have joked about the mouthful of marbles through which Marlon Brando mumbled his every utterance, but Brando's slips and slurs were crystalline in their clarity when set beside Connery's twisted Scots vowels. One of his *South Pacific* co-stars, Millicent Martin (fifty years later a regular on the US sitcom *Frasier*), could understand so little of what Connery said that she believed he came, like Brando's Kowalski, from Poland.[46]

Afternoons, meanwhile, Connery spent studying other touring shows. He watched anything and everything, from mainstream comedies and thrillers through Shakespeare, to the latest avant-garde productions. He was, Henderson would remember, a quick study, picking up a trick here, a tic there and all the while refining that Edinburgh brogue, though never let it be said that Connery is one of those stars who merely got lucky. The popular imagination likes the idea of the untutored star because it means that success is almost accidental and therefore potentially available to all. But regardless of his lack of formal training, Sean Connery worked very hard at his craft.

Come January 1955, just as Henderson was about to leave *South Pacific*, Connery was promoted to a speaking part – the one-line walk-on role of Lt Buzz Adams. Audiences seemed able to handle his accent, and he hung on to the part until the tour came to a finish in Plymouth that September.[47] He had just turned 25 – a rather more advanced age than we would now consider it – when he returned to London, determined to be an actor and not at all sure how to go about it.

2

Treading the Boards

Legend has it that what happened next was a lot of not very much. Back in London, Connery took a basement room at 12 Shalcomb Street, off the King's Road – not then the glitzy spot it would subsequently become – and cycled in to the West End every day to hector the big showbiz agencies, hang around the stage doors, keep up on the theatre gossip, all the while signing on at the Westminster Labour Exchange for the £6 a week dole to which he was entitled. And maybe things did feel tough to Connery. Walls always look high when you're on the wrong side of them. But the fact remains that once in the big city in that famously dry, famously mild autumn of 1955, Connery was almost instantly making a living as a jobbing actor.

To be sure, his first work in London wasn't much to write home about. Nor did it come from out of the blue. Connery wasn't spotted hanging around backstage at the Old Vic by some talent scout on the lookout for a new Hamlet or Macbeth. (Indeed, no less a figure than the artistic director of that very theatre, Michael Benthall, auditioned Connery, rejecting him out of hand because of what he said was his dodgy diction.) No, it was Robert Henderson who came good for his young protégé. In the second week of November, he told Connery, he would be mounting a production of *Witness for the Prosecution* at the Q Theatre in Kew. If Connery wanted it, there was a small part for him.

Small is right. In fact, calling it a part rather over-dignifies the large stretches of silence punctuated by the odd stentorian bark this run-through of the Agatha Christie warhorse required of Connery's court usher. And yet, if he didn't exactly steal the show, he emphatically stole much of its thunder.

It was the usher's full black cape that did it. Connery had likely never been anywhere near such a cape before, let alone worn one. But no sooner was the cloak about him than garb and gait became as one. The cloak brought out the essential Connery, held up to the light his natural theatrical splendour, magnified the grandeur of his muscled form, pointed up the casual elegance of his leonine strut. So there were no two ways about it: the cape would have to go. 'I had to take it off him,' Henderson recalled. 'The main actors were compelling, but Sean's movement across the stage was so eye-catching . . . that it just wiped them out.'[1]

A few years later that eye-catching grace was to find an outlet in James Bond's pantherine stroll. Before then, though, there was much that was graceless and mind-numbing to be waded through. For we are talking of what were still very much the early days of TV, when most people were still getting their narrative fix at their local theatre. Just like the television dramas that would eventually supplant them, most theatrical productions were forgettable rubbish, destined for short runs and shorter memories. But while they were all that was available, Connery had to take what he could get.

And so Henderson, having forgiven Connery his cape-swirling operatics, saw to it that Frederick Farley used him in the next-but-one Q production – *Point of Departure* (Anouilh's wordy, putatively poeticised version of the Eurydice myth). Connery played Matthias while Ian Bannen – who would work with Connery many more times over the coming years – was cast as Orpheus. For a man with an impenetrable accent and no vocal training it must have been a baptism of fire. But a baptism it was, and given Connery's enduring penchant for wordy poetics there are grounds for believing that he has never shaken off Anouilh's influence.

Meanwhile, there was the landlord to pay and in the week

running up to Christmas Connery was back at the Q Theatre for Henderson's next production – Dolph Norman's whimsically titled *A Witch in Time* (aka *Great Great Grandmother was a Witch*). *Bell, Book and Candle* one suspects it wasn't. 'The Scene,' one learns from the theatre programme, 'is laid in the Common Room in the old house of the Rogans, in some rural centre of an Irish county. The time is the present.' Not for the last time, in other words, had Connery, who played one Robert Callendar, been cast as an Irishman.

And then, in the February of 1956, just three months after Connery's arrival, the Q Theatre closed down for want of funds. Its final production, which kicked off on the 19th, was a show called *Who Cares?*. Connery wasn't in it, but there is reason to think he may have been hanging around the theatre while Leo Lehman's play was being put together. Later in the year, when Connery made his television debut, it was in a one-off drama written by that same Leo Lehman.

At Q, Connery would later say, he learned 'enough to know I didn't know enough'.[2] Indeed, while there he stuck to his autodidactic guns, keeping up his visits to the local library in Chelsea, keeping up his self-imposed elocution lessons, keeping up his hopes.

And his luck held. Within a few weeks of the Q closure, he won a part in a Frith Banbury just-off-the-West-End production of *The Good Sailor* – a theatrical version of Melville's *Billy Budd* – that opened on 4 April 1956 at the Lyric in Hammersmith. Connery, who was cast as O'Daniel, found himself playing opposite four men who would all become famous on TV and in the movies: Bernard Bresslaw, Dinsdale Landen, Leo McKern and Ronald Fraser. These last two were to figure prominently in Connery's life over the next couple of years. Through McKern, Connery would meet his first agent – Richard Hatton. Through Fraser, a fellow Scot, he would meet 'failed actress' turned Fleet Street photographer Julie Hamilton, one of the most important women in his early life.[3]

31

This wasn't Connery's first serious affair. During *South Pacific*'s long run he had fallen in love with a dancer called Carol Sopel.* Yet though the romance endured for much of the tour, when it threatened to get too serious, Carol's Orthodox Jewish parents stepped in and called a halt to things. Connery would encounter such negative (though in the circumstances perfectly explicable) sentiments again after he took up with Julie Hamilton.

Hamilton was the daughter of Jill Craigie, a socialist journalist, documentary-maker and authority on the history of feminism – which means that by the time Connery met her she was also the stepdaughter of Michael Foot, at the time the editor of *Tribune*, thirty years later the leader of the Labour Party. The Foots lived in Hampstead, then as now a north London village mocked for what a later resident, the novelist Kingsley Amis, would call its trendy leftiness.

In short, Hamilton was the most well-connected person Connery had so far met – though she is adamant he wasn't on the make. 'He was ambitious but unassuming,' she remembers. 'I've never been able to believe the stories I've heard about him after he became famous. I can't believe he's at all violent, for instance. During the time we were together he was incredibly gentle. Unlike a lot of actors, he was absolutely straightforward, and he is still the most honest man I've ever been involved with.'

Not that she fell for him immediately. They met in Hammersmith, during *The Good Sailor*'s short run. Hamilton's best friend, Lizzie Howe, was engaged to Ronald Fraser and the four of them went for an after-show drink. She was, she remembers, unimpressed. 'It's not that I was this innocent posh girl frightened of this rough-and-ready guy. I'd never have described him as rough – he was bright – though he did have tattoos and gold teeth, just like a navvy. If anything, I thought he was rather large and rather boring. And

* Unforgivably, her name is misspelled Sobel on page 33 of Connery's *Being a Scot*.

32

I think I'd probably only recently broken off my engagement to Leslie Bricusse after finding out he'd been playing around.* So at first I didn't think there was anything attractive about him.'

Connery himself, though, thought enough of Hamilton to make a long, drawn-out play for her. 'Over the next few months he seemed to be at all the same parties, pubs and friends' homes as me. He was always around, smiling that shy "I like you" smile. And I remember one day Peter O'Toole coming up to me in the Buxton Club [a West End club peopled largely by what would then be called theatrical types] and asking why on earth I wouldn't go out with Sean because he was mad about me.'†

Eventually, one Saturday in the late summer of that year, she decided to give him a chance. 'It was the day Ronnie and Lizzie got married. I was a bridesmaid and I thought I looked stunning. When I got to Hampstead church, though, Sean was there in full Scottish dress – kilt, frilly shirt, the whole get-up. He looked devastating! After the wedding I took him back home. That meant walking down Fitzjohn's Avenue to Abbey Road – and because we were dressed for a wedding heads were turning as we went by. After a while, though, I realised it wasn't me they were really interested in – it was Sean. He was so magnificent.'

Not so magnificent, though, that Hamilton could bring herself to appreciate the décor of his 'very damp basement' in Chelsea – which she remembers as being plastered with photographs of its tenant modelling underwear. These last were probably the work of Bill Green, who, under the pseudonym Vince, ran a studio in Manchester Street, north of Oxford Street. It is true that Green lit his work beautifully, the glistening bodies of his subjects seeming

---

* Bricusse later wrote the lyrics to John Barry's themes for *Goldfinger* and *You Only Live Twice*.

† At the time, O'Toole was making a name for himself at the Bristol Old Vic (an offshoot of the London theatre). Over the past few months he had appeared as Cornwall in a production of *King Lear*, as Bullock in *The Recruiting Officer*, as Peter Shirley in *Major Barbara* and as Lodovico in *Othello*.

almost to be carved out of light against the oil-slick black of his backgrounds. But he could be clumsy with his choice of lens and camera position. Though Connery does indeed appear godlike in some of these pictures, he can look Neanderthal too. There is a shot reproduced in *Being a Scot* that gives him a neck as wide as a bucket. And, sculpted as his musculature may be, no thought has been given to Connery's eyebrow (the singular is apt) – a great roll of chaotically wiry hair that lours above his face like some thunderous cloud. No wonder he was cast as a baddie in his first credited movie.

Shot in the summer of 1956, the gangland drama *No Road Back* (1957) was just one of the many monochrome cheapies the British film industry of the day churned out as second-string accompaniments to the bigger Hollywood pictures. Certainly, Connery's appearance aside, Montgomery Tully's movie is of no interest to the film historian – though it should be said that, for a debut, that appearance is more than assured. Connery may, in the words of one of the policemen on his character's tail, be 'a tall dark Scotsman with a bit of a stammer', but in a cast of overacting nobodies he stands out as the man capable of doing nothing but just being in front of the camera.

He plays Spike, the brainless heavy used as muscle by the not significantly brighter Railton (Skip Homeier) and as a faithful lean-on by Rudge (Alfie Bass). Perhaps because his elocution lessons were deemed not to have done enough to his accent, or perhaps because the screenwriter (Tully again) thought such a minor character needed nothing by way of lines, Connery has about as much to say in the picture as Harold Sakata would have a few years later when he played Oddjob in *Goldfinger*. Nonetheless, what he does have to say he says well, Spike's stammer serving to slow down Connery's line readings sufficiently to make them comprehensible to an audience not yet accustomed to the mumbles and grumbles of the Method school.

True, Connery overacts in silent moments – gurning here, trying too hard to look like he's thinking or confused there. But already, padding about on rooftops or stepping silently through corridors on the way to a safe-break, he is moving supremely well. Alas, while pretty much everyone else in the cast gets involved in a scrap, Connery never gets to throw a single punch. A pity, because all the punches that do get thrown are of the limp-wristed variety every actor indulged in before Connery got to show everyone how fights really looked in *Dr No*.

Connery has one big scene in which he has to struggle through his speech impediment to tell the ringleader of the gang (Margaret Rawlings) that Rudge has been killed. What marks the moment out is Connery's expressive use of his hands – rubbing them nervously together, lacing and unlacing his fingers, locking his thumbs against one another – to suggest the torments of a man under pressure. The performance isn't perfect, but there is enough evidence in it to suggest that here was a man who was giving some thought to what he was doing while on screen.

Certainly, the powers that be seemed to believe he had acquitted himself well enough. Hard on the heels of the release of *No Road Back*, in February 1957, he scored both that aforementioned agent, Richard Hatton, and two more big-screen bit-parts. First up was *Hell Drivers* (1957), Cy Endfield's lame-brained *hommage* to Elia Kazan's Oscar-winner of a couple of years earlier *On the Waterfront* (1954), in which Connery was cast as the trucker Robert Henderson had said he resembled.

In the Marlon Brando part, meanwhile, is Stanley Baker's Tom Yately, an ex-con trying to make good. Marshalled against him is the unacceptable face of capitalism in the form of a tight-fisted boss Cartley (William Hartnell) and a brutishly competitive co-trucker known only as Red (Patrick McGoohan). The story requires Yately to take sundry slights from Red and Cartley before coming punchily good toward the movie's denouement. What it requires of Connery is rather less than that. Along with Sid James and Gordon

Jackson, he has to sit at the back of the frame and grin oafishly as McGoohan metes out yet another tongue-lashing to Baker.

Hell Drivers, which began shooting in December 1956, is no better than you'd expect (certainly nowhere near good enough to merit the two-disc special edition DVD treatment it was granted for its fiftieth anniversary), its only interest today deriving from the Connery character's unthinking endorsement of every new bit of hooliganism from McGoohan. A better director than Endfield, a better actor than Connery then was, would have realised how much more bite McGoohan's ritual humiliations of Baker might have had had someone been looking on askance in the background. Since neither the weedy James nor the reedy Jackson could have been expected to test such treacherous waters, the honours would logically have fallen to the Connery character. As it is, Connery looks beefily but brainlessly on, his face forever cracked by a CinemaScope smile – the better to show off a mouthful of suspiciously white teeth.

What really marks *Hell Drivers* out in the early Connery canon, though, is that he remains fully dressed throughout its proceedings. Few are the movies in these early years in which Connery doesn't bare his chest or at least his arms. Showing off his biceps was certainly the order of the day in *Time Lock* (1957), a £100, four-day shoot Connery walked into within days of the *Hell Drivers* wrap. In this clunker, our truck-driver lookalike is cast not at all against type as a welder whose job it is to cut open a bank vault in which is trapped the manager's young son. The picture was the brainchild of Gerald Thomas and Peter Rogers, and is as ripe with tensions, ironies and subtleties as any of the *Carry On* series they were months away from unleashing on the world.

What to say about *Time Lock* other than that life is too short? Certainly, the only possible reason for watching the movie – which still airs regularly on TV – is to watch Connery in action. Not that he has much to do. His most dramatic moment comes when he gets to light the oxyacetylene torch he will try to cut open the vault with and you wonder whether his eyebrow (again, that singular is apt) might go up in flames.

Indeed, what really marks the film out is the extremely un-promising nature of Connery's performance. He has only a handful of lines, some of them spoken in the Scots burr audiences would come to love, others barked out in what might be Kajkavian. Little wonder he blows his big set-piece argument with the boss, where he is unable to dramatise the (admittedly tedious) technical problems a welder's life is heir to.

Most remarkable, though, is his lack of grace. Connery spends his fifteen minutes or so of screen-time shambling and stumbling, a far cry from the matinee-idol elegance he would soon be famous for. His back is arched, his shoulders slumped, his head bent primitively forward – a Neanderthal who has yet to master walking erect. And yet the movie ends with a set-piece composition of all its players – Connery in back of frame glowering motivelessly as the focus racks away from him: Notice me, his face is saying. Somebody notice me.

'I think I must have first met Sean at the weekly poker game a few of us – actors, directors, mostly Canadian directors, like me – used to play,' says Alvin Rakoff. 'We took turns to host it in our respective homes – though since Sean was living pretty much hand to mouth he was excused from that task. Christopher Mann, the agent, was a regular. On the direction side there was me, Ted Kotcheff, Hank [Henry] Kaplan, Silvio Narizzano. The actors were a more moveable feast, though Sean was a regular. And then there was Ronan O'Casey, Madge Ryan – an Australian – Daniel Massey and Adrienne Corri. One night Adrienne showed up and I said, "Sean, do you know Adrienne?" Everyone burst out laughing – because they knew each other all right.

'Understandably, Sean was keen for work so we gave him a walk-on in *Epitaph*.[4] And after that, every time he heard of a production, he would call and ask for work. I liked him. He was keen and wanted to learn. In fact, as a kind of private joke, I used

37

him in multiple extra roles in one show, *The Condemned*.[5] The play ended with a battle filmed at Dover Castle, and we had one shot in which Sean threw a grenade – then cut to another shot of him as another character with the grenade landing by him and he bites the dust.'[6]

We are talking here, of course, about non-speaking parts. For all the work Connery had put in with his Shakespeare and his tape recorder, Rakoff had no faith in his card-game acquaintance as a man to whom he could entrust dialogue. So six months later, when Rakoff's future wife, the actress Jacqueline Hill, suggested he use Connery as the lead in his latest television production, he scoffed at the notion. 'Sean Connery? You can't understand a word he says,' he remembers telling his wife. 'Well,' she told him, 'the ladies would like it.'

The play in question was Rod Serling's *Requiem for a Heavyweight*, and until Friday, 6 March 1957, three days before rehearsals were due to begin and three weeks before the show was due to go out, the lead was to have been played by Jack Palance.* Then the phone in Rakoff's office at the BBC rang and Palance's US agent came on the line to tell him that, sorry, but Jack couldn't make it after all. 'I immediately had a few actors in mind to replace Palance as Mountain McClintock,' recalls Rakoff, 'but after what Jacqueline said I decided to invite Sean in. He came round late on the Saturday, and by the Sunday afternoon I'd narrowed the list down to just two actors: Connery and another then unknown actor called Peter Arne.† By the evening, I'd decided to take a chance on Sean.'

For all Connery's shoo-in potential as a muscle-bound fighter, it is difficult to exaggerate the risk Rakoff was taking with this decision. Connery had rarely said a word to camera – and in *Requiem* he would be required to say many words, all of them in

---

* Who had played the part on US television the previous year.
† Later a heavy in many an ITV actioner, he had a minor part in Blake Edwards's *The Return of the Pink Panther* (1975).

whatever he could muster by way of an American accent. Indeed, as rehearsals progressed, Rakoff was told over and over again that he had screwed up. 'Warren Mitchell, who played Sean's trainer, was always on his side,' he remembers, 'but otherwise he had few supporters. Eric Pohlmann, the play's gangland villain, laughed at me when I told him who was going to be playing the hero of the piece.'

Nor did Rakoff's problems end there. Michael Barry, Rakoff's mentor – and boss – at the BBC, was adamant that he was making a big mistake in using Connery in the lead role. Every day during rehearsals, Barry stopped by to tell Rakoff he wanted Connery fired. 'But I told him, "Yes, I know Sean can't really act. But I've designed the production in such a way that whenever he is really called on to do something big I'll cut away from it to another piece of action."' Eventually Barry laid off, and the show went out on 31 March 1957, as the BBC's Sunday Night Theatre presentation.

An anonymous review in the *News Chronicle* arguing that while Connery 'looked absolutely right as the boxer . . . he did not quite seem able to bring the emotional tenseness of near-punch-drunkenness that Jack Palance must have given to the part in America'[7] aside, the critical response was red hot. The movie producer Roy Boulting, guest reviewing with his brother John for the *Evening Standard*, thought it the '[second-] best piece of television I have seen',[8] while CEH in the *Daily Echo* thought 'the acting . . . of Sean Connery . . . would have been hard to better'.[9] Elsewhere, 'Sean was a knock-out!'[10] claimed the *Daily Mirror*, his casting 'a master stroke'[11] according to *The Stage*, while the *Daily Mail*'s Peter Black wins the prize for 1957's most prescient critic by writing of 'Mr Connery's performance [being] an outstanding demonstration of television acting from the inside. He is star material if ever I saw it.'[12]

'If anyone had told me that Sean Connery was going to go on to become one of the biggest movie stars ever,' says Rakoff, 'I'd have laughed in their face. I remember saying to Jacqueline during rehearsals, "This guy John Atkinson* is going to go far." Well, have you ever heard of John Atkinson? The thing is, though, that Sean was lucky. Because James Bond, the part that made him famous, required so little of him compared to the part I'd given him in *Requiem*.'

One needn't agree with Rakoff's suggestion that creating the part of James Bond took no work on Connery's part to see that he has a point. Sadly, no recording of the Rakoff *Requiem* exists, but a read through Serling's script is enough to know that Mountain McClintock is the lynch-pin of the drama – the character who goes through a process of change during its eighty-minute running time. Little wonder that Julie Hamilton, by then living with Connery in a flat she shared with the actress Meryl McCue in Hamilton Terrace, Maida Vale, remembers he worked very hard at the part.

Whether the part was worth making an effort for is rather more moot. Serling might have thought that in the figure of Mountain McClintock he had created an emblematic vision of the victims of industrial capitalism that could stand shoulder to shoulder with the Terry Malloy of *On the Waterfront*. In fact, his portentous poetics treat Mountain no more kindly than the economic system his drama is out to savage. No actor, not a Brando and certainly not a very young Connery, could have breathed life into Serling's sacred cow – because as written the cow is really no more than a slab of beef. Not that Connery saw things that way. Talking about 'the horrible make-up' the part required him to wear, he told one reporter he regarded it as 'an advantage. If I get fan letters . . . I know they will be for my acting – not sex appeal.'[13]

Half a century on, the critic who knows Connery's oeuvre well feels pretty sure that much of the praise he received must have been

---

* An actor so far down the list that, like Michael Caine – who also appeared in the show – he didn't make the credits in the *Radio Times*. Atkinson had also, incidentally, made a couple of appearances at the Q Theatre during the season Connery played there.

over the top. But if Connery himself imagined the press coverage was part of an elaborate prank, what was he to make of the fact that that same day talent scouts from the offices of both Rank and Twentieth Century Fox called Richard Hatton's office bidding for a stake his client's future? Doubtless stunned, he maintained an admirably level head and said he wanted a few days away in Edinburgh to consider the rival deals.

The Connery family tenement came as something of a shock to Julie Hamilton, who drove Sean to Edinburgh. Joe Connery, then working for a removals firm, was away on a job for the bulk of his son's first trip home in several years. Still, they had a pleasant enough time there – as is evidenced by the famous photographs Hamilton took of her boyfriend laughing and joking with his grandfather over a pint.*

Back in London, Connery had more to smile about as he and Hatton got down to brass tacks on the rival studio offers. Eventually, Connery decided to sign a seven-year contract with Twentieth Century Fox worth around £6,000 a year – whether he worked or not.† Which was handy, because the studio hardly went out of its way to find its new star star roles. The very next month Connery was to be seen modelling slacks and sweaters in the classified pages of *Films and Filming*.[14]

And so, with time on his hands and money in his pocket, Connery set about finding a home befitting his new status. Eventually, he and Hamilton settled on a studio flat above a double garage in Wavel

---

* Legend has it that Hamilton took umbrage at Connery's sneaking off to the pub with his brother – a legend she nonsensed when she came to the pub with me. 'Maybe your average Edinburgh girl of the time would have disapproved, but I went with them – and have the photographs to prove it!' The story, which came from Neil Connery and that previous Connery biographers have relied on, appeared in the *Sunday Express* of 15 August 1965.

† Translating money values across the years is as much art as science. Still, extrapolating from the retail price index, Connery's Fox contract would have been worth a little north of £100,000 in 2007. If you go by average earnings, though, he would have been getting rather more than £250,000 a year.

Mews, NW6, an area that, while it is not quite Kilburn, is not quite West Hampstead either. This being Connery's first property purchase, he had little with which to furnish it, but Hamilton's mother helped out with a few unwanted bits and pieces that filled the place up.

For there is no truth to the claim that Jill Craigie had no time for her daughter's boyfriend. 'It wasn't that she didn't like Sean,' says Julie Hamilton. 'Don't believe the things people have said about Jill thinking him beneath us.[15] She could see he was a fine figure of a man, and she loved it when people deferred to Michael – which Sean was always doing, asking him about Shakespeare and poetry. But she had worked in the film industry. She knew what a rackety business it was, and she knew she didn't want her daughter marrying an actor.' Nonetheless, though Hamilton at first turned Connery's proposal of marriage down, she did in time come round to the idea. The trouble was, she remembers, 'the more I agreed to marry him, the more he backed off'.

Things weren't improving on the work front, either. Within weeks of the couple taking up residence in Wavel Mews, Ian Bannen had helped Connery to get an audition for Cyril Frankel's *She Didn't Say No* (1958).* It wasn't to be, although, as we shall see, Frankel would play a key part in establishing Connery's name a few years hence.

Nor did Connery score the part in the first Hollywood picture he was put up for – Henry Levin's *April Love* (1958). And no matter how bad the picture turned out, the screen test that survives suggests Connery really didn't merit a part in it.[16] To watch him moon and maunder his way through Winston Miller's sub-Tennessee Williams dialogue is to be reminded that the cinema is not the theatre and that actors who forget that fact will soon come a cropper. Bluntly, Connery does far too much, emphasising his lines with a flutter

---

* The film is alternatively known (and was remade) as *We Are Seven*. Connery's failed screen test was made on 28 June 1957.

of his eyes here, a look heavenwards there, and a furrowing of his brow whenever he finds himself with nothing to do. Worse, the balletic grace that would eventually make him famous is nowhere in evidence, so that his manhandling of Dolores Michaels comes across more slapstick than lovestruck – Orpheus galumphing.

Eventually, though, he got something. MGM called Fox to ask whether they'd be interested in hiring out their new boy. They had, they said, an exotic, eastern Europe-set thriller with a part just made for Connery.

So it was that, in the spring of 1957, Connery found himself en route to southern Spain (doubling for Albania) to play Walter Brennan to Van Johnson's Humphrey Bogart in *Action of the Tiger* (1957). This, it needs stressing, was far and away Connery's most important work to date. Not because the picture was going to turn out any good – it is as dull and clunky as anything put out that decade. Not because it gave Connery the chance to get his mouth around more than the odd monosyllable and prove he could handle dialogue. (Though let the record state that when Connery is given more than a grunt to voice he manages to do so in an accent verging on the one with which we associate him to this day. Those self-imposed elocution studies were finally paying off.)

No, what marks this picture out for Connery is that it was directed by Terence Young, a none too subtle second-rater to be sure – but also the man who would go on to direct three of the first four Bond movies. And while he had cast Connery in a role that was on one level very far removed from the 007 the two men would go on to create, still Young came to see in the young man something of the truck-driving Dostoevsky reader Robert Henderson had urged him to be. 'He had a sexual quality,' Young would say of the 26-year-old Connery years later. 'To call it a star quality would be to overrate it, but the sex was plainly there.'[17]

As it needed to be for this picture. Connery plays Mike, the rum-brave and sex-crazed ship's mate to Johnson's Captain Carson, a job whose main duty seems to be behaving badly, the better to point up Carson's sense of honour. Hence Connery spends the bulk of the movie slavering and leering at women, the rips in his T-shirt lengthening and widening as he expands with lust. In other words, he's being asked to play another cut-price Kowalski – 'a dirty man who needs a shave', as Martine Carol's Tracy Malvoisie says of him. 'I don't want to stay here alone with him. He's frightening enough when he's sober.'

All of which is incontestable – though nor is there any denying that five years later such dubious charms would seem a lot less dubious.* Essentially, Connery's Mike – a ravenous sexual predator with a taste for the hard stuff – isn't that far removed from his James Bond. Indeed, in the movie's long, tiresome middle section, in which an unshaven Connery prowls around below deck in his tattered white T-shirt, he could be the Bond of the final act of *Dr No*. He could also, of course, be one of those on-the-make rough-traders that Joe Orton would soon be building plays around. Certainly Terence Young was taken with his new protégé. Just look at the way he lights him in his first scene: we see only a silhouette, Young's backlighting pointing up the godliness of Connery's frame, a small but powerful keylight snooted just so to pick out the grandeur of his facial bone structure.

Connery, who had never been treated like this on a movie set, evidently believed Young's direction could be the making of him. Though he would appear in only fifteen or so of *Action of the Tiger*'s ninety-three minutes, by the end of the shoot he was confident enough – for which, perhaps, read naïve enough – to ask the director whether he was going to be a success in his picture. Young, to his credit, was sufficiently honest to tell his charge that he was afraid not because he (Young) had made a 'pretty awful film'. But,

---

* Indeed, Martine Carol – who in happier days, we should remember, had worked for the likes of Max Ophüls – is said to have had trouble with her motivation in *Action of the Tiger*. Introduced to Connery by Young she turned to the director and said, 'Am I supposed to run away from that?' See Kenneth Passingham, *Sean Connery* (Sidgwick & Jackson, 1983), p. 29.

he told Connery, 'keep on swimming. Just keep at it, and I'll make it up to you.'[18] We all make such promises, of course, but Young would be lucky enough to make his come true.

Still, successful or not, Connery was certainly busy enough by the time *Action of the Tiger* was unleashed to little clamour in August 1957. Only a few weeks earlier, *Hell Drivers* had had its premiere. *Time Lock* was due out a few weeks hence. And he had recently been asked to appear in a television production of Eugene O'Neill's *Anna Christie*. The production was to introduce him to the woman who would become his first wife.

3

Diane

'Ken,' said Tom Stoppard at the memorial service for the theatre critic Kenneth Tynan, 'was part of the luck we had.' Diane Cilento was part of the luck Sean Connery had. She introduced the fledgling actor to new ideas, plays, writers, producers, teachers and lifestyles that would have a lasting impact on both his life and his work. At the most basic level, she helped focus Connery's hitherto diffuse ambitions, goading him into learning more and more about his craft, challenging him to dig deeper and deeper into himself to get as close as possible to (to use the title of a play Connery would be much taken with a decade or so later) something like the truth.

Though their eventual marriage would go through a painfully protracted breakdown that was played out in the blazing glare of a tittle-tattling media, and though, thirty-five years and more after their divorce, their verbal sparring matches still sporadically take place, there can be no doubt that Cilento was an enormously beneficial influence on the actor generations of men and women have come to worship and adore. It would be stretching things to say that without her there would have been no Sean Connery – but there can be no gainsaying that she helped mould the Sean Connery we have. While Cilento's latter-day dissings of her former husband have done her few favours, it remains the fact that she did everyone reading this book a big favour.

'He looked dangerous but fun,' she would many years later recall of her first sighting of Connery.[1] That is hindsight talking, of course, but relationships between actors are fraught with danger anyway. Few marriages can survive the persistent onslaught of twin egos set on the same course, but with actors the situation is stickier still because they have to love themselves more than anyone else. Maybe this is true of all of us, but with actors the pretence that protects us from such self-knowledge is necessarily absent. They don't just want to be loved, they want to be loved by everybody, unconditionally, unconsciously — which is another way of saying thoughtlessly.

More, it is the nature of acting — in its throwing people into close proximity (often putatively passionate proximity) and licensing them freedom from themselves — that it fosters rather than stifles the fantasies of love. I trod the boards only on a very amateur level myself, but I saw enough to know that a mood comes over people who are spending three or four hours a night on stage together. Because it is never enough just to love yourself: you have to know that other people are in thrall to you, too.

And then there is the competitive side of this ludicrous game. At any one time something in excess of 95 per cent of actors are out of work. Such conditions necessarily throw them together for away-from-work hours — those hours in which love affairs can bloom and envies fester. Only watch Bruce Robinson's *Withnail & I* (1986) for some idea of the enmities that can brood over the friendships of resting actors. The end of that movie is touching not simply because it shows us all over again what the loss of innocence feels like and what the limits of male friendship are. It moves us, too, because the I character has had his stroke of luck and the Withnail one has not.

But who, you want to know, was in the driving seat when Diane Cilento was introduced to Sean Connery on the night of 11 June 1957, at the premiere of *The Admirable Crichton*? It is true that photographs of the event show us a Connery in his first tuxedoed plumage. But given that *Crichton* was Cilento's eleventh picture in the past six years, it was likely she who felt in command. This is not to deny that her first ten pictures had given her little to do. But nor can one deny the fact that in those pictures she had found herself working with the likes of John Huston, Stanley Holloway and Kay Kendall — moving-picture luminaries all.

More than that, over the past few years Cilento had been carving herself an impressive little niche on the stage, too. She had played Juliet to packed and appreciative audiences at the Manchester Library Theatre. And she had done more than 200 nights on Broadway opposite Michael Redgrave in Giraudoux's *Tiger at the Gates*. The reason Connery was pointed out to her at the Crichton premiere was that they had been cast opposite one another in a forthcoming TV production of Eugene O'Neill's *Anna Christie* — she in the title role, he as Mat Burke, the sailor who would save Anna from a life of prostitution.

By any reckoning, then, Cilento had a more impressive CV than her new co-star. Added to which, she had actually been trained as an actress, having graduated from RADA a few years earlier. She was more worldly, too. Connery's time in the Navy got him no further than the south coast of England. Cilento was just back from Bermuda, where the bulk of *The Admirable Crichton* was shot. And beyond that, she not only came from Australia — the daughter of a high-flying medical family (her father Raphael would be knighted for his services to medicine) — but part of her growing up was done in post-war New York, that hotbed of jazz, abstract expressionism and the Method. Unlike post-Depression Edinburgh, both were places certain of their place in the world.

RADA, it should be said, was at first a little less sure of Cilento's place. From where, they wanted to know at her audition, had she got that cocktail of vowels? Still, she got in — and despite her parents' return to their homeland during her studies she stayed the course, working hard at the only thing she had ever wanted to do. Acting is a game fraught with chance, and there is never any way of predicting how things will turn out for even the most talented of its hopeful players. Still, Cilento had a game-plan, was following some kind of map. She hadn't just drifted into her work. She had chosen it.

So to Sean Connery's eyes, Cilento looked like somebody he could profit from working with. His part in *Anna Christie* was, after all, his first in an established 'serious' drama. If he were going to do it justice, he would have to get by on rather more than the brawn he had brought to his previous projects. There are pictures of him in a later (1960) stage production of the O'Neill play at the Oxford Playhouse in which he is to be seen smashing the stage up in best Brando/*Streetcar* fashion. But Mat Burke is more than just a hooligan. He has a sensitive side, an intellectual side even. He cannot bring himself to believe that absolutely everything has been preordained by the God whose existence he nonetheless acknowledges.

With his poetry and his piano-playing fantasies, it is fair to say that Connery had something of Mat Burke's serious side about him. And as he was to discover during many a private weekend rehearsal at either his own or his leading lady's home, Cilento had something of Anna Christie about her. She was a woman about whom it was mighty easy to entertain the thought that perhaps she needed saving from herself.

Only a couple of months earlier, Cilento had attempted suicide. On 29 March 1957 she was found in a hotel bath, her wrists slashed, the water turned red. Talking to journalists, Cilento put the incident down to the script changes that were forever holding up production of *Zuleika*, a musical show she was due to star in in Oxford.[2] But there were signs, too, that her two-year-old marriage to Andrea Volpe was in trouble. Volpe, a well-born Italian, had been having an affair with a set-designer who worked for Alexander Korda (with whose British Lion Films Cilento had signed a seven-year deal the year previous, and for whom Volpe was working as a translator) – largely, he claimed, because he was convinced his wife was having an affair with the theatre director Alfred Rodriguez. Such things happen, of course, and we are talking about a couple only in their early twenties. And yet, as rehearsals got under way for *Anna Christie*, Cilento discovered that she was pregnant. Her daughter Giovanna (named for Andrea's father) was born on 10 December 1957.

Meanwhile, both she and Connery were learning that being long-term contracted to a movie studio often meant no more than a regular pay cheque. Just as Fox had yet to find anything suited to Connery's nascent talents (it never would), so was Cilento struggling at British Lion. As her friend and colleague the director Tony Richardson would later argue, the studio never realised what it had on its hands. 'With her long mermaid-blonde hair, her sea-blue eyes, her long, lithe body, her electricity and sexuality, Diane would have been a great movie star,' Richardson wrote. 'She'd been under contract to some of the British film companies but, with their inability to see what they'd got and their lack of imagination, they'd tried to fit her into their own stereotypes – self-sacrificing nurses or jolly barmaids – to all of which her exotic temperament was completely foreign.'[3]

The majority of actors in the age of studio dominance could have defended themselves with similar gripes, of course. Joan Greenwood, for instance, was a seductively suggestive actress that no moviemaker – not even Robert Hamer in *Kind Hearts and Coronets* (1949) – really got to grips with. For talent is rarely enough. What so often counts is luck, and it was to be Diane Cilento's bad luck that during the fair-to-middling stages of her career she took up with a man only a few years away from the biggest stroke of good fortune either of them would ever witness.

And how could it not hurt yet more that Cilento turned out to be a big part of her husband-to-be's luck? For, as Tony Richardson again spotted, 'Perhaps had she gone to America her whole career would have been different. But there was also a quirky, metaphysical side [to her]. She dabbled in Gurdjieffism and worshipped at the feet of the then fashionable movement guru Yat Malmgren. As an exercise teacher Yat was extraordinary (he helped me a lot), but unfortunately he elevated his physical principles into a dogmatic structure for creativity which even as gifted and funny a movie director as Alexander Mackendrick accepted. Diane's instinctual talent looked after her in the end, but she often talked the jargon.'[4]

And one of the times she talked it was during a Sunday lunch at Connery's flat early on in the rehearsals for *Anna Christie*. One of the reasons Cilento had been invited was to give Connery a test-ride on her Vespa scooter so that he could decide whether to buy it from her. (He did.) But they were also meeting to put in some extra-curricular work on the O'Neill production. This, Connery had made plain, was the most demanding role he had yet attempted. He needed all the help he could get. Then why, said Cilento, didn't he come along and meet Yat? (At the time, Cilento says, Connery 'walked like a bodybuilder'.)[5]

Formerly a dancer in the Kurt Jooss Ballet Company, Yat Malmgren has some claim to being the man most responsible for giving the world audience the Sean Connery it adores. For he it was who taught Connery how to move – how to position his body in space in such a way as to make for maximum dramatic impact in any given scene. Swedish by birth, Malmgren was to be Britain's answer to Stanislavsky and the Actor's Studio – an aesthetic theorist convinced that acting was something that came from within the actor rather than from the world's effect on him or her.

What attracted Cilento to Malmgren, one guesses, was the Jungian undertow of much of his less practical, more mystical advice. But Sean Connery, a physical man, a man in tune with his body through years of weight-training and football, was more likely drawn to what Malmgren calls 'the relationship of feeling and form in drama'. Malmgren's self-proclaimed aim was to 'help the actor raise the consciousness[,] and control the forces that determine the expressive qualities of movements, gesture and speech', in order to equip him or her 'with that sensitivity of body to emotional impulse which is the basic condition of every act of transformation'.[6]

Beneath Malmgren's broken syntax is a profound insight into the actorly aesthetic – that the way actors move across the stage or the screen is as replete with meaning as anything a given script requires them to say. And Sean Connery would be the pupil who most eloquently – which is to say silently – demonstrated the wisdom of this truth. 'The dance, to me, is all important,' he would later say of his experiences with Malmgren. 'The place where you stand, how you use your space, is the number-one priority. How you stand in relation to other people in scenes, how you dance with them – that's what it's all about.'[7] And again, 'If you can *show* what people are doing, then the dialogue and the sound effects become like a bonus. Otherwise you'd just be listening, as if to a radio.'[8]

Which doesn't mean he abandoned work on his elocution. Alongside the daily classes with Malmgren (four practical sessions a week, the other three more theoretical), Cilento and Connery attended elocution sessions with Cicely Berry, subsequently the Voice Director of the Royal Shakespeare Company. Berry later claimed that she didn't really approve of helping Connery to lose his Edinburgh brogue – 'more like Irish, really' – but 'he felt it limited his career'.[9]

Beyond those lessons, Cilento, who was fluent in the Italian of her family name, served as another reminder to Connery that there was a world of better-read people than him out there. Indeed, in 1960 the two of them would appear together at the Oxford Playhouse in a production of Pirandello's *Naked* translated by Cilento herself. From now on, it is worth noting, one or more books will figure in the burgeoning number of 'Mr Sean Connery at Home'-type publicity shots – the actor leafing through a weighty-looking tome, while looming in the background are the Complete Works of William Shakespeare and volumes of Proust.*

One stresses all this work and craft because, though Connery and Cilento quickly became close, they did not become a conventional couple for quite some time after their meeting. Though it has been claimed that Connery left Julie Hamilton for Cilento during the rehearsals for *Anna Christie*, Hamilton herself is adamant that their relationship continued quite some time beyond the summer of 1957. Moreover, Cilento maintains that she and Connery had known each other 'a whole year before we fell in love'.[10]

So dating the commencement of their affair is not easy. According to Tony Richardson, both he and Robert Shaw were involved with Cilento as late as the spring of 1959. Many years after rehearsals for his Royal Court production of *Orpheus Descending* (which opened in May 1959, and in which Cilento played the vampish Carol Cutrere), Richardson remembered a comical not-quite date: 'Like many others I was mad about Diane and had been in love with her on and off for years. I had a date with her after one of the dress rehearsals or previews of *Orpheus*. To my fury, Robert Shaw turned up at the end of the show, also with a date with Diane . . . We had a nasty confrontation – as near as I've ever come to physical blows – then we separated.' At which point a disconsolate Richardson did his rounds of the theatre, giving performance notes to actors and technical comments to the lighting crew and backstage team. And then, 'Feeling very sorry for myself, I walked out of the theatre and into the next-door pub. There was Robert, looking equally black and equally convinced that the lady had gone off with me. We both realised in a flash what had happened and started to laugh. At closing time, after a few drinks, there was only one thing to do: we would go together to Diane's and confront her. When we arrived there, we could hear through the door that she was entertaining someone else! We banged on the door, we roared insults and made ourselves as embarrassing as we could.'[11]

So while Julie Hamilton remembers Connery waking one morning and telling her with absolute certainty that he was now in

---

* And much later in his career, in the 1980s and 1990s, many of Connery's characters – the William Baskerville of *The Name of the Rose*, the Professor Henry Jones of *Indiana Jones and the Last Crusade*, the Barley Blair of *The Russia House*, even the John Mason of *The Rock* – are bookish types. 'My first big break,' Connery notes in the Foreword to *Being a Scot*, 'came when I was five years old . . . [when] I first learnt to read.'

love with Diane, it was to be some time before Cilento began to respond to his attentions. Having tried marriage once and found it wanting, she was not about to be tied down again while still only in her mid-twenties. Hence, to hear her tell it, it was Connery who made all the running in what would finally become their romance. 'I've never been the one who pursued,' she would remember years later. 'I've always been pursued, and so what's drawn me to people is them being drawn to me, more than anything.'[12] All of which may be true. But it hardly sounds like the eternal love Sean Connery would be called on to evoke in his biggest picture to date.

The movie was *Another Time, Another Place* (1958), and Connery was booked to play the male lead opposite Lana Turner – a decade earlier one of the biggest names in Hollywood. By the late fifties, though, she was on the slide, which is not to gainsay the import of the line in the movie's press book about 'Sean Connery [being] personally selected by Lana Turner'. When, on Monday, 16 September 1957, he arrived on director Lewis Allen's set, Connery knew that this was far and away his biggest chance yet.

'Introducing Sean Connery', it says on *Another Time, Another Place*'s opening credits, and once they've finished rolling, there he is in the first shot uttering the movie's first line of dialogue. Alas, twenty minutes later he is gone – vanished from the story with one of those melodramatic deaths the movies so love. (With its kindly shrinks and Cornish, coastal setting the movie owes a lot – though by no means enough – to Joseph Mankiewicz's 1947 masterpiece *The Ghost and Mrs Muir*.)

And in between? Well, in between Connery has to chew his way through a lot of overblown romantic fluff – precisely the kind of high-flown rhapsodic fustian his instinctively ironic presence might have come into being in order to discredit. But the movie grants Connery no sardonic distance, so that the look of dumb despair on his face as he once more bleats about his aching heart speaks not of a star having a high old time of it in a cheapie stinker but of an actor who is lost and looking for help. As Turner would remember, 'It was one of Sean Connery's first films, and he often missed his marks or forgot his key lights, to the annoyance of the director. Because I was co-producer, I had to work to smooth things out to ensure that the schedule went ahead as planned.'[13]

Hence, one suspects, the clumsy stresses in too many of Connery's line readings. Nervousness clutches at his throat as he struggles to articulate every vowel and clarify every consonant for the World Service broadcasts it is Mark's job to make. Worse, the untrained Connery's biggest technical shortcoming is his lack of breath control, a lack that means the despairing threnodies he showers on Turner tend to evaporate midway through, condensing cloudily a word or two later in another tone, another pitch.

What the picture lacks above all, though, is any sense of connection between Connery and Turner. For a couple who are meant to be head over heels in love they look an awful lot like two bad actors spouting lines at one another. That fearsome monobrow aside, Connery looks very much the matinee idol, but everything about his performance tells us he is diffident about his appearance. When he takes Turner in his arms he looks less like a comforting lover than a baby in search of the blanket that tells it the world really is as it remembers it. Connery looks, in other words, like he is clawing desperately at the biggest chance that has come his way for fear that if he lets go it will run away. In short, he looks nothing like a star.

But then, despite the presence of Lana Turner, *Another Time, Another Place* looks very little like a movie. The Frank Sinatra assassination thriller *Suddenly* (1954) aside, Lewis Allen spent most of the fifties working in television, and the smaller medium's strictures and short cuts are everywhere apparent in *Another Time* – from its brief running time to its two cardboardy sets.

The bigger shame is that the lead character's essential weirdness – a dead man's lover suffering such a breakdown she insinuates herself into his family home to console his wife Kay (Glynis Johns) and son – is never explored. Only think what a Patricia Highsmith could have done with such a set-up! What a study in perversity a Hitchcock or a Chabrol might have made of it! It is true that Lana Turner wasn't the most versatile of stars, but given her gloriously sleazy turn in Tay Garnett's *The Postman Always Rings Twice* (1946), can there be any doubt that she could have turned *Another Time, Another Place*'s Sara Scott into a study in malignant mourning?

Such questions aren't purely fanciful. For even at this early stage of his career, even in the baggy flannels and V-necked sweaters Laura Nightingale's costume department kitted him out in, Connery's presence (not the same thing as his performance) hinted at murky, ravenous depths. Clumsy as his embraces of Turner are, there is something immoderate about them, too. Michael Caine once said that in British movie thrillers of the forties and fifties you could always tell who the bad guy was: he was the guy who chased the girls. Well, Connery is chasing the girl here, and it is a pity that Lewis Allen for once didn't resort to cliché, because the idea of Connery as the villainous seducer is a potent one.

Bluntly, we never believe for a minute that this man with the thunderous face could ever really have been involved with Glynis Johns's Kay. So mightn't he have been involved in a plot to do away with her – and steal her fortune – instead? Mightn't he have 'come back from the dead' and haunted her at night, even as his lover piled on the more quotidian anguish through the day? No, I'm not suggesting that in Allen's hands such a restructured story would have been any better than the picture we have. But I am saying that the commonplace that *Another Time, Another Place* did nothing for Connery's career is wide of the mark. If nothing else, the picture bodied forth the glowering intensity, the brooding darkness that he had, one suspects, borrowed from the young Olivier.* Within the

---

* Olivier's *Macbeth* was playing at Stratford in mid-1955, just at the time when Connery was playing in *South Pacific* in Birmingham, Coventry and Stratford itself. For much of the rest of his career Connery was forever working on a movie version of the Scottish Play.

terms of the narrative, such smouldering turmoil made no sense. Eventually, though, it would make a star of Connery.

Perhaps because of the on-screen disconnect, the studio was keen to play up rumours of Connery's real-life involvement with Turner. The story was put about that when Connery first escorted Turner out for a night around London town, he turned up in a T-shirt on his motorbike expecting her to ride pillion in her furs and jewels. Well, perhaps. More likely the publicist had seen Marlon Brando in *The Wild One* and got the idea that Connery's rough and ready beauty could be pressed into service in a PR pastiche of the picture.

But it is likely, too, that Turner was using Connery – as she used so many men over the years – to stir her lover, the violently possessive yet curiously uninterested Johnny Stomponato (once a bodyguard to the gangster Mickey Cohen), into a jealous rage. And stirred he was. When Stomponato heard the rumours about what was going on over in London he booked himself on the first flight over. 'And suddenly,' Connery remembered, 'out of the blue this guy arrived . . . We were just going out when he arrived at the door. [Lana] had her chauffeur-driven car and everything. And he comes in. And, shocked, she introduces him to me. We're going to go in the car. And he makes to hand me his coat. And I said, "I don't want your coat." "Just look after it," he says. I said, "Look after your own coat, for Christ's sake." '[14]

From here, the drama (for that is surely what Turner would have regarded it as) escalated. Stomponato wanted his girl off the movie – and if she wouldn't quit he'd take his knife to her face so that the director wouldn't want her in front of the camera. 'We were halfway through the picture,' says Connery. 'He was in the corridor outside her dressing room. She wouldn't come out on to the set . . . I went down to ask, "What's the problem?". "No discussion with you," he said. "Nothing to do with you," I said, "Surely. I'm waiting on the set." ' Stomponato headbutts Connery, and a fight ensues. Eventually what Connery calls 'the guys in Whitehall with the white raincoats' are summoned and Stomponato is escorted from the building and deported.[15]

How different, how very different, from what goes on between Turner and Connery in Lewis Allen's finished movie. And yet we need to grasp that for Turner such incidents were very much part of a movie – the imaginary movie she was never not starring in, the movie that in her warped consciousness stood in for the life she could never get a fix on. This inability to deal with reality is what stardom can mean, and Sean Connery took far more from the episode than he himself has perhaps ever grasped.

So it is that six months later, in May 1958, *Another Time, Another Place* was rushed out in America. A few weeks earlier nobody had held out any great hopes for the movie – but now it was thought that the picture might do well out of sheer notoriety value. Because a few weeks earlier, on the night of 4 April, in the midst of another horrific row at the Turner home, Lana's 14-year-old daughter Cheryl Crane had stabbed Stomponato to death with a kitchen knife. Though the rumours have never gone away that it was really Lana who wielded the knife, a jury decided it was a justifiable homicide. Subsequently, the Stomponato family sued Turner for $7 million – and the word was that Mickey Cohen was bankrolling their legal costs. The case was eventually settled out of court.

None of which would matter much to us were it not for the fact that Connery was unlucky enough to be in LA at the height of the gossip-fest. He was staying at the Hollywood Roosevelt Hotel, though he paid his bill and quit the place the minute Mickey Cohen called to tell him to 'get your ass outta town'.[16] Cohen had vowed revenge on his bodyguard's killer – and he did not believe the guilty party was Cheryl Crane. Connery spent the rest of his time in Hollywood in a small hotel in the backwoods of the San Fernando Valley.

Connery wasn't in Hollywood just for the fun of it. Though in December of 1957 he flunked an audition for the second lead opposite Ingrid Bergman in Mark Robson's *The Inn of the Sixth Happiness* (1958),* he had subsequently come good, winning a part in a Disney movie called *Darby O'Gill and the Little People* (1959). Connery was listed third in the cast on the *first* screen of credits – a big step up.

The director was Robert Stevenson, one of those moviemakers who gropes for what he wants while on set. Twenty and more takes were often required on even the smallest moments of a Stevenson production, and *Darby O'Gill* was no exception. Connery, perhaps overawed by his new surroundings, didn't gripe – and nor should he have. Because it has to be said that no matter how many takes Stevenson gave him for his scenes in the picture, his performance wasn't up to much.

Connery was cast primarily because of his dark Celtic looks and lithe physique. Still, the overriding impression he gives in this half-live action, half-animation movie is one of slowness and stiltedness. In what the movie imagines is its big fight scene, he lumbers around the set like a drugged rhino, utterly devoid of the brute elegance that would characterise his James Bond. His dancing is nervous and arrhythmic, though his singing – of a two-note song called 'Pretty Irish Girl' that was put out as a single in the spring of 1959 – is not entirely merit-free. ('You didn't capitalise on your singing, then?' Connery was once jokingly asked. 'No,' he fired back, 'and nor did anyone else.')[17] And his reaction shots are lumpen – all his smiles and grimaces and looks of startlement or bafflement held not a second but several seconds too long.

All of which said, it is Connery's line readings that must really give us pause. Once again, his lack of technique is letting him down badly here. Too often he stresses the wrong word in a line, and just as often he breaks the rhythm of a sentence for no reason save inexperience. At one point he has to say, 'Oh, we can't let the cutting of the turf stand in the way of good deeds.' What he actually

* The part went to Curt Jürgens.

says is, 'Oh we can't let the cutting of the turf . . . STAND in the WAY . . . of good deeds.' Worse, he says it in the vari-speed vein – racing through half a phrase here, stuttering through a few words there – beloved of actors who don't understand the Shakespeare they have been asked to read.

A few years later, the producer Albert R. 'Cubby' Broccoli's wife would urge him to test Connery for *Dr No* on the strength of his turn in *Darby O'Gill*. Dana Broccoli proclaimed herself much taken with Connery's kissing technique in the movie, the rapine hunger with which he seizes Janet Munro's Katie O'Gill and pulls her close. Even today, after half a century of Connery superstardom, you can't watch the picture and miss that salty greed. Nor, though, can you miss the fact that what Dana Broccoli had essentially spotted was Connery's overblown theatricality. When he yanks Janet Munro towards him for that kiss, Connery isn't acting for a movie crowd but for the back row of the gods. It is a moment that owes very little to the work of the mature Cary Grant the Bond producers wanted to ape, and rather more to the Stewart Granger of *Scaramouche* (1952).

Still, it must have seemed a massive step down when Connery was offered the part of another taciturn heavy in *Tarzan's Greatest Adventure* (1959). Sure, he got to stay in Hollywood a month or two longer, but perhaps to prevent his angle-jawed beauty detracting too much from that of Gordon Scott's Tarzan, the movie required him to wear a heavy beard – his first hirsute appearance on the silver screen. Whatever else this was, in other words, it wasn't the kind of part that was going to lead to greater things. And nor did it. A whole two years and three months would elapse between the release of *Tarzan's Greatest Adventure* and Connery's next picture – far and away the longest cinematic hiatus in what we may begin to call his career.

And so, in September 1958, Connery was to be seen on the Independent Television Network in a one-off drama called *Women*

In Love (not, incidentally, a version of the D. H. Lawrence novel). He spent the remainder of the year resting. Nor did 1959 start promisingly, when John Osborne – casting for his musical drama *The World of Paul Slickey* at the Royal Court – rejected Connery out of hand.

Now Osborne doubtless had good reasons for this decision, but it prompts thoughts about Connery's theatrical career trajectory. How come, in the age of the angry young man, in the age of the torn T-shirt and the guttural vowel, in the age of the muscle and the mumble – how come he was being cast in none of the plays of the moment? How come the man the movies clearly saw as a potential British Brando was being cast on stage only in historical dramas and charming Celtic brews? How can it be that in May 1959 he found himself back at the Oxford Playhouse ('by permission of Twentieth-Century-Fox' it said in the programme) playing Pentheus in a new production of *The Bacchae*? Such versatility is not to be sniffed at, but we ought not discount the notion that it bespoke a talent that knew not what to do with itself.

Because another peripatetic period was upon Connery. Come the summer, as *Darby O'Gill* was given its June premiere at the Theatre Royal in Dublin, he was back on television in another boxing drama, ITV's *The Square Ring* – and this time he wasn't even playing the lead fighter, an honour that went to George Baker.

From late October through November, he was on tour again. Hank Kaplan, one of Connery's poker-playing pals, had put together a new show – *The Sea Shell* by Jess Gregg – with Sybil Thorndike as its star. Here, then, was a chance for Connery to stretch himself against a real stage actress. What the two of them were like together we shall never know, of course – though we do know that despite Connery's fervent hopes that the show would go over big ('It better be a success,' he told one reporter, 'we've all turned down screen parts to be in it. That's how good we think it is'[18]), it never made it to London.

In November, as *Tarzan's Greatest Adventure* failed to live up to

61

its title around the cinemas of Europe, Connery played the part of John Proctor in a live ITV production of Arthur Miller's *The Crucible*. No small part, yet as the fifties became the sixties there was no sign of a greater focus in Connery's work. In the first month of the new decade he appeared in Anouilh's *Colombe*, the start of a relationship with the BBC that would take him through the rest of the year.

A couple of months later, in March 1960, he returned to the Oxford Playhouse for another production of *Anna Christie*, playing Mat Burke again, though this time opposite Jill Bennett. Come Easter, he appeared as Hotspur in the early episodes of *The Age of Kings*, a television version of Shakespeare's history plays that takes us from the age of Richard II to that of Richard III and sounds Wellesian in ambition if not achievement. According to one critic Connery was 'physically relaxed, not at all fazed by the verse speaking, and . . . considerably more dynamic than the leaden Shakespearean actors around him'.[19]

In September came two more productions for the BBC: *Without the Grail*, a Maughamian tea-plantation drama in which Connery came up against Michael Hordern, and J. M. Synge's *Riders to the Sea*, in which he was once more working with the redoubtable Sybil Thorndike. The next month he was back on ITV for *The Pet*, a one-off drama adapted from a novel by – and starring – his old rival for Cilento's affections, Robert Shaw.

At which point he got his biggest movie offer in three years. Samuel Bronston wanted him to play Count Ordóñez, the second lead opposite Charlton Heston in Anthony Mann's three-hour epic *El Cid* (1961). Astonishingly, he turned Bronston and his cheque for some £15,000 down,[20] the part was given to Raf Vallone, and Connery took himself off to Oxford, there to appear in the Cilento-translated production of Pirandello's *Naked* on which we have already touched. For his efforts he was paid precisely £25 a week.[21] Dressed in a morning suit, Connery played an aristocratic diplomat given to self-aggrandising outbursts of emotion. So emotional, apparently, that during one opening-night explosion 'there was a loud PING! and his collar stud flew out in a great arc, landing noisily halfway into the stalls'.[22] 'Mr Sean Connery,' an anonymous critic wrote, 'makes a curiously unforgettable impression.'[23]

Why, though, had Connery chosen to rebuff the Hollywood machine by electing to take this role? On a personal level, at least, his motivation can be easily grasped. For the past year and more Cilento had been terribly sick with tuberculosis, and though she was by now on the mend, Connery did not want to leave her for a long shoot abroad. Truly as noble an act as anything done by El Cid himself, and one that looks all the nobler in the light of the movie role Connery ended up taking instead – as the support act heavy in another black and white British B-picture. True, the role was as big as supporting roles get, but nobody could ever have imagined that *The Frightened City* (1961) was the stuff of which cinematic dreams are made. Nonetheless, throughout December and the first half of January 1961, Connery was to be found pounding the streets of Soho – and looking very proto-Bond-like in the process.

Certainly, all the visual elements of the Bond series are in place in John Lemont's movie. When we first meet Connery's small-time hood Paddy Damion he is showering down in a gym after a boxing match and his musculature has never looked more magnificent. For later scenes he dons a three-piece suit as well as various silky lounge numbers, the trim fit of sixties tailoring pointing up his snake-hipped grandeur. Moreover, those movement classes of Yat Malmgren's have given Connery's whole body the lethal grace that would characterise Bond's every twist and turn. Toward the end of the picture we watch him climb the wall of a house, and he does so with the daunting effortlessness of a big cat. All in all, and despite the fact that the movie requires him to act afeared of tubby old Alfred Marks (as gangland boss Harry Foulcher), Connery looks every inch the noble anti-hero in *The Frightened City*.

And yet, and yet . . . Kinetically satisfying as Connery's playing is, his handling of dialogue still leaves a lot to be desired. Too many of his line readings are blank and uninflected, as if he has no grasp of their import as elements within an overall narrative structure. In the Bond movies such vacuous incomprehension came into its own, bestowing an ironic knowingness on the two-dimensional tailor's dummy that Connery invented. But the character Connery was asked to put together for *The Frightened City* was rather more complex than that – by some measure, indeed, his most complex yet. Paddy Damion may not be the flawed Shakespearean hero the movie's publicist claimed him to be,[24] but in asking Connery to play a villain who comes to see the error of his ways and decides to put things right, the movie required rather more from him than he had hitherto ever been asked to give. True, *The Frightened City*'s pat moral schema might have been designed to ensure that Damion's volte-face seems trite. But Connery's affectless delivery does nothing to render it any more real.

In that affectlessness one detects the dead hand of John Lemont (whose first and only picture as director this was). Though none of Connery's earlier movie performances had been vocally satisfactory, they had suffered not because he underplayed them but because he had tended to overdo the billowing rhetoric. Lemont had sensed, correctly enough, that such high-blown melodramatics were hardly of a piece with his low-life gangland thriller. The problem was that neither he nor Connery had anything to put in their place.

And so, strange to relate, Connery's next movie project, a slight, polite army comedy, turns out to have been more suggestive of the greatness that was just around the corner. As the dumb sidekick to Alfred Lynch's wised-up con artist, Connery acquits himself well in *On the Fiddle* (1961). For the first time in his working life the big, inane grin that can split his face wide open is being used in the service of a story that requires it. When Connery had cackled at some co-worker's mishap in *Hell Drivers* or laughed as he drunkenly assaulted a fragile blonde in *Action of the Tiger*, the grin had seemed like the nervous reflex of an actor unsure of the tone of a scene and

utterly uncertain of his effects. In *On the Fiddle*, though, the smile
– borrowed, like so much of the performance, from Stan Laurel –
comes into its own as the synecdochic expression of a benign fool,
the kind of holy innocent that the Connery of the post–Bond years
would return to over and over again.

With this newfound beneficence comes a new attractiveness.
Though the Connery of *On the Fiddle* is rather less hewn, rather
less groomed than the Connery of *The Frightened City*, the women
in the movie take to him more openly than they have in any of
his previous efforts. When he strips his top off in a hot kitchen it
is to reveal a chest not delicately embroidered with a subtly styled
crucifix of hair (as James Bond's will be) but one covered in unruly
outgrowths of bum-fluff. And yet the girls see through this hirsute
wildness. 'He's gentle as a baby,' one girl says of Connery's Pedlar
Pascoe, and a key point in the plot is built around the Pascoe's faux-
naif beauty.

His best moment in the picture, though, comes when he has to
pretend to be a hard-nosed villain and the distant, Brechtian, ironic
Connery audiences would shortly come to love is first spied on the
big screen, tipping the wink to those on the *qui vive* that we're all
having fun. Indeed, Connery takes so well to comedy in *On the
Fiddle* that the misfires of the past five years and more stand revealed
as (at least in part) the product of his desire to be taken seriously.
Like many an autodidact before and since, Connery finds it difficult
to believe that comedy can be just as serious as tragedy.

Seriousness was what kept on coming at him, though. In June
1961 he played Alexander the Great in a BBC production of Terence
Rattigan's *Adventure Story*. It's his biggest role so far, and the show –
and Connery – make the cover of the *Radio Times*. Does he deserve
the attention? Happily, yes. Rattigan's Alexander is a moon-ruled,
mood-swinging myth of a man, and Connery rises to the challenge
with a performance full of variety and invention.

It is true that his Alexander is just a little too gesticulatory, just
a little too theatrical for the confines of the TV screen. On the

other hand, Connery is here utterly in command of his voice, and he beautifully conveys the king's boyish impetuosity and excitable lustiness with a snap of his wrist here, a tremble of his hand there. As *The Times*'s anonymous critic thought, 'Certain inflexions and swift deliberations of gesture at times made one feel that the part had found the young Olivier that it needs.'[25]

So it shouldn't come as too much of a surprise to learn that Connery's next job was playing the lead in *Macbeth*. For one thing, he had been offered the part before. A couple of years earlier, during Cilento's long fight with tuberculosis, Joan Littlewood had wanted Connery for her Theatre Workshop production of the play, but he had turned her down (Richard Harris ended up taking the part). For another, Paul Almond's production was not destined for the West End stage. Instead, it was being made for Canadian television as a broadcast for schoolchildren. The play's acts were to be broadcast separately over five days in late November and early December. Before then, there were ten days of rehearsal, and a day to shoot it. Connery received a free hotel room and 500 Canadian dollars.

How did he do? Given that he claims to have been suffering terribly with a cold, not too badly – at least on the evidence of the three-minute snippet that can still be found on the web. True, he fluffs the last line of the scene ('False heart must hide what the false face doth know'!), but otherwise he is speaking well, and moving superbly about Rudi Dorn's Caligariesque sets.

Once back home, he got his biggest challenge yet, in a television version of *Anna Karenina* on the BBC. No recording survives, unfortunately, though according to our anonymous friend in *The Times*, Connery was the 'most successful' of the three leads as the 'headstrong, passionate Vronsky'.[26] No small achievement, considering that the title role was occupied by Claire Bloom and that Karenin himself was played by that scene-stealing old hand Marius Goring.

Given that on the movie front he had been reduced to taking a

bit part in *The Longest Day* (1962) – a bit part so small it occupies less than a sixtieth of the movie's running time – Connery could by now have been forgiven for imagining that television and the theatre were where his future lay. One of the remarkable things about Connery's apprenticeship, after all, was the old-fashionedness of its emphases. Here is a man whose career proper began in 1956, the same year that modern British theatre was born with the production of John Osborne's *Look Back in Anger*. And yet five years later Connery had done no Osborne, no Pinter, no Wesker, not even any Brecht – nor expressed a jot of interest in the work of such writers. It is true that he had done a little Pirandello, but Pirandello's emphatically humanistic modernity bears no relation to the more abstract angers of the newer writers. It would be ridiculous to suggest that Connery had had a classical theatrical training. (A couple of years later he would recall these 'prentice years as being like 'walking through a swamp in a bad dream'.)[27] But it is vital to grasp that the tradition of heroic stage acting he had taken so much from was being assailed from all sides even as he was committing its lessons to memory. He was beginning to look, that is, like a man out of time.

Indeed, a few weeks earlier, after several months of discussion about a new adventure picture a couple of hack producers were knocking together, and after a test shoot and interviews with the high and mighty, he had been told that the projected picture's American backers were unimpressed with his test footage. 'New York did not care for Connery,' reads a memo from co-producer Cubby Broccoli to his partner Harry Saltzman. 'Feel we can do better.'[28]

And so the search for an actor to play Ian Fleming's James Bond went on.

4

Bondage

Take a look at the list of the names of prospective leading men Saltzman and Broccoli were conjuring with over the months it took them to put together *Dr No* (1962) and one thing is clear: these guys hadn't a clue what they were about. A measure of the project's lack of focus can be found in Richard Maibaum and Wolf Mankowitz's original screenplay for the picture, in which the villainous Dr No turned out to be . . . a spider monkey. What, one wonders, would the Ian Fleming who 'was not sure if a working class Scotsman had the social graces to play his hero'[1] have made of such a casting coup?

Then again, a large number of the problems confronting Saltzman and Broccoli were to be found in their source material. Taken straight, Fleming's novels were pretty much unfilmable. In many ways, Fleming's original Bond was an insufferable bore – priggish, snobbish, public-school effete and almost gruesomely uncultured. A shoo-in for Richard Todd (whom Fleming fancied for the role), in other words, or maybe Dirk Bogarde.* Which is a way of saying that a Fleming-style Bond would have been a one-picture flop.

Yet for a while, at least, Saltzman and Broccoli persisted in the fantasy, talking one minute of Michael Redgrave as a potential 007, the next of Trevor Howard. Both, it hardly needs saying, were

* Bogarde had, astonishingly, been suggested to Fleming as a possible Bond as early as 1959. See Robert Sellers, *The Battle for Bond* (Tomahawk Press, 2007), p. 54.

fine actors; neither would have been right for the part in hand. A Redgrave Bond would have spoken far too beautifully to be taken seriously as a man of action – Redgrave's transformation from musicological aesthete to scrapper in Hitchcock's *The Lady Vanishes* (1939) had rightly been played for laughs. A Howard Bond, meanwhile, might have had a suitably maverick loner quality, but there was no denying that Howard's fight scenes down the years had shown him to be rather more convincing as the punchee than the puncher. At one point in Ralph Thomas's *The Clouded Yellow* (1950), even that old flouncer Barry Jones gets the better of Howard's secret service man.

Still, either of those two would have been better for Saltzman and Broccoli's prospective movie than any among Messrs David Niven, James Stewart, Richard Burton (surely the model for the illustrated Bond that adorned so many 007 paperbacks in the late fifties) or Rex Harrison – four more men Ian Fleming believed to be cut from the kind of cloth suited to playing his hero. (Fleming, by the way, thought that his friend Noël Coward should play the movie's villain. The answer, said Coward in a justifiably famous telegram, was 'Dr No? No! No! No!')

Nor would Cary Grant, an actor much favoured by Broccoli, really have cut the mustard as Fleming's secret agent. To be sure, Grant's classless mid-Atlanticism (he was born in Bristol, though came across as the epitome of East Coast breeding and West Coast style) was an essential aspect of what the Bond of the movies would eventually embody. But there is no evidence that the producers and writers had realised such worldly anonymity was what they were after. Moreover, while the Hitchcock/Grant comedy thriller *North by Northwest* (1959) was plainly a key inspiration for the look and feel of Saltzman and Broccoli's finished picture, Grant had never convincingly played an *uncompromised* hero. It may be that a Grant Bond, a Bond conscious of his own worldly, amoral game-playing, would have been a fascinating invention – a kind of Hamlet with a handgun. Still and all, it is a fact that sales of Fleming's books dropped off markedly as they moved toward an awareness of the Hyde lurking beneath their hero's Jekyll.

One of the more thoughtful suggestions for Bond was the actor who had played opposite Grant in *North by Northwest* – James Mason. Cruelly good-looking *à la* Fleming's original, Mason was as chilling and charming as the British cinema had ever got. Smoky with suggestion, his voice – Oxbridge hauteur laid over north country flat – remains one of the most distinguished the movies have ever had, and he looked as good in a suit as anyone ever has. But like all the actors mentioned so far, Mason was rather too old for the part. He was 52 even as Broccoli and Saltzman's search for a Bond began, would have been well into his fifty-third year by the time their projected movie came out, and nearing 60 by the end of the five-picture contract they had in mind for whomever they eventually signed up.

All of which said, there is no reason to believe that any of these actors – Grant, Redgrave, Howard, Harrison, Niven, Mason – would have agreed to play Bond. For the key point about all these men is that by the early sixties they were established stars – in one or two cases, indeed, established *actors*. As such, they were unlikely to handcuff themselves to a series, especially considering the peanuts Saltzman and Broccoli were offering for what the man eventually cast as Dr No – that stately Method actor Joseph Wiseman – took to calling 'just another Grade-B Charlie Chan mystery'.[2]

For *Dr No*'s budget was not a grand one. At just over $1 million* (then worth somewhere in the region of £350,000), the movie was set to cost a mere sixth of what had been spent on the picture Connery had recently turned down – Anthony Mann's *El Cid*. To clarify further: three years after the making of *North by Northwest* – the film that had in many ways engendered the idea of a cinematic

---

* Incidentally, the same amount of money Dr No tells Bond it cost to have installed in his underwater hideout the inches-thick plate glass through which he watches the creatures of the sea.

Bond – *Dr No* was set to come in at little more than a quarter of the budget Alfred Hitchcock had been allotted.[3]

In other words, all this talk of big-name stars was just that – talk: talk designed to make the idea of James Bond in the movies the subject of further talk. Indeed, a wise-after-the-event Broccoli would always subsequently claim he had been adamant that the part of Bond required 'an unknown actor, not a star'.[4] A nicely mealy-mouthed way of saying that what the part of Bond required was someone prepared to work for not very much money.

Hence the only three names that really counted in the search: Patrick McGoohan (the broodingly suggestive Celt who had played opposite Connery in *Hell Drivers* and had more recently made a name for himself on TV in *Danger Man*; but, having qualms about what he saw as Bond's amoral ways, he felt obliged to say no); Roger Moore (an affably light comedian who had also recently made a name for himself on TV in *The Saint* – and whose contractual commitments to that show rendered him unavailable for *Dr No*'s lengthy shoot); and Sean Connery. All three of these men were in their early thirties – the right age for Fleming's hero. More importantly, while all three of them had been around for a few years, moving slowly up the cast-lists of the pictures or TV shows they found themselves in, none had appeared in anything like a major production, much less taken top billing anywhere. Each of them, in other words, could be had on the cheap.

Who decided on Connery as Bond? The likelihood is we will never really know. Over the years, pretty well everyone involved in the picture save Ian Fleming has claimed to have had some say in his being cast. But simply because he would go on to direct the only Bond movie of any distinction, *On Her Majesty's Secret Service* (1969) – constructing in the process a more than passable performance from the not at all actorly George Lazenby – Peter Hunt, *Dr No*'s editor, is the man I am most minded to credit with bringing Connery to the project. Hunt had recently done the cutting and splicing on *On the Fiddle* and, much taken with the insouciant comic timing of its leading man, had urged Harry Saltzman to check the picture out.

This Saltzman did, although all his life he would remain adamant that the actor who played Bond mattered little in the scheme of things. What mattered was the character of Bond himself. He was what audiences fantasised about, Saltzman said. Like Tarzan or Sherlock Holmes, it followed, anyone could play him. In this view, *Dr No*'s director Terence Young would remember, Saltzman had the backing of Ian Fleming. Despite his protestations about David Niven and Cary Grant, Fleming was most taken with the idea of an unknown actor incarnating his hero. That way the movies could be sold as 'Ian Fleming's James Bond, played by Norman Nobody' rather than 'Sid Somebody IS James Bond' (the poster-line formula that would eventually accrete around Connery's name).

Cubby Broccoli, meanwhile, maintained that throughout all his discussions with Saltzman about who would make the perfect James Bond, 'one face kept coming back into my mind. It belonged to an actor I had met briefly a year before in London. He was Sean Connery.'[5] More 20–20 hindsight, I'm afraid. Though Broccoli claims in his autobiography to have been knocked out by what he calls Connery's 'animal virility', Terence Young has remembered that Broccoli's first reaction to Connery was that 'he look[ed] like a bricklayer'.[6] As we have seen, it was only after Dana Broccoli chanced, very late in the day, to see a reel or two of *Darby O'Gill and the Little People* and told her husband that Connery was to die for that he began to wonder about using him for Bond.

At least initially, Young himself had other ideas, too, petitioning for a television actor named Richard Johnson to be given the part of Bond. When, however, it became clear to Young that Connery was seriously in the running for *Dr No*, he thought enough of the young pup he remembered from the *Action of the Tiger* shoot to offer him some advice for the meeting Saltzman and Broccoli had invited him to. 'I knew how he dressed,' Young remembered in the eighties, '[so] I said, "Sean, come wearing a suit." He came without a tie on and wearing a sort of lumber jacket.'[7]

In fact, Connery seems to have approached the interview almost like a Method actor approaching a role. Those scruffy, unpressed clothes, the unadulterated Scots burr, they might have been put on in order to goad the producers into telling him he wasn't quite what they were looking for. That way, Connery could slam their desk with the palm of his hand and tell them that they either took him as he was or they didn't take him at all. Was he acting up, or was he just acting? Certainly, he had planned the whole thing out. 'I shall establish myself on Overpowering,' he told Yat Malmgren a few days before the meeting, 'and take the interview like that. That would be a good thing, don't you think, sir?'[8] Indeed Malmgren did, adding that Connery ought to be 'think[ing] about cat animals' during the proceedings because 'they are very loose'.[9] 'I think he walked into that audition very self-assured, very large, very secure,'[10] Malmgren would say years later. Or, as Connery himself would put it: 'I put on a bit of an act, and it paid off.'[11]

In putting on that act, Connery was giving Saltzman and Broccoli all they needed to know about how he'd play Bond – with macho, devil-may-care menace backed up by a Brando-style sense of relaxed rebellion. Indeed, the casting interview sounds like nothing so much as that Bond movie staple – the meeting 'twixt our surly, mocking, ironic hero and Bernard Lee's irascible M. As Harry Saltzman would recall: 'We spoke to him and saw that he had the masculinity the part needed. Whenever he wanted to make a point, he'd bang his fist on the table, the desk, or his thigh, and we knew this guy had something.'[12]

And so, after he left their West End offices, Connery's prospective producers went to the window and looked down as he crossed the road to where he had parked Diane Cilento's sexless little Fiat. 'He's got balls,' Saltzman said.[13] 'In 30 minutes he sold us both,' Broccoli would remember. 'It was the sheer self-confidence he exuded. I've never seen a surer guy . . . It wasn't just an act, either. When he left we watched him through the window as he walked down the street. He walked like the most arrogant son–of–a–gun you've ever seen – as if he owned every bit of Jermyn Street from Regent Street to St James's. "That's our Bond," I said.'[14]

Or was he? Over in New York, United Artists, who were backing Broccoli and Saltzman, insisted that screen tests would have to be made. Connery protested, arguing that the brief snippets he would be asked to read through would give him no chance of imbuing the character of Bond with the flip humour he believed necessary. 'How could I get over in a few moments the comedy I knew to be essential?' he would rhetorise a couple of years later. 'I knew the thing couldn't be taken seriously and got the script worked around that way.'[15] It was a fair point, though one that managed to elide Connery's fears about his less than scorching track record in America. Lana Turner, Walt Disney, Tarzan: all had taken him to Hollywood; all, he could have been forgiven for thinking, had let him down. And indeed, his worries turned out to be well founded. As we have seen, New York's response to his screen tests was subdued, to say the least. Nonetheless, a couple of months later, on 3 November 1961, United Artists announced that Sean Connery was to be their James Bond.

Which is not to say that that famous memo was wrong. In many ways, Broccoli and Saltzman *could* have done better. To say that the lumberjack-shirted, tatty-trousered Sean Connery was nothing like the Bond of Ian Fleming's original novels is to state the most banal truism. (Once Connery was signed up, the decidedly dandyish Terence Young became a Method director, dragging his young charge around the bespoke outfitters of Mayfair and St James's and kitting him out in high style. Young even claimed that he ordered Connery to sleep in one of his new Savile Row suits, so that he might get a feel for what it is like to be beautifully dressed. 'I had a very clear idea of what an old Etonian should be,' Young remembered, years later. 'I was a Guards officer during the war, and I thought I knew how Bond should behave. So I took Sean to my shirtmaker, my tailor and my shoemaker, and we [fitted] him out.')[16]

Even more importantly, though, Connery was nothing like the Bond so plainly envisaged in the *Dr No* screenplay. That screenplay, finally knocked together by Young and his assistant Joanna Harwood in a week-long session at the Dorchester Hotel, was written for precisely the kind of old-fashioned public-school hero Connery's instinctively insolent creation was about to do away with. Early on in the movie, in fact, just such an (uncredited) haw-hawing bore turns up at Les Ambassadeurs gaming club and asks to see 'Mr Janes Born' in old Etonian tones so piping and strangulated that not even Peter Sellers could have come up with them.

The real joke, though, is that the dialogue Young and Harwood give Mr Janes Born himself is not very different from that given to this old-school caricature. 'But of course!' Connery's Bond is required to say at one point in the action (as he will be throughout his pictures in the series; Roger Moore – on whom such stuffed-shirt inanities might have sat rather better – was never asked to utter the line). Hitherto, such stockbroker Sheridan would have been sayable only if dressed in the exclamatory high camp British cinema specialised in. Connery, though, played the line for laughs by uttering it in the mocking, unshockable, dignified yet dressed-down drawl that would come to be one of the hallmarks of his Bond. It is impossible to overemphasise how central to the movie those democratically satirical inflections were. Without them, the Bond of *Dr No* would have been as insufferably snobbish as the Bond of Fleming's original novels. Without them, there would have been no *From Russia with Love*, let alone any *Quantum of Solace*.

Which is a way of saying that all the claims about the template for the cinema's James Bond being Terence Young himself are slightly wide of the mark. To be sure, Young, an Old Harrovian aesthete with a taste for the finer things in life, had much in common with the Bond of Ian Fleming's original novels. But the movie Bond owed as much and more to Connery's languorously insurrectionary take on what he saw as this jumped-up imperialist bore.

Both Young and Connery have claimed authorship for the movie Bond's flip, amoral humour. 'When I flew out [to Jamaica] with Sean, before anyone else came,' Young told a TV documentary, 'I said, "For Christ's sake, Sean, we've got to make this picture a little bit amusing – it's the only way we're going to get away with murder." Because a lot of the . . . sex and violence, I think, (a), they're objectionable and, (b), we'll never get them past the censor.'[17]

Connery, for his part, was always insistent that humour was essential to the movie Bond. Indeed so, though it should be pointed out that humour was about as essential to the Fleming Bond as a light ale and a roll-up. The Bond of the novels never cracks a joke, and Fleming himself was so humourless that fancy the idea of Alfred Hitchcock turning his novels into movies though he did, he also worried that Hitch might treat them with insufficient seriousness. Advised by a friend keen on growing the Bond business into the cinema to see *North by Northwest*, Fleming subsequently pronounced himself baffled as to why 'the master of suspense, having got us on the edge of our chairs', derailed his thriller by making 'us dissolve in screams of laughter . . . while the mixture is delightful, he really does throw away the most wonderful plot. We need a few touches of comedy but, unless we treat this story with an absolute straight face and with a desperate sense of urgency, the film will collapse. Personally, I'm for keeping the jokes to a minimum and getting people really sweating.'[18] Note to Mr Fleming: *North by Northwest* was from the off conceived as a comedy, as the casting of Cary Grant ought perhaps have alerted you.

So yes, perhaps the humour did originate with Connery's chippy insolence. Still, when first interviewed by Saltzman and Broccoli, he had been asked whether he was really interested in playing a character like Bond. Hadn't he just spent the past five years or so working his way through chunks of the classical repertoire on stage? Connery defended himself by saying that he had merely gone where the work had taken him. There was, to be sure, something to this line of argument though it is also true that the move towards more serious stage work had followed both his meeting Diane Cilento and the disaster that had been *Another Time, Another Place*.

The key point, though, is that Saltzman and Broccoli were plainly sufficiently clued up about the light touch they thought their movie Bond would need to have wondered whether a classical wannabe like Connery could ever summon the requisite humour for a hero even Fleming in one of his less solemn moments had dismissed as a 'cardboard booby'. And on the evidence of a scene early on in *Dr No*, when, rather than talk, one of the villain's ill-shaven heavies suicides in Bond's arms, the producers were justified in their fears. Connery reacts to this untimely death with smouldering repugnance, as if he were playing Horatio in the closing moments of *Hamlet*: a sweet prince's noble heart has cracked, and as Connery eases his form to the ground flights of angels sing him to his rest. Like all the location work in Jamaica, that scene was shot early on in the production, when Connery was still struggling to find his stride. Only as the shoot returned home to Pinewood Studios did he relax enough to let his ironic instincts come to the fore.

Young, on the other hand, directs with a deft comic touch from the off. How else but by laughing can one react to his calculatedly slow build-up to the introduction of the screen's James Bond? First we get a close up of Bond's dinner-jacketed shoulder, then of his back, then his shirt cuff, his hand, his cigarette case, his lighter (the cuts from close-up to close-up a nicely proleptic summary of the commodity fetishism the Bond movies would make their own, as well as a reminder that Fleming himself once disarmingly confessed to not having created a character so much as a tailor's dummy on which his readers could hang their fantasies). Only then are we allowed a shot of Bond himself, Young's camera following the hand and lighter up to his mouth, holding tight on them as they torch a cigarette and then pulling back to give us our first sight of Connery as he drones drily what was to become the series' most immortal line: 'Bond. James Bond.'

Young was always honest about having based this scene on the one in William Dieterle's *Juarez* (1939), in which Paul Muni's titular character is introduced in exactly the same manner. The difference is that Dieterle was teasing his audience by delaying the first appearance of an actor many of its number had paid good money to see. Young, on the other hand, was pump-priming the first appearance of an actor nobody had heard of playing a character many of them knew back to front.

It worked, too. When Young's camera finally does give us a view of Connery, his mouth half-twisted in its habitual Edinburgh slur (there is something of Elvis Presley in its asymmetric impudence) as he lights a cigarette, it is of a man so assured of his gorgeousness that almost half a century on it still takes your breath away. When, moments later, Bond waves his cigarette hand nonchalantly in the air as he says he has 'no objections' to the stakes being raised in the game of *chemin de fer* he is playing, he looks like a man who has never had to object to anything in his life simply because everyone is always willing to do things the way he wants them done.

They say that if you want to be a star you have to act like one, and despite Connery's doubts about the picture he had got himself involved in, he and Young were going to put the theory to the test. They did so largely by abandoning the screen-acting tradition of which Muni had been one of the last examples. Muni, who was born into a theatrical family, came to the movies blithely unaware of how radically different the medium was from that which he had grown up with. The big gestures and gurning faces of the stage were utterly unsuited to the chamber-piece qualities of even the biggest movie. Muni never grasped the fact, but there is no need to act to the back row when the back row, just like the front row, is looking at a 40-foot-high picture of your face.

One of the things that had recommended Connery to Alvin Rakoff five years earlier was what the director called his 'stillness',[19] his ability to hold back while also holding the attention of whomever was in his presence. At a very basic level that is a definition of the screen actor's trade. What really marked Connery out, though, was that that stillness could coexist with the dynamic tensions he brought to even the tiniest gesture. 'The difference with this guy,' Broccoli would tell an interviewer a couple of years later, 'is the difference between a still photograph and film. When he starts to move, he comes alive.'[20] (I know of no photograph of Connery, incidentally, that has ever truly captured his fatal elegance.)

Connery's silky mobility could animate the dullest of scenes. Witness in *Dr No* Bond's padding around his hotel room on his first night in Jamaica – stretching upwards from the balls of his feet to peer out of a window like a dancer at full height, dipping gracefully down to his knees like a dying swan to booby-trap a wardrobe door. It was for such seemingly insignificant moments that Connery came to be worshipped by a zillion men around the world. The men who had wanted to be Ian Fleming's James Bond hadn't really wanted much more than to know their way around a menu and a wine list. Connery's Bond mocked and deflated such social-climbing antics while appealing to the human instinct for grace that men had hitherto been able to allow themselves – and even then only surreptitiously – at fights and football matches. Connery's Bond moved almost as well as Fred Astaire, but the context in which he did so – the context of Ken Adam's gleaming, hard-edged sets and John Barry's pulsing, dissonant, brassy jazz scores – was so thoroughly heterosexual that he became balletic only when you sat back and thought about it.

Earlier generations of British actors had never been able to move like this. Laurence Olivier's famed physicality was never less than dreamy, but it was never less than androgynous either. As Guy Burgess (Alan Bates) says of Laertes (an actor we never see) in Alan Bennett's *An Englishman Abroad* (1983), 'He goes well in tights.' Olivier went well in tights, too. But while in many ways he looked the part of Ian Fleming's original, an Olivier-style Bond would have been almost as camp as John Gielgud's Ashenden in Hitchcock's *Secret Agent* (1936). True, the blue satin and soft leather shoulder holster the Bond of *Dr No* wears is a fetishist's delight, but on Connery it suggests neither a hidden taste for bondage nor for cross-dressing lingerie — as it might have done on Olivier, and absolutely would have done on Dirk Bogarde.*

And camp would have cut away Connery's Bond's only real claim to seriousness — the violence bubbling just beneath the surface of his dandyish hi-jinks. 'The proper sadist,' Connery had told the journalist Susan Barnes (now Susan Crosland) mere days before shooting on *Dr No* began, 'is always partly aware of what he's doing. He is never completely passionate. His mind is always working.'[21] Connery's mind was working there, too, of course, bent as he was (for just about the only time in his career) on giving an interviewer good copy. But that interview also served notice of Connery's intention of playing Bond as a proper sadist — the kind of man who can make the sound of a camera-strap being tugged forcibly from a phoney photographer's neck like that of a whip being viciously cracked.

So it is that when he finds Eunice Gayson's Sylvia Trench playing golf half-undressed in his living room, Bond (who has entered the apartment wearing a frock-coat that makes him look very Heathcliff with a haircut) doesn't just take the golf club from her before taking the poor thing herself. Rather, he takes the club from her and holds it behind her waist, a hand at each end, the better to tug her toward him as he moves in for a violent, devouring kiss. Read Ian Fleming and it quickly becomes clear that he got his kicks not from describing his hero's bedroom action (the sex scenes are chastely romanticised fluff) but from itemising the violations his body suffers at the hands of the villain. By contrast, the Bond movies (at least until recently) have no interest in making us share their

---

* Intriguing to note that while Connery sports chamois leather atop his hand-cut shirt, Jack Lord's Felix Leiter wears a sleeveless vest under his polyester off-the-peg number. In the world of early Bond, Americans lack not only class and taste, but sex appeal too.

hero's sufferings. Whatever tortures he endures, Connery's Bond always comes out of them unscathed. Not, it needs stressing, that the sado-masochist heartbeat of Fleming's prose has been stopped in the movies. Rather, it has been transplanted into Bond's every encounter with the opposite sex. Terence Young and Peter Hunt jump cut from Bond's manhandling of Sylvia Trench with that golf club to his flight landing in Jamaica. But while we don't see what ensued in Bond's bedroom, we have, thanks to his repeated threats to take Lois Maxwell's prim Miss Moneypenny over his knee, a pretty good idea.

Later on in the movie, Miss Taro (Zena Marshall), wearing only a silken dressing gown and a towel round her neck, welcomes Bond into her hilltop apartment. As she turns away from him saying something about drying her hair, Bond grabs the towel and uses it to pull her towards him for another in the movie's series of savage kisses. Eventually he releases her, but holds on to one end of the towel so that as she turns round and walks towards the bedroom it slips from her shoulder – at which point Bond raises it to his face and sniffs it: a wild animal scenting its capture. Pity poor Miss Taro, because moments later the animal is toying with its victim: having had his wicked way with her, Bond sends the poor girl off with the police, pushing her head down into their car with sadistic glee.

Little wonder Young's camera lingers so lovingly on Connery's broad, pelted torso – a pelt altogether more coiffed than in his earlier pictures. Hitherto, Connery's chest hair had been as all-over as the paint in a Jackson Pollock. From *Dr No* on it would be an altogether more structured affair, squared off below his pectorals, but with a thin line arrowing down to his navel and pointing beyond, like the zip in a Barnett Newman. 'Sex without affection puts you in the animal category,' Connery once said.[22] It was an insight he put to good use in the construction of the affection-free Bond audiences held so dear. Cradling his conquests in his arms, Connery is careful never to let Bond's hands rest on female flesh.

Instead, they dangle claw-like in the air, in readiness to swat away their prey after they have given of their pleasure.

If such carnal brutishness had its roots in the Brando of *A Streetcar Named Desire* (as, surely, does the inexplicably tattered T-shirt Connery wears during *Dr No*'s torture scene), it recalled, too, the seductive sadism of Christopher Lee's Count Dracula in the then ongoing Hammer horror series of pictures. Whatever else those movies are about, they are about the expression of hitherto unmentionable desires – chief among them the unmentionable desires of women. For the past few years, that is, the British cinema had been moving towards an accommodation with the more somatic urges of its prospective clientele. For all the emphasis on screams and scars in the titles of Hammer's movies, what stays with you when you watch them are the close-ups of the women as Dracula has his wicked way with them: far from fighting him off, they're revelling in his attentions. For such sins, of course, these women were punished by their transformation into vampires – and at the end of the pictures Dracula himself was always dispatched to yet another gruesome death. Not so Connery's Bond, whose every lascivious urge audiences not only didn't disapprove of but actively cheered on.

And what went for sex went for death, too. Olivier's Richard III had dispatched his victims with gay abandon, Lee's Dracula with venal lustiness, but neither could have pumped six bullets into Anthony Dawson's treacherous Professor Dent with the detached, scornful calm Connery's Bond brought to the task. The British tradition of murder had been either screamingly histrionic or low-rent nasty. But when Connery's Bond killed people he did so with a kind of resigned contempt. Murderous ennui has been a movie cliché ever since, but it was one minted by Connery.

While patriotic to the point of self-mockery, Connery's Bond seemed not at all tied to notions of history and tradition, but merely to the self-aggrandising conspicuous consumption that was the true hallmark of the decade which spawned him. Bond's affectlessness

– when he learns the detail of Dr No's plans he neither laughs nor cries but merely sounds weary at what he calls 'the same old dream: world domination' – chimed with a post-Suez British public wary of imperial overreach. Hence the movie's pop art elements, which tipped the wink to the audience that they weren't meant to take this stuff seriously. Everything they were watching, Connery's sly, sideways-on performance kept reminding them, was all part of a big joke.*

Not, for all its self-consciously modernist game-playing, that the performance was faultless. While the voice Connery found for Bond was a masterpiece of classy classlessness – pitched low and guttural yet eerily precise in its enunciation, it was surely an attempt at sounding like both James Mason and Richard Burton – his handling of dialogue in *Dr No* can be quite as woeful as it had been in his earlier pictures. He is still emphasising words and even whole phrases uneasily ('Do you play any other games?' he asks Miss Trench at the end of the movie's opening scene, 'I MEAN besides *cheMIN DE fer*'), with no sense of their relative dramatic importance, and he is singularly ill-at-ease whenever Bond is called upon to get priggish or moralistic. It is true that in essence the script gives Bond little to say beyond the baldest expository points. Still, there is enough evidence in the movie to suggest that the fears of those American executives who had difficulties with the idea of Connery as a potential star were not groundless.

Then again, the man himself held out no great hopes for *Dr No*. 'Oh, it'll just be another job,' Connery had told fellow actor

---

* Nobody saw this more clearly than François Truffaut. 'For me,' the director told an auteurist worshipper, 'the film that marks the beginning of the period of decadence in the cinema is the first James Bond – *Dr No*. Until then the role of the cinema had been by and large to tell a story in the hope that the audience would believe it. There had been a few minority films which were parodies of this narrative tradition, but in the main a film told a story and the audience wanted to believe that story.' Don Allen interviewing Truffaut, *Sight and Sound*, Autumn 1979.

Anthony Newley* shortly before filming began. 'Then I'll be waiting for the phone to ring as usual.'²³ And surely nobody who was confident about his cinematic future would have been in talks with Michael Winner about appearing in his next picture, *West 11*.²⁴ Nor would an actor who thought he was about to become a star have signed up for a three-month stint as the token muscle in Christopher Fry's translation of Giraudoux's *Judith* within days of the *Dr No* wrap.²⁵

Cast as Holofernes in the play, Connery had few lines and fewer clothes. He spent his time on the stage of Her Majesty's Theatre in a loincloth that might have been stolen from the set of *Tarzan's Greatest Adventure*. (He would wear a mighty similar outfit, a decade and more later, in John Boorman's *Zardoz*.) One anonymous reviewer pronounced himself so unmoved by Harold Clurman's production that all through it he kept recalling how little he had thought of Connery's performance in *Requiem for a Heavyweight* five years previous.²⁶ *The Times*'s similarly anonymous critic, meanwhile, thought Connery played the part 'with a stolid narcissism rather too crude for the vision of pagan freedom against which Jehovah's discipline loses its power',²⁷ which may or may not have been the case, but tells us everything we need to know about why Connery was cast: his rippling sexuality.

It is a mark of how low down the pecking order Connery still was that no picture of him appears in the programme for the show. (It does manage to find room for likenesses of Michael Gough and a very young Barry Foster.) And yet the pictures we have of Connery's near-naked Holofernes are remarkable for their satanic sensuousness. Certainly they fully endorse Robert Henderson's oft-made claim that 'never before . . . had the legitimate stage seen such remarkably graceful masculine physical beauty'.²⁸ On the other hand, the show's opening date of 20 June 1962 rather gives the lie to Henderson's concomitant belief that 'out of that came

---

* Who would, in a year or so's time, help pen the lyric to 'Goldfinger'.

84

Bond'.[29] Truer to say that out of Bond came Connery's Holofernes: so uncertain was he of *Dr No*'s prospects that he remained an actor who would apparently accept any role provided the pay was right.

Sure enough, when a few weeks later *Dr No* was released, the reviewers were no more bowled over than they had been by *Judith*. 'Perhaps,' wrote another of *The Times*'s anonymous critics, 'Mr Sean Connery will, with practice get the "feel" of the part a little more surely than he does here.'[30] 'Well,' a corporate honcho in America told Harry Saltzman after a private preview screening of the picture, 'all we can lose is $950,000.'[31] United Artists money man Ilya Lopert, meanwhile, counselled Bond's producer that the movie 'simply won't work in America, Connery will never go over'.[32] Hence when *Dr No* did finally open in the USA, in May 1963, seven months and more after its debut in the UK, it did so not in New York but at the drive-ins of Texas and Oklahoma. United Artists, Cubby Broccoli was to recall, 'expressed some doubt that they could sell a picture in the major US cities with a "Limey truck driver playing the lead"'.[33]

Hardly surprising, then, that Shelley Winters, who attended the first US press showing of *Dr No* with Connery in early 1963, would remember how, though she was bowled over by the picture, its leading man was somewhat less than enamoured of it. After the screening, Connery insisted the two of them dine at Schwab's drugstore, arguing that nobody was likely to come looking for him there. 'He was very nervous about the film,' Winters would recall. 'In fact, he hated it.' *Dr No* was, he told her, 'glitzy, mannered and dangerous'. So much so, apparently, that he wanted nothing more to do with the series Saltzman and Broccoli were now certain they were going to produce. 'Sean,' said the admirably down-to-earth Winters, 'if you truly don't want to do any more Bond pictures, just ask for some outrageous sum like a million dollars a picture for three pictures.'[34] Sage advice, as things were to turn out.

On the other hand, Connery's lack of confidence in the movie remains easy to understand. Certainly, his performance as Bond having gone over no better than his performance in *Judith*, he can be forgiven for wondering whether the £6,000 he had been paid for *Dr No* might be the biggest money he would ever see.* Like any canny man then or since, he decided to invest in property. For the now-amazing sum of £9,000 he bought a five-bedroom villa – once home to a convent of nuns – in the less than trendy west London area of Acton, and set about convincing Diane Cilento it was time she married him.

* Over the years various figures have been quoted, but Connery himself told Gloria Hunniford around the time of *Never Say Never Again* (1983) that 'I think I got £6,000'. (*Sean Connery talks to Gloria Hunniford*, ITV, 6 January 1984.) On the 'Inside *Dr No*' DVD documentary, associate producer Stanley Sopel says Connery was also paid location expenses of £25 a week. Incidentally, those other prospective Bonds, Richard Burton and Rex Harrison, had just signed to do *Cleopatra* (1963) for, respectively, $250,000 and $300,000.

5

Behind the Mask

Connery's proposal of marriage didn't come out of the blue. For one thing, though he and Cilento's relationship had hardly been marked out by its exclusivity, it had by now gone on more than five years. For another, since early April, Cilento had been pregnant with Connery's child. (Take a close look at her as Molly Seagrim in Tony Richardson's *Tom Jones*, which was filmed in the late summer and early autumn of 1962, and it's clear that Albert Finney's titular lead has every right to fear she is carrying his child.)

Even now, though, with Connery and Cilento 'melded together as an alloy',[1] Cilento was not sure she wanted to marry again. Instead, she proposed that they live together in 'a largish house in an inexpensive area of London . . . in a sort of loose community of artists'. In this commune – which sounds uncannily like the Acacia House Connery had just put his money into in Acton – 'we would live together and bring up the children but not impinge on each other's lives', a well-to-do Iris Murdoch-style fantasy several years ahead of its time.

For all these proto-hippy dreams, Cilento likely had other qualms about the wisdom of marrying Connery. While such a union made perfect practical sense for him, she would have had grounds for believing there would be rather less in it for her. For one thing, there was the memory of her failed first marriage. For another, her star was still emphatically on the rise. Despite having been paid only £1,500 or so for *Tom Jones*[2] (as we have seen, a quarter of the money Connery had been paid for *Dr No*), Cilento could at the time have been forgiven for thinking that hers was the career that was going places. Wasn't she the one who had been working with Tony Richardson – the hot and happening maestro behind such zeitgeist-defining pictures as *A Taste of Honey* (1961) and *The Loneliness of the Long Distance Runner* (1962)? Wasn't she the one from whom the Royal Court had just commissioned a new translation of Pirandello's *Rules of the Game*?[3] And as if all that weren't enough, she had as little faith in *Dr No*'s being a success as Connery had.

Nonetheless, as the pregnancy progressed and the birth loomed, she came round to Connery's proposal. On 29 November 1962, two months after the opening of the Bond movie, and only one month after the annulment of her marriage to Volpe, Cilento and Connery were married in something like secrecy in, of all places, Gibraltar. It wasn't until two days later that the news broke at home. The *Daily Telegraph* ran a one-column brief headlined 'Diane Cilento marries'.[4] Not, be it noted, 'Sean Connery marries' or even 'James Bond marries'. So much for what Cilento would come to call the overnight success and 'worldwide acclamation' of *Dr No*.[5]

By early February, mere weeks after Cilento had given birth to their son, Jason (on 11 January), Connery was back on set for the second Bond movie. Though *Dr No* had yet to be released in America, United Artists were pleased enough with its performance in Europe to have doubled its budget on *From Russia with Love* (1963). Connery's salary take, meanwhile, had more than tripled, to some £20,000 plus £65 a week expenses. Big money, to be sure, but as we have seen, nothing like the sums the properly established stars of the time were commanding.

For all that, the movie kicks off with an audacious send-up of Connery's Bond's starry status – a night-time sequence set in an ornate, statuary-strewn garden in which 007 is killed off by Red Grant (Robert Shaw) before the credits have even rolled.* Except, of course, he isn't. As the camera closes in on the dead man, we see that it isn't Bond at all. It's some poor sucker wearing a rubber mask that makes him look like Sean Connery. In cinemas the scene always gets a big laugh — but the laugh is of the uneasy variety, the kind that more usually accompanies the spookier moments of a horror movie. That's because this is a moment that both endorses the newfound celebrity of Connery's Bond (what possible practical purpose can be served by having agents dress themselves as 007 in order to have other agents practise their killing techniques?), and threatens to end it by suggesting that he can always be replaced with a rubber-faced lookalike.

Then again, the whole plot of *From Russia with Love* is premised on the starry nature of Connery's Bond post-*Dr No*. SPECTRE, the shady Eastern-bloc gangster outfit Dr No had been working for, want revenge for the death of their man and are determined to kill Bond in return. But they intend to do so in such a way as to compromise his reputation as an upstanding representative of Her Majesty's Secret Service. Clearly apprised of all that had recently been going on in London (namely, that Secretary of State for War John Profumo had admitted to the House of Commons that he had been sleeping with a prostitute who also numbered among her clients one Yevgeny Ivanov, a senior attaché at the Soviet Embassy), they intend to have agent 007 caught *in flagrante* with a Russian agent. Right from the off, then, the picture treats Connery's Bond as an emblem of Britishness, a secret agent so well known that he is more like a matinee idol, a movie star. 'I suppose,' Bernard Lee's M half scoffs, 'girls do fall in love with men from a photograph'.

Hence, as they are with all big stars, the audience is made to wait for the man in the photograph's appearance. In Fleming's original novel Bond doesn't make an entrance until almost halfway through

---

* Terence Young, back at the helm, has laughably claimed he modelled the scene on those of Alain Resnais's rather more stately — some might say statuesque — *L'Année dernière à Marienbad* (1961). See James Chapman, *Licence to Thrill: A Cultural History of the James Bond Films* (I. B. Tauris, 2007), p. 76.

proceedings. The movie version doesn't go quite that far, but it teases things out nonetheless. If the build-up to Bond's appearance in *Dr No* had been delayed by that series of fetishistic close-ups of his accoutrement, here the agony is prolonged a whole seventeen minutes, so that the picture is a full sixth over before anyone gets to see the man they have paid over their money for.

This is all, it should be said, canny gamesmanship on the part of Saltzman and Broccoli. The producers had chosen to film *From Russia with Love* – in the Fleming canon, the novel that *precedes Dr No* – in a bid to break the American market that looked like being so singularly unswayed by their first Bond outing. Why *From Russia with Love*? Because a couple of years earlier, in March 1961, America's then very glamorous President John F. Kennedy had placed the novel at number nine in his top-ten favourite reads list for *Life* magazine. And what was good enough for Kennedy was good enough for Americans as a whole – because it was only after that announcement that Fleming's novels began to sell big-time in the States.

For all that, Connery takes even greater pains in his second outing as Bond to sound rather more like the gentlemanly heroes of English cinema than he had in his first. 'Everybody knows,' Edwin Muir once claimed, 'that the Scotsman who tries to be English takes on the worst English qualities and exaggerates them to caricature'.[6] Certainly, Connery does so here. During moments of comic seduction with Daniela Bianchi's Tatiana Romanova he stretches vowel sounds with an ironic, throaty drawl that sounds here like the baritone rumble of George Sanders, there like the nasal haughtiness of Richard Burton. Called upon to utter the dread line 'Most inconsiderate,' Connery does so with a deflationary élan that tells you that, for all Bond's taste and tailoring (Broccoli and Saltzman had considerably upped the budget on Bond's clothes for *From Russia with Love*, granting the spending of £1,000 on his shirts and suits), he really has no time for this old-world stuff. It's as if Connery has come to see the part he has been called upon to play as his chance to kick back at the stuffed-shirt strictures of a culture he instinctively mistrusts.

As early as the press interviews for *Dr No* Connery had signalled that he had little time for the cruelty that underlay so many of Bond's appetites. 'He's a man who makes his own rules,' he said at the time of *Dr No*'s release, 'and that's fine as long as you're not plagued with doubts. But if you are – and most of us are – you're sunk. Women . . . by their nature, are indecisive – Shall-I-wear-this? Shall-I-do-that? – so a man who is absolutely sure of everything comes as a godsend.'[7] Unluckily for him, nobody was listening. So closely would Connery come to be identified with Bond that, despite the liberal instincts he discoursed on in interview after interview, the reactionary mud stuck. Over the years he would pay heavily for this character-conflation. Even this early into proceedings, though, Connery seems to have sensed something was awry. As the *From Russia with Love* shoot moved back to England after two months on location in Turkey, he was to be heard telling *Time* magazine he would play Bond for no more than seven years.[8]

Hence, during the closing weeks of the shoot (on location around Lochgilphead in Scotland – 'the first time I've managed to get home in more than a year', Connery told an interviewer[9]), he signed up, script unseen, for Basil Dearden's next picture. The movie was called *Woman of Straw* (1964), and Connery would later say that the prospect of working with his co-stars had been enough to get him on board. Gina Lollobrigida was to be his leading lady, while Connery's uncle cum employer was to be played by Ralph Richardson, an actor he had long admired. 'An audience is never safe with him,' Connery would say of the twentieth century's greatest Falstaff. 'You don't know what he's going to do next.'[10]

Connery was impressed, too, with Dearden's reputation as a safe pair of cinematic hands. Certainly *Woman of Straw* was shot with all Dearden's customary efficiency, in a matter of weeks – after spending the bulk of August 1963 at Pinewood, the production moved to

Majorca in September for a fortnight's location work. Connery, who would come to resent the ever-lengthening shoots the Bond films required (*From Russia with Love* had taken sixteen weeks, significantly longer than the time spent on *Dr No*), was cheered by such professionalism. Alas, he was thoroughly disappointed with the finished movie, especially after the critics pounced on it.

The consensus on Connery's work in *Woman of Straw* boiled down to two very similarly flavoured stocks. There were those critics who felt that Connery's performance argued for a limited range and that he'd better get back to doing what he did best. And there were those who credited him with a little more nous by arguing that the Connery of Dearden's picture looked like a man desperate to get back to what he knew he did best. Quite how much such comments were designed to hurt Connery it is hard to know. But hurt him they must have. 'I don't want to be Bond all the time,' he told a reporter in late 1963. 'It riles me when people call me Bond off the set . . . That's why I'm making pictures like *Woman of Straw*, in the hope audiences will accept me in other parts.'[11]

But even that early on in the Bond saga such hopes were pipe dreams at best. This was not, it should be said, because Connery wasn't actor enough to burst out of the 007 matrix. Rather, it was because no movie director in his right mind wanted to cast Connery for any other reason than the fact that having James Bond in his movie was bound to generate publicity and, with luck, money.

Moreover, movies are and have always been written – and emphatically *re*written – with specific actors in mind. Just as with the original Ian Fleming Bond books, the central character of Catherine Arley's pot-boiler novelette on which *Woman of Straw* is based bears little resemblance to Connery. But once Connery was on board, the script was rewritten *around* his presence – rewritten, in other words, to fit the actor who plays James Bond. Nowhere in the original novel will you find an exchange like this one between Lollobrigida and Connery:

MARIA MARCELLO: Do women always do what you want?
ANTHONY RICHMOND: Invariably.

Though you will find such exchanges – especially variants on that single adverbial response – in all the Connery Bond movies.

For all Connery's hopes, then, the part of Anthony Richmond, the weakling nephew cum secretary to Sir Ralph Richardson's irascible patriarch Sir Charles, turned out to be little more than a reflection of and comment upon the figure of Bond. Indeed, the movie tie-in paperback edition of the Arley novel trades on the Connery/Bond iconography. On its front cover is a picture of Connery in a white tuxedo, a Martini casually in hand; on the back is a picture of Connery in a black tuxedo lighting Lollobrigida's cigarette. Meeting Richmond in the movie proper, we are introduced to a man dressed exactly like the James Bond of *From Russia with Love*: light grey, narrow-lapelled suit; pale blue shirt; black, knitted tie (although, unlike Bond, Richmond favours a single rather than a double Windsor knot*).

What Dearden and his screenwriter, Robert Muller, have made of Arley's plot, moreover, is entirely premised on the steely, Bond-like chill of Connery's Richmond. All that is different is that this time round the steely chill is pressed into malignant service. Our anti-hero Anthony enlists the aid of Lollobrigida's Maria to knock off Sir Charles because the old man is keeping the younger ne'er-do-well from the family fortune. Moreover, it is difficult, after the examples of *Dr No* and *From Russia with Love*, not to read Richardson's Sir Charles as an older – and even more irate – version of Bernard Lee's M. The old man isn't at war with his nephew just because he is young, after all. He also hates the fact that he spends far too much time and money on clothes and manicures and

---

* Fleming aficionados will remember that in the original novel of *From Russia with Love* Bond twigs who the Russian heavy is thanks to his faux aristocratic habit of knotting his tie with a double Windsor. In the movie, the cad gives himself away by drinking red wine with fish.

haircuts – just the kind of decadences M is forever upbraiding 007 about. (A year later, Fleming himself would open his final Bond novel, *The Man with the Golden Gun*, with a scene in which his now much troubled hero attempts to enact an Oedipal revenge on the man he plainly conceives of as his monstrous father.)

As *Woman of Straw*'s troublesome patriarch, Richardson has a lot of fun, gurning and hamming and generally stirring things up with actorly mischief. Connery's performance is no less good, though he looks distinctly less comfortable in the giving of it, largely, one suspects, because he was so eager to impress Richardson. And so, by a quaint irony, the least convincing aspects of Connery's Anthony Richmond are those moments in which he is called upon to fawn uncomfortably around his uncle, the fawning seeming driven less by the narrative than by the actorly pressures of the world outside the movie script.

Elsewhere, though, he is on cracking form – literally so when he manhandles Lollobrigida's lingeried temptress before fetching her a good slap about the chops. Gossip columns at the time were full of rumours to the effect that Connery, less than impressed with La Lollo's talent and temperament, really had slapped her and she had ended up with a swollen lip.[12] And perhaps she did. But at worst, the incident was likely no more than an accident of the type that happens on movie sets, at best a stunt put together by a cunning press agent. Such stories are always useful when it comes to publicising a film, and the legend that had accreted around *Dr No* and *From Russia with Love* would have told the PR powers that be that one of the things people found most attractive about Connery's Bond was his passionate, animalistic violence.

On the other hand, it's possible that there might have been something to the rumours of on-set enmity between Dearden's two stars. Connery said that he had mistimed the slap, a claim that would have been rather more convincing had he ever mistimed a punch on the set of a Bond movie. Worse, in the build-up to the release of *Woman of Straw* he was to be found arguing that all that really mattered in acting was timing. It was, he said, 'very much like playing golf. It's a matter of timing, enjoying what you're doing and doing it in an easy way.'[13]

What matters about *Woman of Straw* is its commentary upon the character of Connery's Bond, its suggestive perception that the 007 figure is little more than a violent, sexual predator. There is a lovely scene in Dearden's movie when Richmond and Maria are interrupted during a furtive kiss and he is obliged to violently shove her away. The point is that it is the push that plays far more convincingly than the passion: Richmond seems to enjoy strong-arming Maria far more than he does pulling her near. With any other actor in the part (and certainly with the more chivalrous actors Dearden might have cast before the advent of Bond – Nigel Patrick, say, or Dirk Bogarde) the scene (and the movie) would have been ludicrous.

Nobody is arguing that *Woman of Straw* is at all realistic, but thanks to Connery's frosty charms it is earthed with a touch of something approximating realism. Quite simply, his casting changed the terms of the movie. It wouldn't be the same without him. *Woman of Straw* might not have done good box office, but it would have done no better with anyone else in the lead role. Moreover, as we shall see, it is a moot point whether anything Connery starred in away from Bond at that time would have done well financially. Audiences wanted to see him in one part and one part only.

As Connery himself noted just as the *Woman of Straw* shoot was coming to a close and as *From Russia with Love* was opening, he was already being talked to in public as if he were 007. 'When I walked into a Mayfair restaurant the other day and a waiter called me "Mr Bond",' he told one reporter, 'I almost had his head for hors d'oeuvres.'[14] It is true that this statement was made the week *From Russia with Love* went on general release (in those days, movies opened in major cities first before moving to the provinces), and may be another of those second-wind boosting stories dreamed up by PR agents. But it is also true that Connery sounded not at all disingenuous when he claimed to be already tiring of the part: 'One more Bond will be enough,' he said. 'I would hate to become identified with him completely.'[15]

So the call from Alfred Hitchcock came at a good time. Would Mr Connery, Hitchcock's agent Harry Friedman wanted to know, consider appearing in the master of suspense's next picture, *Marnie* (1964)? Of course, said Richard Hatton, but Mr Connery couldn't even begin to look at offers under $200,000. That's fine, said Friedman. At which point Hatton came back with a surprise late punch: Mr Connery would also need sight of the script before he could make a final decision.

What was shocking about this insistence, as Hitchcock himself later joked, was that not even Cary Grant asked to see one of his scripts before signing up for the movie. 'The thing is,' Connery explained at the time, 'Cary's big enough to be able to insist on changes after a film starts. But I can't. So I must be happy with it before I begin.'[16] And anyway, as he told another reporter, 'For the first time in my life, I can ask to read a script, and if you had been in some of the tripe I have, you'd know why.'[17]

Which is fine, as far as it goes. But how to account for the fact that Connery had asked to see the script of a Hitchcock picture but not that of *Woman of Straw*? The answer, surely, is precisely because he was being asked to work in a *Hitchcock* picture. *North by Northwest* had been, as we have seen, one of the key inspirations behind the Bond movies. And in reality it was Messrs Saltzman and Broccoli, who had Connery tied to a multi-year/multi-movie contract that allowed them to veto such extra-curricular work as they saw fit, who were asking to see the movie script. They needed to be sure their boy wasn't going to be appearing in any movie that came too close to the cinematic territory they were marking out for themselves.

Certainly, it was Saltzman and Broccoli who, on 14 October 1963, cabled Hitchcock's agency to spell out the terms of the deal:

Mr Connery gets top billing; he gets a fee of $200,000 as previously discussed; he gets expenses of $1,500 a week for the picture's twelve-week shoot (which must end no later than 7 February 1964); and his wife and son get a round-trip air fare. Hitchcock replied by return. Everything was fine, save for the stipulated end date and the top-billing request. On the end date, Mr Hitchcock would do all he could to meet it (in fact, he anticipated being through with Mr Connery's services by the beginning of that month), but he could not guarantee it. On the question of billing, Mr Hitchcock was happy for Mr Connery to be top of the bill in the United Kingdom, but the director would decide nearer the time whether he was to be first or second on the bill throughout the rest of the world. A couple of days later the deal was done, with the shoot set to start in mid-November.

Granted all that to-ing and fro-ing, it is important to grasp that this was a mighty big break for Connery. Not only would *Marnie* be his first picture in Hollywood since *Darby O'Gill and the Little People* five years and more earlier, it would be his first picture ever with a well-known director. In these days of universal film-buffery, when everyone knows the name of the key-grip and the dog wrangler, it is easy to forget that in the early sixties Alfred Hitchcock was pretty much the only film director the man in the street could name. Indeed, in that autumn of 1963 he may have been at the height of his fame – personally introducing a weekly series of grand-guignol shockers on television, and with a decade of non-stop hits (*Rear Window* (1954), *The Man Who Knew Too Much* (1956), *North by Northwest*, *Psycho* (1960)) behind him. His last picture had been *The Birds* (1963), an enigmatic adaptation of an apocalyptic Daphne du Maurier short story that was made for the hermeneutic autopsies the then just-being-born field of film studies so adored.

According to one of Hitchcock's biographers, Connery had been on the shortlist for the male lead in that film, though his schedule hadn't permitted him time.[18] Well, perhaps, though it seems unlikely. Since *The Birds* was filmed during the early part of

1963 it might well have crunched into the production time of *From Russia with Love*, though Hitchcock was always a practical man and could doubtless have found ways around things had he wanted. The bigger problem with the claim is that in the second half of 1962, when Hitchcock was putting *The Birds* together, Connery was far from being a star. Indeed, as we have seen, *Dr No* hadn't been released in the USA until May 1963 – the same month *The Birds* made its debut at the Cannes Film Festival. If Connery was beeping on Hitchcock's radar as *The Birds* was being worked on, then his genius for inspired casting deserves even more celebration than it has already had.

That genius may yet prove to be Hitchcock's most lasting contribution to the craft of movies. No director, it seems fair to say, has ever been quite so alert to the reef of meanings the mere presence of a given actor can bring to a given picture. Anyone going to see *Notorious* (1946) in expectation of another Cary Grant light comedy, for instance, was in for a shock. And though it was Anthony Mann who, in a series of triumphantly tragic westerns (*Bend of the River* (1952), *The Naked Spur* (1953), *The Man From Laramie* (1955)), had first exposed the neurotic sociopath simmering beneath the seemingly relaxed hick of so many Jimmy Stewart characters, it was Hitchcock who refined and polished this image of derangement and degradation by bringing the character up-to-date in the Eisenhower years of post-Freudian America. No movie subverts the Stewart persona of down-to-earth self-possession like Hitchcock's *Vertigo* (1958). A couple of years later, Hitchcock took the technique even further, casting Anthony apple-pie/boy-next-door Perkins as the momma-fixated serial killer in *Psycho*.

With Connery, though, Hitchcock's strategy was rather different. Instead of casting him against type, Hitchcock seems to have been using him in order to dissect and analyse the make-up of the chill, sex-charged monster that was his Bond. On the strength of Connery's performance in *Dr No*, that is, Hitchcock had seen through the glitz and glamour of Saltzman and Broccoli's technocratic hero to the barely socialised psychopath underneath. Like so many of the Bond audience, Hitchcock had thrilled to the animal grace of Connery's Bond. Unlike them, he had thought what fun it would be to put that kind of wild, self-regarding behaviour under the microscope. He only half got his way.

For *Marnie* is a picture that Connery's presence ends up seriously destabilising. Though he does indeed take second billing in the opening credits of every print of the picture I've seen (after the title card for Tippi Hedren – an actress who, save for her troubles with Hitchcock away from the camera, is now all but forgotten), the movie is less an investigation of its titular character than it is an analysis of Connery's Mark Rutland.

Ostensibly, of course, the picture tells the story of Hedren's Marnie, an icy blonde secretary with a penchant for breaking into the safe of whichever firm she has presently inveigled her way into and making off with the money therein. Rutland is an urbane young publisher and amateur zoologist who has recently lost his wife and is keen to evade the attentions of her sister Lil Mainwaring (Diane Baker). Not that that is sufficient motivation for his falling for Marnie when she comes to work for his father's firm. From the off, Rutland is on to Marnie as a wrong 'un, and it is a moot point whether he is more attracted to her for her beauty than he is for her kleptomania. Whatever, after she has broken into his safe and gone on the lam, he hunts her down and blackmails her into marriage. After a hellish honeymoon he vows to get to the bottom of the animal he has 'tracked and caught'.

Alas for Marnie – and, unfortunately, *Marnie* – a wilder animal is about, in the guise of Sean Connery. The bestial imagery the picture is structured around has a long tradition in Hitchcock's work. Only think of the preening cats in *Sabotage* (1936) or the stuffed birds that people (the word is not inapt) the world of Norman Bates in *Psycho*. Tippi Hedren's delicacy of movement and gesture in *Marnie* is similarly birdlike. The trouble is that Connery's putatively gentleman publisher, fascinated though he may himself be with predators, can't help but come across as the movie's big beast.

This is not just a question of star wattage, nor one of actorly acumen (Connery is a far more supple performer than Hedren, yet despite her shortcomings it is difficult to gainsay her casting here). It is simply the case that by dint of his panther-like gait and mocking, feline face, Connery cannot help but be the movie's wildest animal. Watch him in the storm scene, in which Marnie is shocked and alarmed by a lightning-struck tree smashing through the window of Mark's office, and Connery's Rutland moves to protect her like a big cat pouncing. For all Tippi Hedren's efforts to give Marnie what film scholar Robin Wood has called the air of a 'dangerous yet terrified animal',[19] it is Connery's Mark who prowls and preens his way through the picture, the wild master of all he surveys.

As Wood says, Mark is, 'of all Hitchcock's male protagonists . . . the one most in charge of situations, most completely master of himself and his environment, most decisive and active and purposive'.[20] Exactly so, though Wood seems blind to how much effect that means the casting of the very un-neurotic Connery had on Hitchcock's Freudian melodrama – how much his star persona's sexual overdrive unbalanced the picture. When watching Connery's Rutland attempt to psychoanalyse Hedren's highly strung heroine, one feels in the presence not of a gently coaxing medic but of a dictatorial brute. Watch the film again and see how Connery never really talks to Marnie. All he does is bark orders at her: 'Clean up your face!' 'Come on!' He could be James Bond on the beach at Crab Key in *Dr No* telling the hapless Negro Quarrel to 'fetch my shoes!' And so, *pace* Raymond Durgnat's talk of Mark's 'invincible smugness',[21] the chief virtue of Connery's performance is its grasp of the perverse desires that motivate the grieving Rutland.

Would that Hitchcock had followed Connery's lead. Certainly the director later worried that he had failed to sufficiently dramatise Mark's fetishism. 'A man wants to go to bed with a thief because she's a thief,' he told François Truffaut. 'Unfortunately, this concept doesn't come across on the screen . . . To put it bluntly, we'd have had to have Sean Connery catching the girl robbing the safe and show that he felt like jumping at her and raping her on the spot.'[22] Such rapacious sexuality was the very stuff of Connery's Bond, of course, and given that Hitchcock spends much of the rest of the movie directing Connery to play up to his Bond persona, there seems no reason beyond his (Hitchcock's) box-office fears that he could not have put this notion into practice.

And yet, he had no such fears over the movie's actual 'rape scene', which takes place midway through Mark and Marnie's disastrous seaward honeymoon. Mark, momentarily angered by his bride's pride in her own frigidity, tears her nightgown from her. Seconds later, appalled at what he has done, he wraps Marnie in his own robe and moves to comfort her. To watch Connery modulate from lusty roughhouse to stricken romantic, as he does here, is to marvel at the progress he has made in the past few years – as well as to remember that anonymous critic's comment about Connery's having provided 'the young Olivier' he thought Rattigan's *Adventure Story* needed: Mark Rutland's closest relative in the Hitchcock canon is surely the tortured Maxim de Winter (Olivier) in *Rebecca* (1940).

Difficult as that scene must have been to play, it had proved even more difficult to write. Indeed, Evan Hunter, the writer of the movie's first draft screenplay, was sacked from the picture for telling Hitchcock that the scene was unfilmable. No actor, he argued, not Sean Connery, not Rock Hudson (who'd also been in the frame for the part, presumably on the back of the post-Freudian sex comedies he'd recently made with Doris Day), could survive having played in such a scene. Jay Presson Allen, the woman Hitchcock subsequently hired to finish the screenplay, had no such worries. Stars have by definition, she argued, sufficient charisma to charm their way through the most despicable moments.[23] Or, as Tippi Hedren rather more bluntly put it to Hitchcock, how was any woman, no matter how frigid she might be, meant to resist the advances of Sean Connery?[24]

Certainly as far as Hitchcock was concerned, Connery was already a star. (True, *Dr No* had not done great business in Hitchcock's adopted homeland, but it had done very well indeed in the country in which his dramatic interests – as opposed to business interests – lay. Watch *Marnie* again and see how much of its iconography – the country manor, the pink-coated hunt, the docks that back on to tight terraces of red-bricked houses – derives from Hitchcock's British pictures.) That is why the character of Mark Rutland is introduced far earlier in the finished picture than he was in the original drafts of the screenplay.

In fact, Connery is in there from the first, ambling into the movie's opening moments and standing in back of the shot looking mockingly on. Throughout the scene, in which Strutt (Martin Gabel) impotently expostulates at having been robbed by a secretary he clearly fancied something rotten, Connery does no more than look coldly amused in a way that evokes not only the sardonic ironies of his Bond but also of the audience's clucking laughter at Strutt (the name says it all) and his posturing. Whatever else this scene is, it is an invitation to the audience to both ogle and identify with the picture's leading man, a real moment of Hollywood's insatiable need to get the goods up front.

You get more of the same a few minutes later, when Marnie turns up at Rutland Publishing hoping to bag a secretarial vacancy. As Sam Ward (S. John Launer) – who has already, as far as he is concerned, found the right woman for the job – asks Marnie a series of questions about her background and career, Connery stands in back of frame again, silently surveying the scene. Again and again Hitchcock cuts from the banalities of a job interview to the amused contempt that plays across Connery's face. For despite the disguise, Mark is on to Marnie – has realised she is the same girl who is forever 'pulling her skirt down over her knees like they were some national treasure' that so rattled Strutt – and is privately smiling at the girl's brass neck. You don't have to share Andrew Rissik's belief that the 'scene demonstrates Connery's mastery of the close-up'[25] – isn't he just a little *too* ironic here, a little *too* mannered? – to see that Connery has already stamped his authority on the picture. From now on, whatever Hitchcock and Hedren do, the movie is Connery's to lose. Hence, as Raymond Durgnat has argued in a telling criticism of the finished picture, 'Mark seems to impose himself on Marnie rather than Marnie to impose herself on Mark'.[26]

All of which is a way of saying that *Marnie* is a confused and confusing piece of work, which – no matter how many exculpatory attempts are made to find its contradictoriness fruitful[27] – never really gets to grips with its leading man. Hitchcock famously said he thought acting no more than a question of casting. What he meant was that if he'd chosen the right actor for the part he would need give them very little direction. 'If I'm paying you as much as I am,' Hitchcock told Connery, 'and you don't know what you're doing, then I deserve what I get in the way of performance.'[28]

And indeed, Connery has remembered that the only direction Hitchcock did give him was to keep his mouth closed when he wasn't talking and to slow his speech down a little (presumably with the American audience in mind). Since Hitchcock had a habit of treating actors like their characters so that they might identify more closely with them, it could be that he left Connery on a long leash the better for his Mark Rutland to become the Lord of the Jungle Marnie describes him as. What Hitchcock didn't foresee was that the leash he had on Connery was so long it let him run away with a movie with which the director had hoped to cement the reputation of his latest blonde amanuensis. So it was at best mischievous (at worst, actively malicious) of Hitchcock to later confide in François Truffaut that Connery was miscast in what he had now decided was no more than a retelling of the prince and beggar-girl myth and that he (Connery) wasn't sufficiently a gentleman.[29]

Whatever, in America *Marnie* turned out to be the first Hitchcock flop in a decade. It did rather better in his country of birth – coming twelfth in the annual UK box-office list – though this was largely on the back of what was increasingly coming to be called the Bondwagon: *Goldfinger* (to which we shall shortly turn) did the biggest business in Britain in 1964.

Until almost the close of the *Marnie* shoot, though, Connery was to be found playing hard to get on the Bond front – so hard that in late January Broccoli flew out to Hollywood to try and smooth things out. (Saltzman didn't tag along because he and Connery had never really got on and were getting on less well with each passing day.) Contracted though he was to make three more 007 pictures, Connery was threatening to quit unless he was given a bigger say in the action. 'I don't want to go into details,' he told a young Barry Norman toward the end of his three months on the Hitchcock movie, 'but it concerns my artistic control of the picture . . . If we cannot come to terms, I don't know that I will do the film.'[30]

Connery certainly wasn't lacking other offers. Only a couple of weeks earlier he had been approached by no less a director than John Ford (like Hitchcock, another moviemaker just becoming a figure of artistic legend thanks to the efforts of the French and English auteurist critics). Ford had thought to cast Connery in *Young Cassidy* (1965), a biopic of the Irish dramatist Sean O'Casey based on the firebrand idealist's autobiography *Mirror in My House*. Ford's shoot, though, would clash with that for *Goldfinger* (1964).[*]

What to do? Connery wasn't helped when his wife told him that she was being Oscar nominated for Best Supporting Actress in Richardson's *Tom Jones*. 'I think,' she would later tell an interviewer, 'Sean got a bit sort of shirty at that.'[31] And maybe he did, though not, one suspects, because he was jealous but because he knew instinctively that, no matter how well they did at the box office, pictures such as *Goldfinger*, to whose Midas touch he had eventually succumbed, were never going to be nominated by the Academy.

Not even if they starred Orson Welles in the title role – as

---

[*] In the event, Ford fell ill and the project was handed to Jack Cardiff, so it is a moot point whether Connery missed out on the chance of working with another serious auteur.

Goldfinger was at one point going to do. What a shame the old scene-stealer didn't make it, and put the aesthetic frighteners on the picture's leading man. (Like Connery, Welles held out for rather more money than was on the table. Unlike Connery – who was paid £50,000 for *Goldfinger*, plus 5 per cent of the profits – he didn't get it.) Instead, the honours went to Gert Fröbe – an actor who spoke barely three words of English, yet one against whom all subsequent Bond villains have been measured.

Indeed, for all the upset and ennui on the part of its star, *Goldfinger* itself became the movie by whose standards all later Bonds have been judged. There is good reason for this. Despite Terence Young's oft-made claim that he leavened the Fleming mix with humour, *Goldfinger* – which was directed by Guy Hamilton – was far and away the most soufflé-like Bond yet.*

Hamilton had by some measure the biggest Bond budget to date to work with – a princely $2.9 million (three times the money Young had had to spend on *Dr No*) – and boy does it show. One miscalculated gag aside, *Goldfinger* looks remarkably undated. Ken Adam's glittering sets and what John Barry would later call his 'million-dollar Mickey Mouse' music grant the movie a timelessness its B-picture-indebted predecessors had lacked. By such means – as well as by dint of its having a plot that actually took him there – *Goldfinger* became the picture that finally broke Bond big in the USA.

Indeed, forty-five minutes of thrilling hi-jinks in, Bond is captured – spending the bulk of the picture's remaining hour in

---

* Young had been told his services were surplus to requirements after he had decided, a trifle tardily perhaps, that the offer the producers had made him on both *Dr No* and *From Russia with Love* of a lower salary with a percentage of the profits might not be a bad idea for his work on any future Bonds. Though Young would return for *Thunderball* (1965), no subsequent director would make more than one Bond in a row until Hamilton returned for the Connery swansong, *Diamonds Are Forever* (1971), which he followed with *Live and Let Die* (1973) and *The Man with the Golden Gun* (1974).

Goldfinger's Kentucky fastness as an emissary between the villain and the CIA. We can laugh, as so many people have down the years, about the fantasy (the essential fantasy of Fleming's original series of novels, of course) of post-imperial Britain's having any assistance at all to offer the American intelligence services. But there is a paradox here (and not just the fact that Connery himself never set foot in America for the making of *Goldfinger*).* For while Bond's producers plainly accepted that if they were to make it big they would have to do so on American terms, it was also the case that with their third picture together, Messrs Broccoli and Saltzman effectively invented the modern adventure movie. Without *Goldfinger* there would have been no *Star Wars* (1977), no *Raiders of the Lost Ark* (1981), no *Die Hard* (1988). With *Goldfinger* and its successors, the Bond series induced the birth of the mass Hollywood audience of the post-studio era.

Certainly, like the Hollywood blockbusters of old, the Bond movies were fantasies built around dreamy stars. Hence Connery's increasing ire. He had seen that the movie posters were starting to feature his own name in rather bigger type than that given to the character he played. (His name had barely been visible on the posters for *Dr No* and *From Russia with Love*.) He had seen the lines of punters eager to hand over their money to see not any old James Bond but his James Bond. He had seen how, the previous year, Ian Fleming had given the hero of his eleventh Bond novel, *On Her Majesty's Secret Service*, a Scots background – in thankful homage to the 'overgrown stuntman' who these days brought home so much of the Old Etonian's bacon. He had seen the fans hanging around outside his home in Acton – or, more creatively, stealing a ladder from the builder's yard next door and climbing up to take a peek through what they hoped might be agent 007's bedroom window.

---

* The Kentucky scenes were actually shot at Pinewood – witness some of the clumsiest back projection in the entire Bond series.

And yet, even as Connery was becoming more and more recognised as the true force behind Bond, he was becoming less and less important to the on-screen action. *Thunderball* (1965), which we will come to shortly, is rightly held up as the movie in which the character of movie Bond is put to death by the thousand and one gadgets and gewgaws Messrs Saltzman and Broccoli have thought to put forward for our delectation. But the move towards mechanised tedium is in fact well in place in *Goldfinger*, with its ejector-seated Aston Martin, its laser guns and murderous bowler hats. The James Bond of this picture has little to do beyond getting captured by the bad guys so that he might escape by means of his fabulous toys – all ponderously described before the fact by Desmond Llewelyn's irascible Q.[32] As Penelope Houston presciently pointed out, this third Bond movie 'perfects the formula . . . so conclusively that it is hard to see what Mr Broccoli and Mr Saltzman have left themselves in hand for the future'.[33]

One card they were holding, of course, was a by now extremely competent leading man. Though little more than two years had passed since the *Dr No* shoot, the nervy, imbalanced, control-free Connery of those days had been vanquished by the time he came to work on *Goldfinger*. Even as the ejector seats and smoke-screens came to the fore, that is, Connery was at last demonstrating that he had the wherewithal to make of Bond something rather more than Fleming's 'cardboard booby'. His then oft-heard claim that he had 'learned to play Bond by playing Macbeth' was perhaps always going to sound fatuous.[34] Nonetheless, there is a roundedness and a depth to the Bond of *Goldfinger* that doesn't entirely belie the parallel. Just watch him during the scene when he finds Jill Masterson (Shirley Eaton) dead on the bed in his Miami hotel suite – 'covered in gold paint' as he disgustedly tells Felix Leiter (Cec Linder) on the telephone. In a medium long shot designed to take both Bond and victim in, Connery manages to fill the frame with feelings of guilt, loathing, anger, disgust and contempt – all with the merest twitch of a nostril, the tiniest clutch of his throat.

Otherwise, though, Connery has a whale of a time in the picture, ambling through its proceedings with a look of perpetually amused contumely on his face. Though it was rumoured that Connery rubbed along rather less well with Guy Hamilton than he had with Terence Young, there is no gainsaying that Hamilton's more insouciant style allowed Connery's instinctive irony to come to the fore in *Goldfinger*. This is, for instance, the first Bond movie in which Connery puts his hands in his pockets when talking to his superiors. Connery's Bond wasn't aggressively anti-authoritarian, much less was he committed to the idea that to be youthful was intrinsically to be on the side of progress. Nonetheless, his jaunty devil-may-care cheek embodied the age's new permissiveness. And still the producers failed to register the insurrectionary spirit of the character their star was creating. In a crucial misreading of the times, Bond compares drinking champagne at the incorrect temperature to 'listening to the Beatles without earmuffs' – a cultural glitch not rectified for the best part of a decade, when Paul McCartney was hired to write the theme tune for the first post-Connery Bond picture, *Live and Let Die* (1973).

Elsewhere we are on surer ground. The fights in *Goldfinger* are among the best in the entire Bond series. The pre-credits sequence – which is so good you wonder why the picture doesn't just end there and then – features a marvellous bedroom scrap involving a full bathtub and an electric heater, while the long slow knockabout with Oddjob (Harold Sakata) that all but ends the movie summons from Connery some of the subtlest close-up work of his career. Guy Hamilton has claimed that, while he had enjoyed *Dr No* and *From Russia with Love*, he was worried that they had made something almost superheroic of Bond and that 'consequently there [was] no suspense in whatever predicaments were dreamt up for him'.[35] Prophetic stuff, and yet, a couple of scaredy-cat moments in that fight with Oddjob aside, the Bond of *Goldfinger* is memorable chiefly for the *joie de vivre* he brings to every punch and parry. However much fun you're having in the audience, Connery seems constantly on the point of saying, it isn't half as much fun as we're having up here.

At times, as John Barry's brassy, overblown, kitschy score pulses and pounds, and as a black-satin jumpsuited Connery glides through Ken Adam's burnished sets, you could almost be watching Gene Kelly warming up for the French Impressionist sequence of *An American in Paris* (1951). Watch Connery's Bond in the pre-credits sequence, in which he dispatches a heavy with a single kick – the kick delivered entirely by the shin, the thigh remaining horizontal, in a more than passable *petit battement*. The only comparable instance I know of such grace under pressure is that moment in Howard Hawks's *Rio Bravo* (1959) when John Wayne combines a kick and a twirl (the strangeness of the movement underlined by Hawks's uncharacteristically self-conscious on-high camera angle) to remove a spittoon from Dean Martin's shameless reach.

All of which is, perhaps, a way of saying that, for all its pleasures, *Goldfinger* is curiously short on action. One reason for this is that Richard Maibaum and Paul Dehn's script allows Bond to be captured rather too early on in proceedings. More signally, though, for all Hamilton's protestations about ensuring Bond is up against the type of villainy he merits, the movie is played largely for laughs right from the off. There is a lovely moment when Bond temporarily escapes his abductors, in which, for the first time since his pre-007 days, Connery gets to mug and grin for the camera. Winking and waving at his Oriental guard through the bars of his prison door, Bond suddenly slides down out of sight, as if in preparation for a magic trick.

Later, Connery extracts some Cary Grant-style comedy from the fact that his seduction of Pussy Galore (Honor Blackman) converts her not only to righteousness (she dishes the dirt on Goldfinger) but heterosexuality (hitherto she has been 'immune' to men). Bond fans, Nina Hibbin noted in the pages of the *Daily Worker*, 'must gurgle with relish whenever their nonchalant hero . . . rolls a girl he's hardly met and certainly hates into the nearest bed'.[36] And perhaps they did, though nobody gurgled more amusedly than Connery himself – laughing up his sleeve at the absurd ease with which Bond arranged his conquests.

Silly to argue, of course, that Connery made of Bond anything like a proto-feminist. But nor is his 007 quite the unreconstructed male chauvinist pig the more air-headed critics took him for – if only because Connery's brazenly Brechtian performance is forever foregrounding its highly constructed status. Moreover, Connery, who spends more time near-naked in the Bond pictures than any mainstream actor since those who played Tarzan, is quite as much an object of desire as the women the various movies showcase. As J. Hoberman observed of *Dr No*, Connery's Bond 'always gets a reaction shot' from the women he meets.[37] In other words, he is quite as much the object of what Laura Mulvey would later call 'the gaze' as any of the women themselves.[38] What, after all, is the long sequence in the bathroom on Goldfinger's private jet, in which Bond is subjected to one intrusion after another on the part of Mei-Lei (Mai Ling), but a jokey reference to the pleasure women found in watching Connery?

The only man not laughing, unfortunately, was the star of the show. True, Connery might not yet have come to loathe making the Bond pictures, but nor was he willing to accept that they were the big deal everyone else was taking them for. *Goldfinger* might be a pleasure to watch, but for Connery it was rather less of a pleasure to make. For almost three years now he had been the face of a man who, in his darker moments, he saw as a snobby imperialist authoritarian, and he was fast becoming tired both of being taken for that man and of the stranglehold the character was coming to exert over his career.

He was becoming tired, too, of being asked fool questions by dumb reporters. One of them – a girl from France or from Italy, depending on who's telling the story – turned up on the set of *Goldfinger* so unbriefed she apparently didn't even know the title of the film she had come to discuss. When, in short order, she asked Connery which member of Pussy Galore's Flying Circus was incarnated by Gert Fröbe and, worst of all, the name of his own character, he stormed out on her. Who could blame him for not showing up for *Goldfinger*'s London premiere on 17 August 1964?

Not that his problems stopped there. Further goading Connery during the *Goldfinger* shoot had been the fact of his wife's working on *The Agony and the Ecstasy* (1965) with Carol Reed. As it turned out, this biopic of the life of Michelangelo was carved from purest corn. But Reed, though his career had faltered these past few years, had in his time directed some masterfully gloomy pictures – *The Fallen Idol* (1949), *The Man Between* (1955) and *The Third Man* (1951) among them. Even had Connery not spent the previous six months playing second fiddle to an in-car ejector seat, he would have to have been an unusually ambitionless actor not to have looked on the opportunity Cilento had been afforded in Rome without envy.

In fact, Connery had a burning ambition to be known as rather more than a muscleman with what he called 'the constitution of a rugby player'.[39] Hence the schizophrenic CV he put together in the latter half of the sixties, the annual Bond extravaganza counterpointed by the rather more self-consciously arty productions he hoped would seal his reputation as an actor. Matters weren't helped, it should be said, by Cilento, who envied her husband's international success even as she knocked the movies on which it was based. (Adding insult to injury, she also claimed – like pretty much everyone else involved with Connery at the time – responsibility for his slyly mocking take on the Bond character.)

Still, such tensions failed to prevent – and perhaps encouraged – husband and wife from discussing working together during Cilento's down time from the Reed shoot. A few months earlier, Terence Young had suggested that the Connerys might like to star opposite one another in his version of *The Amorous Adventures of Moll Flanders* (1965). The idea was sound: Connery's Bond had, after all, been part of the inspiration for Albert Finney's dick-swinging take on *Tom Jones*. On the other hand, Defoe's original story is, if not exactly feminist, then very female-centred. Bluntly, Connery wouldn't have had enough to do to please Paramount Studios. The same problem dogged Cilento's idea for a film of D'Arcy Niland's *Call Me When the Cross Turns Over*, a story that centres on a female wanderer in Cilento's native Australia.

Meanwhile, in Rome, Connery befriended Rex Harrison – who was playing Pope Julius II to Cilento's Contessina de'Medici in *The Agony and the Ecstasy*. Over several rounds of golf (one of them played in honour of Ian Fleming, who died on 12 August 1964), the two men shared gripes about the pressures of being married to fellow actors (in Harrison's case the alcoholic depressive Rachel Roberts). Not long afterwards, Connery told a reporter that 'Diane and I are often asked why we don't make a film together. Frankly, it would be a bloody disaster. I don't go along with husband and wife double acts. I want a wife to go to bed with, not a script conference.'[40]

Golfing aside, Connery filled his days in Rome by studying Ray Rigby's screenplay for *The Hill* (1965), to whose shoot in Almeria, southern Spain, he and Cilento would fly in September, once her work on the Reed picture was through. The script, which began life as a (never produced) play, is a harsh chamber-piece that for all its emphasis on outdoor action fails to ever quite shake off its stage origins – and over the past year or so, Connery had more than once turned it down. Now, though, Rigby had reworked it, and while Connery was still not being offered the part he wanted, he found himself rather more taken with the drama's earnest abstractions.

The plot, which Rigby claimed was based on incidents from his own wartime experience, is simplicity itself: five court-martialled naysayers – Joe Roberts (Connery), George Stevens (Alfred Lynch), Jacko King (Ossie Davis), Jock McGrath (Jack Watson) and Monty Bartlett (Roy Kinnear) – are sent to a compound in North Africa where harsh punishments are meted out until the inmates break. Chief among these punishments is the movie's titular hill, a man-made pile of sand and rubble 50 or 60 feet high, which our band of troublemakers is made to march up and down, up and down, all day long, in the scorch of the equatorial sun.

The part Connery had fancied himself for in this Sisyphean drama was that of Sergeant-Major Bert Wilson, the movie's martinet military man originally conceived by Rigby for Trevor Howard. Howard, though, thought the role rather too similar to the Captain Bligh he had played in Lewis Milestone's remake of *Mutiny on the Bounty* (1962), and turned it down. Subsequently, it was given to Harry Andrews (fresh from working with Cilento on *The Agony and the Ecstasy*).

Why did Connery want the Wilson part so much? In order, surely, to comment on what he saw as the sadistic undertow of the character the public so closely identified him with. Because while Terence Young's suggestion that Connery's Joe Roberts is 'James Bond in the glasshouse' is a little overemphatic,[41] still there is a sense in which the part subjects the Bond figure to the kind of in-depth analysis the 007 movies might have been created in order to render impossible. Roberts's refusal to obey what he sees as lunatic orders from on high is quite of a piece with Bond's indifference to the diktats of the powers that be. What marks the hero of *The Hill* out, though, is his wish to win through while renouncing violence.

What marks Connery out, meanwhile, are the histrionics Sidney Lumet's treatment of Rigby's drama calls for. While the whole construction of the Bond character was predicated on a seemingly seamless link 'twixt actor and part, so that for vast swathes of those adventures Connery seems to be doing no more than breezing through a succession of colourful set pieces armed with a quip or a pick-up line, Joe Roberts is a man given to endless argument and debate. True, Rigby's screenplay is overly wordy, line after line of dialogue hammering home points made quite well enough the first time around. But what matters here is that Connery, after a string of movies in which he had done little but crack wise, proved himself well equipped to handle such tempestuous loquacity.

He did so, moreover, up against Harry Andrews, one of the British cinema's most powerful presences, and an actor who had gained his spurs on the stage of the Old Vic in its justly famous post-war years. While the Ralph Richardson of *Woman of Straw* had treated that whole melodramatic fiasco with the kind of contempt Connery would reserve for post-*Goldfinger* Bond, Andrews took his role as *The Hill*'s domineering sadist very seriously indeed. Which meant that for perhaps the first time in his career Connery found himself up against an actor properly engaged with his work. The result was the raising of the Connery game by a significant margin, so that Rigby's and Lumet's rather too diagrammatic arguments about authority and rebellion found a concrete embodiment in the very texture of the drama.

What neither Connery nor Andrews nor anyone else on *The Hill* could best, though, was Oswald Morris's overemphatic camerawork, a mishmash of self-conscious compositions completely at odds with the movie's putatively *vérité* Steadicam style. As Connery noted at the time, 'We even use a special sort of film that gives it a rough, documentary look. There are no little lights under your face to take away lines; in fact we use natural lighting as much as possible.'[42] For all Connery's overly proprietorial air there, *The Hill*'s aesthetic follies can hardly be laid at his door (though there would be evidence over the years to come that he did indeed go in for such stagey, puffed-up visuals), and it would be a harsh critic who found him wanting in Lumet's picture.

Indeed, the unbearable heat of the Spanish desert aside, Connery's professional experience on *The Hill* was almost wholly positive. Terence Young would later argue that his protégé's turn as Joe Roberts reminded him of Spencer Tracy, while an anonymous critic in *Time* magazine was only the first of many to wonder whether Connery 'may be the screen's new Gable' – an unimpeachable hero in an increasingly impeachable age.[43] Unsurprisingly, Connery himself was mighty pleased with the picture. 'Even before being shown,' he told an interviewer, '*The Hill* has succeeded for me, because I was concerned and fully involved in the making of it. The next stage is how it is exploited and received, and that I have absolutely no control over . . . But whatever happens to *The Hill*, it will not detract from what I think about it.'[44]

Audiences, however, were rather less willing to be impressed. No matter what the intrinsic qualities of *The Hill*, they felt badly let down by its emphatically glamour-free subject matter and brutally naturalistic treatment, by its deliberately rough-looking monochrome photography, by its at times inaudible soundtrack. (In parts of America, both Connery's and his co-stars' accents were deemed so impenetrable the picture had to be subtitled.) Most of all, they felt let down by the efforts of its leading man to act not at all like a leading man. Comparisons with the work of Spencer Tracy and Clark Gable were all very well, but did Connery really have to go rug-free and wear a moustache in the picture? They wanted their favourite movie star to look like their favourite movie star. Fortunately for them, *Thunderball* – and with it, further Bondage – now loomed large on Connery's horizon.

6

A Not So Fine Madness

Connery was paid £140,000 for his work on *The Hill* (almost as much as the rest of the cast together),[1] and he had just signed up for the then massive pay cheque of £200,000 for the fourth Bond movie, *Thunderball* (1965).* Only Elizabeth Taylor, who around the same time was being paid a straight $1 million (then around £300,000) for *The Sandpiper* (1965), was pocketing more up front.

Not, Diane Cilento has remembered, that Connery was at all relaxed about his new financial status. 'The more successful Bond became,' she notes in her memoir, 'the more insecure Sean felt.'[2] Curiously, though, she also says that Connery did feel comfortable enough to want her to become a stay-at-home wife and mother. 'Ever since we had married,' Cilento recalls, 'Sean had become progressively more disapproving of my working.' Indeed, she writes that shortly before she had signed on for *The Agony and the Ecstasy*, Connery told her he would give her no more housekeeping money if she insisted on continuing to act.

Whatever the truth of such now quaint-sounding memories, they are the essential background to the big set piece Cilento has claimed took place towards the end of *The Hill*'s horrifically realistic, sickness-ridden shoot: 'Unlike any other set I had been on,' she has remembered, 'the violent and oppressive nature of the

---

* The first three Bonds were by then said to be earning £1,000 every hour of every day.

film spilled over into ordinary life at the hotel I was staying at with Sean. It was against this backdrop that our lives together began to unravel.'

One weekend, towards the end of Connery and Andrews's macho grandstanding on the Lumet picture, Cilento found herself befriending some of the guests at a wedding in Almeria's Aguadulce hotel. 'My glass of sangria seemed to be bottomless,' she remembers, and soon enough she was dancing the flamenco with the local wedding celebrants. 'Then the music and dancing stopped . . . I looked around but couldn't see Sean anywhere. I went searching for him at the snooker table and out on the terrace overlooking the sea, but he was nowhere to be found. Yet, later, I could strangely recall seeing his face scowling at me through the blur of faces, although I couldn't be sure.'

The story now moves upstairs to the Connery suite. 'It was late when I climbed the stairs to our room . . . I was a bit drunk. Once inside, in the darkness, I felt a blow to my face and was knocked to the floor . . . another blow sent me flying . . . I spent the rest of the night sprawled on the bathroom floor . . . whimpering.' In the morning Cilento looked in the mirror and, seeing that her 'face had ballooned out like a giant puffer fish',[3] decided to jump in the car and drive 100 miles or so west, to Malaga. 'I had to hide,' she says, 'from the actors, the crew and, above all, the press.'

Alas, she hid herself away so well that no one has ever been able to corroborate this story. What we do know is that several months later (and many years before Cilento ever mentioned the incident), Connery granted an interview to *Playboy* magazine in which the following, now infamous, exchange took place:

DAVID LEWIN: How do you feel about roughing up a woman, as Bond sometimes has to do?
CONNERY: I don't think there is anything particularly wrong about hitting a woman – although I don't recommend doing it in the same way that you'd hit a man. An open-handed slap

is justified – if all other alternatives fail and there has been plenty of warning. If a woman is a bitch, or hysterical, or bloody-minded continually, then I'd do it.[4]

Several matters bear scrutiny here. First, this is 1965, and what Connery says here would have seemed little out of the ordinary to the vast majority of people (by which I do not mean solely men) in the Western world.

Second, David Lewin is really asking Connery to comment on the question of violence towards women within the context of the James Bond pictures. To be narrowly legalistic about it, Connery is being asked whether he feels at all uncomfortable about being called upon to hit a woman *on set*. (*Thunderball*, during whose shoot this interview took place, actually opens with Bond socking a woman in widow's weeds on the jaw – in the process revealing that said woman is really a man in disguise.) It is Connery who opens the question out on to real-life issues, in doing so being absolutely candid about his belief that hitting a woman is not 'particularly wrong'. In other words, though he accepts that it is wrong, he does so on a relative scale – there are, he implies, wrongs he considers rather more damaging to a relationship than 'an open-handed slap'. 'In my book,' he would tell another interviewer almost thirty years later, 'it's much more cruel to psychologically damage somebody . . . to put them in such distress that they really come to hate themselves.'[5]

Third, Connery nowhere *advocates* the hitting of women. Finally, even if Connery had suggested that he thought it was generally a good thing for men to beat up their womenfolk, it would neither prove nor disprove Cilento's claims about what took place that night on the Costa Almeria.

All we can safely say about the Connerys' marriage at this time – a time when Connery, who was regularly in receipt of more than 200 fan letters every day of the week and was arguably the most famous man on the planet – is that we are here dealing with a couple under the immense pressure of worldwide fame and acclaim.* Indeed, a few months later the Variety Club of Great Britain granted a special award to Connery (in absentia) for 'creating the role of James Bond'. Note the phrasing. Connery wasn't being lauded for playing James Bond but for having *created* him. Those words are grimly symptomatic of the slippage that was taking place whenever anyone came to discuss Connery's Bond: it hadn't simply become difficult to work a cigarette paper between character and actor, it had become impossible – the two were now considered one and the same.

Woody Allen famously joked that his one regret in life was that he wasn't someone else. Most people feel something similar, and those people who become actors feel it all the more. Acting is a form of camouflage, after all – although, paradoxically, if the camouflage is applied sufficiently well it will tell us something about not just a single character or a single actor but about everyone, about what it is to be human. Unsurprisingly, there are stories of actors failing to come out from behind the camouflage. In George Cukor's *A Double Life* (1947), Ronald Colman plays an actor who can't help bringing his work home with him. When he's playing in a comedy he's a pleasure to be with, but cast him in a tragedy and he's hell on earth. So what will happen to his marriage when he's cast as the lead in *Othello*?

The many wives of Peter Sellers lived through similar scenarios for real. Sellers didn't pretend to be a hard-line workers' representative or an over-protective lover only when in front of the cameras. He lived those parts all day long, and for as long as he was that jealous lover or that tyrannous shop steward he seems to have acted accordingly both on and off screen. It sounds like madness, but perhaps any kind of serious actor is by definition a tiny bit crazy.

---

* 'It was around the same time as the Beatles,' Connery once said. 'The difference of course was that they had four of them to kick it around and blame each other.' Mark Cousins, 'Kiss Kiss, Bang Bang', *Scotsman*, 3 May 1997.

Sean Connery, at least, was one of those actors who didn't take their work home with them. Or, rather, when he did take his work home with him, it was not in order to carry on living it but in order to bemoan the fact that he had to pretend living the stuff in the first place. From pretty much the first day on *Dr No*, after all, he had been keen to stress the fact that he was *not* James Bond. He was an actor who was playing a part.

The problem was, the part was so damnably attractive to everyone. 'James Bond: The man every man wants to be and every woman wants between her sheets.' So ran the sell-line on a million Ian Fleming paperbacks of the fifties and early sixties. Why was Bond so attractive? Even as Connery had been girding his loins for *Goldfinger*, Kingsley Amis had been writing a light-hearted yet learned treatise called *The James Bond Dossier*, in which he argued, surely correctly, that unlike the fantasy of the western hero or the sci-fi epic 'the secret agent fantasy is marked by being totally portable'.[6] What Amis meant was that it was the secret agent's very secrecy that could have even the most anonymous office drone or municipal dullard daydreaming about being a spy. The fantasy needed nothing by way of special preparation or equipment. The more average you looked, the less you stood out from the crowd, the better a spy you would make.

Moreover, Amis went on, when Fleming did require his hero to become more of a superhero, he was careful to make him go into training. Essentially, Amis argued, Fleming was writing about a man who we could all, provided 'we took the trouble to keep fit, if we started the day with twenty press-ups and enough straight-leg lifts to make our stomach muscles scream', imagine being.[7]

Connery's James Bond, though, was a horse of a rather different colour. For starters, his sublime good looks carried him off into the matinee-idol stratosphere that very few men can ever ascend to. More, his body, for all the beautifying effort of his weightlifting, never actually looked as if it had been worked on. Rather, Connery's physique (which obeyed every diktat of Classical norms:

it's a dead-ringer for Michelangelo's David or Leonardo's Vitruvian Man) seemed utterly natural rather than hard-earned – not fought for, just a fact of life. In short, he looked less like a man than he did a Greek god.

Hence the fact that the Bond movies, though infantile in their plotting and dialogue and characterisation, could appeal to people older than children. The young fans merely wanted to be Bond, master of all those gizmos and gadgets. Their fathers, though, wanted something different: they wanted to be Sean Connery as James Bond. 'All I and the directors [of the Bond movies] did,' Connery once said, 'was add a sense of humour that was lacking [in Fleming's work], and a quality of effortlessness. Which doesn't mean it wasn't hard work to achieve that appearance of ease.'[8] One doesn't doubt him for a minute (as Gene Kelly once said, 'If it looks like you're working, you're not working hard enough'), but nor is there any denying that the sense of ease Connery brought to Bond helped audiences greatly in their conflation of actor and character. There seemed to be no distance between them, especially since all Connery said away from the camera was that he wasn't Bond. A secret agent would say that, wouldn't he?

And so, as marketing and PR departments, as journalists hungry for an angle and interviewers desperate for an intro, talked more and more as if Connery and Bond were one, he became increasingly angry. In Paris for the French premiere of *Goldfinger*, he agreed to arrive at the cinema in 007's Aston Martin. Unfortunately, as Connery drove down the Champs-Elysées, a more than usually obsessive female fan took a dive into the car (which was travelling slowly, in a movie convoy) and tumbled in next to him. Understandably shaken by what he saw as a lunatic act, Connery refused to take part in any of the grandstanding that took place for the opening of subsequent Bond pictures.

As Terence Young told a reporter as he and his leading man geared up for *Thunderball*, 'Sean could be the biggest star in movies since Gable. But he won't be. He doesn't give a damn for the ancillary assets of being a star. It's not that he's ungrateful; it's just that he's too concerned with personal integrity. A hell of a lot of people don't like Sean because of this.'[9] No indeed, especially when the man in question is given to declaring that, in his view, 'to get anywhere in life you have to be anti-social . . . but if I've ever been actually rude, a good 50 per cent of it has usually been provoked by other people's attitudes'.[10]

And yet, infuriating though much of the Bond hoopla must have been, it's difficult to look back at it all now without asking: what was the beef? 'Sean,' one wants to say to him, 'you're an actor. That means you're a guy who gets a kick out of pretending to be someone other than yourself. And now people are taking you for somebody else! Their loving confusion means you've done your job well! And since we know you value your privacy, this confusion only makes it easier for you to hide from the fans. All you need do is play up to their fantasies in public! But by lecturing reporter after reporter that you aren't James Bond, you only make them and the fans more desperate to find out who you *really are*.' And so one gets to wondering whether what really goaded Sean Connery was the fact that he had been made famous by a part and not that he had made a part famous . . .

The *Thunderball* shoot kicked off at a villa forty minutes' drive from Paris on 16 February 1965. From there it moved to Pinewood Studios, and a month or so later, on 22 March, the cast and crew travelled to the Bahamas – though a few days before Connery flew out there it was reported that he and Cilento had agreed to a trial separation and he had moved out of Acacia House and was bunking up at the flat of a golfing friend, the singer Ronnie Carroll.[11] Cilento, it should be said, has subsequently claimed that it was she who walked out on Connery: 'It has always been reported that it was Sean who left,' she writes, 'as it would have created a bad image for Bond had the girl walked out on the mighty macho man'.[12] All of which may be true, though assuming that it is it rather implies that the angry feminist was for some reason happy enough to have her own image besmirched.

Whatever, by mid-April the Connerys were reunited at Nassau airport for the closing weeks of the location work on the fourth Bond.[13] Still, not everything was right with the marriage, as Ken Adam has remembered: 'Competition was part of it, of course, but it was rather more serious, too. It was like the relationship in *Who's Afraid of Virginia Woolf?* The rows were vicious.'[14]

Well, all marriages have their arguments (and Adam overlooks the fact that in Edward Albee's play it is the rows that work to keep the couple dependent on one another). But a marriage between two actors is likely to have more than its share of rows simply because actors are born to revel in the oxygenating afflatus of such anguished, attitudinising mini-dramas. Which is a way of saying that maybe actors ought not marry one another. Before they love anything else, actors must be self-lovers – and as such they necessarily find it difficult to credit that anyone else might love them quite as much as they do themselves. And if the anyone else in question is a fellow actor, well, the chances of their being properly worshipped are vanishingly small. Better to marry somebody with no designs on stardom than a somebody proper.

More than that, acting is a highly competitive game, and it is in the nature of competitions that not everybody comes out a winner. Galling enough if your partner turns out to be first past the post in the fame and money stakes. Worse than galling if you were the one in the driving seat in the early days. Tempting, then, to rubbish your partner's successes. Or as Connery himself put it, thirty-odd years later: 'The film business lends itself towards marriage breakdowns. You're constantly separated from each other because of location shoots, and if one party in the marriage suddenly gets more successful, the other partner can't always accept.'[15]

With a budget almost ten times as big as that for *Dr No*, *Thunderball* was the biggest Bond movie yet – and as we have seen, Connery's salary had gone up accordingly. Where did the rest of the $5.5 million spend go? Largely on Ken Adam's production designs – SPECTRE's stainless-steel and leather boardroom, an awesome, Churchillian war-room (complete with 30 ft-high paintings that at the flick of a switch become maps of the world), the villain's leisure cruiser that, at the flick of another switch, can jettison half its length and become said villain's high-speed hydrofoil. And yet for all that, *Thunderball* suffers rather because Adam isn't really given his head. No sooner have we been introduced to one or other of his marvellous sets than we have been whisked somewhere else.

'Well, Kutze,' the villain of the piece Emilio Largo (Adolfo Celi) asks of the weaselly boffin he has inveigled to mastermind SPECTRE's use of the nuclear warheads they have hijacked, 'are you pleased with your new toys?' Whether George Pravda's Kutze is pleased or not hardly matters, of course. What matters is that the movie itself is blissed out with its new toys. Barely a minute of the picture goes by without some ludicrous gizmo or other being pressed into service. The movie's pre-credit sequence makes use of both a military jet-pack and – such a hit in *Goldfinger* – Bond's Aston Martin, this time kitted out with a whole new arsenal of gadgets. And yet, these opening moments aside, Bond does very little driving in *Thunderball* – an ominously neat synecdoche for a movie in which our hero is chauffeured around from one set piece to another in order that he might react to whatever gizmo is now being passed in front of him. Far from being the man in charge, James Bond is here the man being told what to do by a series of mechanical inanities.

Despite all the glitz and the gunmetal, *Thunderball* is without question the weakest of the Connery Bonds – and may be the worst edited of a series never known for its emphasis on continuity. Aficionados have long compared notes over the variety of different *Thunderball* prints that have done the rounds over the years – a scene missing here, a line of dialogue changed or dubbed there – but such faux pas are as nothing when set beside the basic ineptitude of the storytelling. If Terence Young's newfound penchant for the wipe/ dissolve recalls the early films of François Truffaut, his mix-and-match approach to the basics of narrative reminds us of Jean-Luc Godard's observation that while a story might have a beginning, a middle and an end, there is no need to parcel them out in that order. The number of narrative non-sequiturs in *Thunderball* is astonishing – as if nobody gave a fig for logical development so long as things appeared to be moving at a brisk pace.

Connery himself knew things were going wrong. Despite the return of his favoured director, and the fact that *Thunderball* boasted John Barry's most hummable Bond score yet, he suspected that all would not be well with the series. As he told David Lewin part-way through the shoot, 'We have to be careful where we go next, because I think . . . we've reached the limit as far as size and gimmicks are concerned . . . all the gimmicks now have been done . . . What is needed now is a change of course – more attention to character and better dialogue.'[16]

Some hope. Emitting a suggestively guttural purr here, a broken-backed moan there, Connery sounds more and more like Cary Grant in the picture. But the dialogue he has been given to play with has a yobbish charmlessness that is new even to Bond. Setting off a health farm fire alarm in the middle of the night, Bond is asked by a panicked woman what on earth is going on. 'I don't know,' he replies, 'could it be the front doorbell perhaps?' This and other such asininities made for a new low in the series, a low Connery, who was reading Saul Bellow's *Herzog* during the shoot,[17] looks distinctly pained by. Perhaps that is why, though Connery had apparently been sufficiently discontented with Guy Hamilton's direction of *Goldfinger* that he insisted Terence Young be brought back for *Thunderball*, the Hamiltonian Bond – the mocking, sardonic Bond of rapier irony and devil-may-care ease – is the Bond he still talks most about in interviews.

It is true that there are moments of pleasure to be had in watching the now highly polished Connery bluff and baloney his way through a movie he is so patently bored by. But at over two hours, *Thunderball* is the longest yet in the Bond series – and it drags virtually from the off. Connery looks listless even during the opening pop art gun-barrel sequence, his ambling gait relaxed to the point of boredom. Nothing, Connery's insouciance suggests, can threaten this James Bond character – so what's the point of watching him, let alone caring about him? Claude Mauriac was defending Connery when he described him (in *Goldfinger*, but the point still stands) as being 'a robot [rather] than a statue, since marble seems insufficient today to celebrate the god mortals – Hercules, Roland, Superman, Tarzan, and James Bond',[18] but the rest of us must wonder how much fun is to be had in watching Connery turn into a parody of the rubber-masked villain we saw killed off at the beginning of *From Russia with Love*.

But then, while previous Bonds had set the template for the dozens of rival spy pictures that were being released at the same time as *Thunderball*, this fourth entry in the series often seems little more than an inventory of all too recent influences. The funeral scene with its widow in disguise that opens the picture cannot help but recall the phoney mourning of Flora Robson in the Margaret Rutherford Miss Marple comedy thriller *Murder at the Gallop* (1963), while the shooting of Luciana Paluzzi's Fiona during a particularly frenzied bongo dance is a straight lift from the second Inspector Clouseau movie, *A Shot in the Dark* (1964). Even the movie's famous torture scene – Bond being almost torn to pieces atop the health farm's back-stretching machine as Young has his camera repeatedly zoom in and out on the rack's greasy pistons – looks like footage from a cheapie bump 'n' grind flick.

Elsewhere, Young tries to ape the Hitchcock touch. The scene on the beach in which Bond and Domino (Claudine Auger) are spied on by a pair of hoods draws heavily on a mighty similar scene in *To Catch a Thief*. Alas, it also points up the fact that Miss Auger is no Grace Kelly. And though the rooftop chase at Largo's villa proves that Connery has all the gymnastic grace of Cary Grant's cat-burglar, Young – unlike Hitchcock – hasn't a clue about where to put the camera to milk the suspense.

And yet, and yet. Knock *Thunderball* as one does, there is no gainsaying the fact that it took a worldwide gross of $141 million (more than 25 times its budget).* Nor, though, is there any denying that *Thunderball* would turn out to be the high-water mark for the Bond box office.[19] *You Only Live Twice* (1967), the fifth in the series – which, significantly, audiences had to wait two years for instead of the by now customary one – would end up with global takings less than not only those of *Thunderball* but also of *Goldfinger*. We are still talking megabucks, of course, but after this fourth Bond we are no longer talking about growth and increases in market share. Nobody could argue that Martin Ritt's movie version of John le Carré's *The Spy Who Came in from the Cold* (1965), which opened just a couple of weeks after *Thunderball* and took a minuscule fraction of its box office, meant the espionage movie's time was up. Still, that was a serious picture (adapted from a yet more serious novel), and if it didn't exactly serve notice on the Bond franchise, it cannot help but have had Messrs Saltzman and Broccoli wondering where their hero's future lay.

Connery, too, of course, was sensible of what was happening. While he was adamant he had no worries about being typecast – 'One is not Bond . . . one was functioning reasonably well before Bond, and . . . one is going to function reasonably well after Bond,'[20] he said as *Thunderball* was released – he was also certain that he must keep trying his hand at other things. Not, he was keen to stress, that he was ashamed of his work on Bond. 'Quality is not to be found only in the Old Vic, and portraying Bond is just as serious as playing Macbeth on stage.'[21] Who could demur? Let the record show, though, that Connery had only just turned down an offer to play Macbeth at the 1965 Edinburgh Festival.[22]

---

* Big money, though small beer percentage-wise when set against *Dr No's* eventual 60-plus-fold take on its original $900,000 budget.

And let it show that a few months later Connery made his first big mistake, turning down Michelangelo Antonioni when the director offered him the lead role in what would become *Blow-Up* (1966). 'I said I'd like to see the script,' Connery recalled, 'and it was only seven pages long and hidden in a Woodbine packet somewhere I think, and Antonioni was highly offended with me and gave the part to [David] Hemmings.'[23] What is most startling about Connery's decision is not just that in Antonioni he had turned down the most recent winner of the Golden Lion at the Venice Film Festival, but that, even sketched out on a cigarette packet, *Blow-Up*'s debts to the works of the Pirandello Connery so admired must have been clear. Here, on a platter, was the chance to take time out from the glittering consumerfest that was Bond and sign up for the other London of the Swinging Sixties – the London of the Beatles and Polanski, the London of Joseph Losey and John Schlesinger.

For *Blow-Up* was a movie that would have stretched Connery in precisely the way he wanted to be stretched. The part of Thomas, after all, with his love of surfaces and visuals, his photographer's desire to turn the world into a sequence of abstract compositions, can be read as a critique of the vacuous greed of the Bond figure. Who else does Hemmings look like as he glides through the pop art London the city was fast becoming by 1966? Wouldn't it have been eye-opening to see the ur-Connery figure reduced to a dithering wreck as he came to doubt what he had previously taken for the reality in front of his eyes?

But Connery had his own personal doubts – chief among them, one suspects, doubts about Antonioni, a director well known for not offering his actors anything by way of direction. And as the return of Terence Young to the Bond fold on *Thunderball* had illustrated, Connery liked direction. And he would certainly have liked some direction in what is a pretty directionless movie, a movie whose plot goes nowhere and whose lead character is as blank and affectless as James Bond yet who is unredeemed by the simplistic virtues of Bond's good-guy versus bad-guys structure. Connery's qualms vis-à-vis *Blow-Up*, then, can be understood readily enough. Still, there can be no denying that, just as the numinous profundity of Antonioni's picture challenges us to wonder precisely what perception is, so Connery's appearing in it would have done more to change the public perception of him than any number of Shakespeare productions.

On the other hand, *Blow-Up* would have done nothing for his placing in the *Motion Picture Herald* survey of US box office draws. In January 1966 Connery topped the list, ahead of John Wayne, Doris Day, Julie Andrews, Jack Lemmon, Elvis Presley, Cary Grant, James Stewart, Elizabeth Taylor and Richard Burton.[24] Not, he was quick to point out, that he wanted to rest on such laurels. 'When I got to 35,' he said, 'I promised myself I would do only things that excite me.'[25] To start with, he was going to direct a play on Broadway – Ted Allan's *The Secret of the World* – with his old friend Shelley Winters in the lead role. As things turned out, that play never came off, but Connery and Allan would work together before the decade was out.

Meanwhile, he agreed to star in Irvin Kershner's *A Fine Madness* (1966), the latest entry in that sixties staple the New York sex comedy, and a calculated slight at all things Bond. For one thing, Connery's Samson Shillito is a poet – for all Kingsley Amis's claims about 007's Byronic inheritance, a distinctly un-Bondlike thing to be. Moreover, Samson is a blocked poet. 'He's writing this big poem,' says his wife, Rhoda (Joanne Woodward), 'and it just won't come out.' Bond, as we know, has never been blocked by anything.

And yet, for all that Kershner's picture does to abstract Connery from the mechanised mayhem of 007, for all his movie's emphasis on spontaneity and the lunatic joys that are to be had from life, there is something curiously Bondian about Samson Shillito. Girls just fall into his arms – and those that don't are forever chasing him down the street. At one point, while he is seducing the secretary of the man whose carpet he has been hired to clean, Samson's hoovering apparatus goes into overdrive, spewing foam at just the moment he brings the girl to ecstasy. Later, with no more than a drawl and a raised eyebrow, Samson will seduce his shrink's wife, Lydia West (Jean Seberg), in a ripple-bath that might have come from the health farm in *Thunderball*. At the end of the picture, nothing daunted by the lobotomy Lydia's husband Dr Oliver West (Patrick O'Neal) has performed on him, Samson socks his pregnant wife on the jaw before gleefully trashing their home – for all the world like Bond taking on that widow cum SPECTRE agent in his last assignment.

But Shillito is a version of Connery himself, too. A poet in the romantic mould, he loathes the idea of giving public readings of his work (forty years ago writers met their audiences rather less frequently than they do today), and is appalled by the apparatus of PR. The same went double, of course, for Connery, who from *Thunderball* onwards would turn down the bulk of the many interview requests he received. More than that, in his tattered corduroys and fraying shirts, Samson dresses an awful lot like the Connery who turned up for his first chat with Saltzman and Broccoli. While one acknowledges Andrew Rissik's suggestive linking of this 'sleek proletarian rebel' with a 'well-known American tradition'[26] (there is indeed something of Brando's Stanley Kowalski in Samson's animalistic grace), Connery's conception of the role owes rather more to the character who had made his Bond a possibility: John Osborne's Jimmy Porter. The trouble is that the movie lacks any real sense that the pricks Shillito kicks against are worth getting all that worked up about.

What the movie does have is a winningly comic performance from its star. Connery's Bond had plainly owed big debts to the chilled smoothness of Cary Grant, but the lessons had not stopped there. Connery's Samson has a Grant-like implacability at the humiliations the world visits on him. (Four decades on, Leonard Mosley's suggestion that if Connery 'wants to continue to be accepted as a serious actor, I suggest that he keeps out of comedy from now on'[27] looks even more fatuous than it did then.) Though it is impossible to imagine Grant ever having played so openly insurrectionary a character as Shillito, it is still impossible to escape the feeling that this is how such a creation would have looked had the master light comedian ever felt able to really dismantle his image.

Connery, of course, did feel like dismantling his image. And yet, despite the creation of characters like Samson, despite his 1966 narration of Prokofiev's *Peter and the Wolf* for Decca records, the image clung. Connery described the reaction of the London critics to *A Fine Madness* as 'mixed',[28] although Mosley aside few of them took issue with the quality of his performance in the picture. What they did take issue with was what they saw as Connery's feather-brained idea that such off-the-wall films were going to do much for his future prospects.

Because no matter how keen Connery was to demonstrate his variety as an actor, the public refused to accept him as anything other than James Bond – the physical incarnation of their fantasies of virility. That was why the public park that bordered the front and side of Acacia House was regularly occupied by obsessives keen for a sighting of their hero. That was why the ladders in the builder's yard next door to the Connery home had more than once been 'borrowed' by crazed fans desperate to make their presence yet more visible to the godhead.[29] A couple of times, while the Connerys had been away on location, their house had been broken into and Cilento's jewellery stolen – as well as a shotgun and cartridges.[30] These last incidents might, of course, have been no more than common burglaries, but in the febrile, neurotic world of Bondmania it must have been mighty easy to believe that something more sinister was going on.

And so, while the Connerys were in America, Sean filming *A Fine Madness*, Diane Martin Ritt's *Hombre* (1967),* Acacia House

---

* Coincidentally, as Connery filmed opposite Joanne Woodward in New York, Cilento was starring opposite Paul Newman, Woodward's husband, in Hollywood.

went up for sale with the Roy Brooks estate agency:

> RESIDENCE OF DISTINCTION. Those who know
> ACACIA HOUSE only as a convent may not know that the Rev
> Mother, ascertaining that their Patron Saint's Day coincided
> with the birthday of Mr SEAN CONNERY, graciously
> allowed him to take over. Now, with Vacant Possession, he
> must sell this fine detached great Victorian house. It retains its
> air of cloistered calm, although the Nuns' changing room is
> now given over to body building appliances and a bar billiards
> table. Central Heating. Splendid Value. £14,995 Freehold.[31]

Splendid value indeed, at least to someone of Connery's means.
At the time, after all, he had just struck a deal for the fifth Bond
film that would earn him $750,000 before the 25 per cent take
he had coming on net merchandising profits. When all was said
and done on *You Only Live Twice* (1967), Connery could expect
to be $1 million richer. Add this to the loot he had just trousered
for *Thunderball* and you could be forgiven for imagining that
the Connery coffers were satisfyingly full. Not so, according to
Cilento. Her husband, she would write four decades later, 'was
convinced that he would never feel safe until he had a million
pounds in the bank'.[32] Oh, well. Another Bond picture or two
should put that right.

Except that Connery then announced that *You Only Live Twice*
was to be his final Bond picture. In July 1966, as he arrived in Tokyo
for the start of the shoot, he told the assembled press conference
that his contract with Broccoli and Saltzman was for five films and
that he would not be appearing in the projected sixth, *On Her
Majesty's Secret Service*. (There had, in fact, been talk that Connery
might not even appear in *You Only Live Twice*. Terence Stamp, fresh
out of his turn as Willie Garvin in Joseph Losey's Warholian parody
of mondo Bond, *Modesty Blaise* (1966), had offered his services to
Saltzman, suggesting that he play the whole picture in Japanese
disguise as a way of getting 'over the self-consciousness of there

suddenly being a different 007. He didn't like the idea, and the discussion ended.')[33]

Did Connery really want out, or was he just playing another hand of poker with what he was by now calling 'fat slob producers living off the backs of lean actors'?[34] Was he just waiting to see how much they would up the ante for the next round of pay talks? Quite possibly, though it was also true that not only had he had enough of Bond – he was beginning to wonder whether the public might have had enough of him, too. In 1966, after all, a spy picture was released at the British cinema almost every week of the year. True, not many of those movies were much good. But given such a surfeit of product, how long could the craze sustain itself?

And how could a craze that, for all its cawing irony, was premised on the old-fashioned virtues of honour and noblesse oblige – 'The things I do for England,' as Connery will drawl during one of *You Only Live Twice*'s more outrageous seduction scenes – survive the onslaught of the burgeoning counterculture? Indeed, just as Connery and co. arrived in Tokyo for the fifth Bond shoot, the Beatles' fifth album, *Revolver*, was being released. With its impenetrable lyrics, its weirdly dissonant harmonies, its emphasis on the alienation and disconnectedness of contemporary life, *Revolver* both posited and was posited upon a great change in the mindset of the culture that had produced (and would consume) it. Bluntly, the album makes even a howling rebel of a poet like Samson Shillito seem as staid as a stockbroker. How could a stuffy establishment figure who only a couple of years earlier had poked fun at the idea of listening to the Beatles hope to keep up?

Hence Broccoli and Saltzman's increasing emphasis on broadening their brand with the kind of spin-off trinkets – toy cars, pillow cases, belts, even underpants – we now take for granted on big movie releases but that were, four decades ago, something quite new. Though *You Only Live Twice* would fare less well at the box office than either *Thunderball* or *Goldfinger*, the moneys taken from its sidelines turned out to be hefty indeed. Understandably enough,

Connery was irked by what he characterised as hucksterism: though it was his face that adorned a gazillion *Goldfinger* gewgaws, he saw not a penny in income from any of their sales. 'What I do not like,' he rasped at the time, 'is all the junk that goes with them [the Bond pictures]. All this merchandising of the Bond name on toy guns, deodorants, underwear. It's cheap, and I dislike it intensely.'[35]

Truth be told, Connery would have had cause enough to resent such gimmickry even if he had been realising a profit from it. If the Bond of *Thunderball* had had little enough to do, the Bond of *You Only Live Twice* has almost nothing to do: here is Connery looking silly in a helmet and a helicopter not much bigger than a bicycle, here is Connery looking absurd in a fibre 'Japanese' wig and what look like sticking-plaster eyelids. Indeed, for the second half of the movie he just has to stand there and let himself be dwarfed by Ken Adam's stupendous volcano interior with built-in rocket-launch pad. At the start of the picture Bond is putatively killed off by a gang of vengeful Japanese, and though once the credits are over it is made plain that he has in fact survived the incident, it would be an adventurous critic who called him alive and well.

What of Connery's suggestion during the promotional work for *Thunderball* that more thought needed to be put into Bond's dialogue and more time given over to developing Bond's character? What indeed? Aside from the fact that he has mysteriously taken to preferring his Martinis stirred rather than shaken, the only change to Bond's character in Roald Dahl's script for *You Only Live Twice* is that now instead of smirking facetiously at Q's latest gizmos he actually rings head office and asks for them to be sent over. As for the dialogue Connery is given to work with on the movie, it is virtually non-existent. He spends the bulk of the film being filled in on various people's back-stories and firing whatever name they have just mentioned back at them: 'Tiger?' 'Osato?' 'Little Nellie?'

Only once does Connery seem to be enjoying himself, during the scene in which he meets the chemical magnate cum SPECTRE villain Mr Osato (Teru Shimada). The dialogue, which centres on

Bond – pretending to be an entrepreneur foodie who needs an export licence for monosodium glutamate! – is as bad as any the series has given us, but just watch Connery sit down on Osato's leather upholstery and cross his legs, languorous as a lion after lunch. Elsewhere, though, Connery practically slouches his way through the movie, a look of bored contempt never far from his face.

A somewhat rounder face than hitherto. Though the Bond of *Goldfinger* had seemed slightly more beefy than that of *Dr No* and *From Russia with Love*, the Bond of *You Only Live Twice* looks heftier still. The naval uniform he wears in some early scenes aside, none of his jackets sits comfortably on him in the movie. In which case, was it really wise to dress him in a wrinkly jumpsuit for the final set piece in Blofeld's volcano? Since Connery has always prided himself on his fitness (and looked in fine fettle in *A Fine Madness*, as he would in his next picture, *Shalako* (1968)), the suspicion arises that this less than sleek new self was another affront to the character he had come to loathe. Though Connery successfully sued the newspaper *France Soir* for suggesting that he had lost his Bond contract due to an increase in his waist size, there is no denying that Connery's girth increased considerably since *Dr No* and that the man in *You Only Live Twice* has forgotten that you only eat once. As Cubby Broccoli, perhaps seeking revenge for Connery's jibe about fat slob producers, was to insinuate as the search for a new Bond took hold in the summer of 1967: 'There's a perfect parallel with the *Tarzan* series. When the first Tarzan, Elmo Lincoln, got so fat that it was considered he'd get laughed off the screen, lots of people thought a new face wouldn't be accepted.'[36]

Which is fair enough. Still, the fact remains that despite Saltzman and Broccoli's oft-made claim that audiences were less interested in who played Bond than the figure of Bond himself, many of the poster designs for *You Only Live Twice* were the first to use the formulation 'Sean Connery IS James Bond' rather than the hitherto customary 'Sean Connery as Ian Fleming's James Bond'. Other ads were even less ambiguous about the existential link between actor and character, not even deigning to name Connery: 'This man IS James Bond' they bellowed, for all the world as if Connery were on a Police Most Wanted list.

And wanted he most certainly was. At one point during the pre-publicity for *You Only Live Twice* Connery snuck off for a quiet pee only to find the gents' loos full of newspaper photographers desperate for a shot of him. Connery fled the scene and, while Broccoli was forced to confront the mass of hacks and snappers and beseech them to leave his man alone, Saltzman, with more than usual solicitousness, urged them to respect his star's privacy because 'Sean has a terrible feeling of loss of personal identity'.[37]

But Connery mania was not so easily assuaged. Director Lewis Gilbert (drafted into the Bond series after his success with Michael Caine in *Alfie* a year or so earlier) has described filming *You Only Live Twice*'s exterior scenes as a nightmare plagued by the unwanted attentions of hordes of fans. Connery himself would later talk of 'a terrible pressure, like living in a goldfish bowl'.[38] The television reporter Alan Whicker, who made a documentary on the Bond phenomenon during the *You Only Live Twice* shoot, argued that Bond's appeal resided in his near-singular status as a non–neurotic man. It's a telling insight, though there is no denying that the man so many people identified with Bond was rather less at ease in the world.

All of which said, the Connery who was shot on set by Ken Adam for his own private film records of the making of the movie seems relaxed enough, joking and gurning and striking body-building poses atop the volcano in which Blofeld's mission HQ is putatively sited. Perhaps he was happy that this whole fiesta of banality was coming to an end.

'By the time of *You Only Live Twice*,' Connery would remember a decade and a half later, '[I thought] . . . they'd peaked and the decline would start . . . I was wrong.'[39] In fact, the non–stop action of *On Her Majesty's Secret Service* and the comic delights of *Diamonds Are Forever* (1971) aside, Connery was quite correct. From here on in the Bond pictures, while still performing well enough, would take progressively less at the box office. From here on in the Bond pictures would descend into humourless travesties as Connery's scalding irony was substituted for Roger Moore's pantomime charm school, as Connery's lethal physicality was substituted for Moore's stiff-kneed waddle, as Connery Bond's smouldering cigarettes were substituted for Moore Bond's Freudianly effete cigars. As Terence Young, whose services we should remember had not been retained for this fifth Bond picture, remarked at the time: 'I simply couldn't go on with Bond. I mean, where do you take him? You'd simply have to parody a parody of a parody.'[40] Such would be Connery's near palindromic achievement in *Diamonds Are Forever*.

What, though, had been his achievement in the first five Bond films? Above all, to remould Fleming's character into a new, cheekily comic-book yet chicly corporeal shape. As Connery has never tired of pointing out, 'in playing Bond . . . I had to start from scratch. Nobody knows anything about him, after all. Not even Fleming. Does he have parents? Where does he come from? Nobody knows.'[41] Yet it is not mere historical accident that explains why every new movie Bond must be measured against Connery's original. Whatever Broccoli and Saltzman's belief that it was Bond himself who was the star of their movies ('Somewhere in a rep company in a place like the Midlands,' Saltzman was heard to say as Connery quit the series, 'we're going to come across an actor who will fit the role perfectly'[42]), there is no gainsaying the fact that had they not cast Connery in *Dr No* there would have been no later Bonds – and no subsequent series – to argue about. Had, say, Roger Moore been cast as Bond in *Dr No*, he wouldn't have played him in *From Russia with Love*, much less *Live and Let Die* (1973). To be sure, Bond had made Connery, but it is equally certain that it was Connery who made Bond.

Convincing as the socio-historical argument is in Simon Winder's *The Man Who Saved Britain* – essentially, that Fleming's original books offered solace to a country getting used to its new lowly status in the post-imperial world – it goes nowhere towards explaining the success of the movie series.[43] It's understandable that misty-eyed nationalists, distraught at what the Suez debacle had done to their dreams for their country's future, should find solace in the patriotic certainties of the Fleming version of *Dr No*. Five years later, though, when the movie came along, the whole world knew Britain's imperial fantasies had turned to dust. And even had anyone bought a ticket for *Dr No* in the hopes of seeing the aftershock of Suez put right, the star of the show took great pains to send up the supremacist fantasies that putatively motivated Bond.

Transforming Fleming's colourless blade into a self-consciously mocking drawing-room comedian was no mean feat. Whatever else such double-edged ironising required, it required a far better actor than the Connery of even the late sixties was still too often taken to be. Unfortunately for Connery, the seemingly snug fit between character and actor fooled too many people into believing that he was just playing himself. By taking such pains to ensure everything Bond did looked effortless, Connery contrived to convince audiences that he wasn't doing much either. 'When people saw Sean doing Bond they thought that was just flip, easy stuff,' Sidney Lumet has said. 'But that's one of the hardest kinds of acting; only a real actor can do that.'[44] It takes 'talent and ability . . . to play that kind of character', Lumet believes. 'It's the movie equivalent of high comedy and he did it brilliantly.'[45] Men and women all around the world concurred.

One of the reasons the Bond movies travelled so well is that you didn't need to understand a word of what Bond was saying to know what he was thinking and feeling, let alone doing. Recalling his training under Yat Malmgren, Connery has argued that 'the first question a spectator asks at a play or a film is, "What are they up to?" It is visual, initially . . . If you can *show* what people are doing, then the dialogue and the sound effects become like a bonus.'[46] Connery, though, served up his own added bonus: he didn't just move eloquently – he moved majestically. Lethally economic in even the most innocuous movements and moments – watch him pad around the health farm in *Thunderball* in a (rather nasty) sports coat and twill pants or steal a hotel maid's key in *Goldfinger* – Connery remains the most physically watchable film star the British cinema has ever produced. You have to go back to the young Burt Lancaster or even as far back as the James Cagney of the thirties and forties to find someone so dangerously motile. However ludicrous the acts of derring-do Bond was called on to perform, they were made momentarily real simply by dint of Connery's lavish, near gratuitous grace.

The problem was, the movies were never anywhere near good enough to live up to the standards set by Connery's air of lethal cool. Ken Adam's pop art sets, John Barry's lazily jabbing scores and Maurice Binder's still remarkable credits aside, too much of the Bond series was put together on the cheap and in a hurry. If it is true that the Bond movies inaugurated the modern action-adventure genre, it is also the case that – as with so many recent British innovations – the concept had to be adopted and adapted by foreign powers to really come good. Save for the contributions of Connery, Barry and Adam, no Bond movie is a patch on, say, an entry in the Bruce Willis *Die Hard* series.

Not that such aesthetic niceties troubled Connery as, back home in London after the *You Only Live Twice* shoot, he moved his family to a Victorian house in the middle of Putney Heath. A little more secluded than his previous residence, Connery's new home came with an acre or so of land and was surrounded by walls rather higher than those he had failed to hide behind in Acton. The golf courses of Surrey were close at hand, many of his friends lived nearby, and if he didn't yet have that million pounds in the bank, still he was well on his way to it. Having turned down Terence Young's offer of the part of Audrey Hepburn's husband in *Wait Until Dark* (1967), Connery sat back to contemplate not just the future, but the past . . .

7

Intermission

In the spring of 1967, Connery wrote to George Leslie, the Scottish National Party's candidate in a by-election in Pollok, a southern constituency of Glasgow. 'I am convinced,' Connery declared in his note, 'that with our resources and skills we are more than capable of building a prosperous, vigorous and modern self-governing Scotland in which we can all take pride and which will deserve the respect of all other nations.'[1]

Forty years on, and Connery is still convinced – though his efforts at the time of that Pollok by-election came to little, with the Conservatives winning the seat. Then again, in November of that same year, the SNP's Winnie Ewing did succeed in capturing what had hitherto been the Labour stronghold of Hamilton. And a year later, Connery's fealty to the Nationalist cause prompted the party to ask him whether he would like to be a candidate at the next election.[2] This was decidedly clever branding on the part of the SNP, although Connery, doubtless smarting at the reviews his first post-Bond picture had just received, was wisely fearful of further diluting his own brand, and spurned the party's advances.

But the taste for intervening in matters of the real world stayed with him. In May 1967, just as the Summer of Love was beginning to heat up, Connery and Cilento were among the signatories to a letter to Prime Minister Harold Wilson urging immediate action to lift the Egyptian blockade of the Gulf of Aqaba (the cause of what became known as the Six-Day War).[3] Not quite a John and Yoko-style bed-in, but the spirit of the counter-cultural age seems to have infused the Connery household. Though Connery might not have taken himself off to India to find his way towards enlightenment with the Maharishi, he had other ways of finding himself nonetheless. A year or so earlier, in the build-up to the testing times of the *You Only Live Twice* shoot, he had begun working with R. D. Laing, an existentialist psychiatrist who had been making a name for himself with his then radical thoughts on the causes of schizophrenia. Laing had had a huge success with his first book, *The Divided Self* (1960), a title that might have been designed to appeal to the Connery of the dog days of the Bond years.

Because though Bond the character was never remotely self-conscious, the actor playing him increasingly came to resemble the double-agent hero cum anti-hero of Derek Marlowe's debut novel *A Dandy in Aspic* (1966) – a man pretending to be another man, a man taken for someone he was not by everyone who was not him, a man increasingly uncertain of who he was and where his place in the world might be. In Marlowe's thriller of ideas, the titular dandy Eberlin is tasked by one of his spymasters with assassinating an enemy agent who turns out to be, in a delightful twist, none other than himself working under a phoney name. It would be fanciful to suggest Connery ever entertained similar fantasies himself. Still, both *From Russia with Love* and *You Only Live Twice* kick off with mini-dramas that end with Bond seemingly being killed off. No subsequent Bond has suffered such a fate. Could it be that something in Connery's playing of the role suggested to screenwriters that his Bond had a death-wish? Whatever, Connery would later say that the three or four one-on-one sessions he had with Laing helped 'me to look at everything more objectively'.[4]

The two men came to work together thanks to the efforts of Cilento, who had herself met Laing and told him of what she regarded as her husband's travails. Connery, she would remember years later, was immediately taken with the idea of meeting Laing simply on the strength of what most people would regard as his lordly terms – a limousine to and from consultations, a bottle of single malt whisky to be on hand at same, and a dauntingly large hourly fee. 'Sean was pleased at the arrangement,' according to Cilento. 'He knew no one could ask for that much loot without being sure of his skills.'[5]

What did Connery and Laing talk about? Who can say, though given that these were the High Sixties, when Connery was drawn more and more to matters of state and Laing was writing *The Politics of Experience/The Bird of Paradise* (1967), it is likely that they touched on the divided society quite as much as they did on any notional divided self. Indeed, according to Cilento, Laing had difficulty in picking the lock of her husband's psyche. Eventually, in order to break through what Cilento describes as her 'emotionally blocked' husband, Laing became adamant that his patient must take a tab of LSD.[6]

For Laing, though, acid was more than just a way of tuning in, turning on and dropping out. Like those doctors in the US who had been treating Cary Grant with the drug since the late fifties, he was convinced that the drug could lower anxiety levels and shed light on hidden or repressed memories.[7] And yet, according to Cilento, Connery's 'enormous reserve and armouring' allowed him to resist the journey into the past his first trip offered him, though she does claim that he was forced to spend the next few days in bed recovering from the side-effects of the trip.[8] In time, though, Connery did open up to Laing – to talk through memories such as the childhood shoplifting incident we touched upon earlier.

And as Connery opened up, so he and Laing became friends, 'knocking about together', in the words of Laing's then girlfriend, the journalist Sally Vincent. They were, she says, 'two Glaswegian [*sic*] boys out for a good time'.[9] Laing was a couple of years older than Connery, but like his client he came from humble stock. And though he did not play the golf that the tranquillity-seeking Connery – by now playing on a handicap of 14 – had become addicted to, he did play tennis and generally keep in shape. Indeed, for all his emphasis on the beneficial effects of acid, Laing's diaries of the time show that he was concerned about the burgeoning hippie movement's reliance on the drug.[10] It was through Laing, then, that Connery found a route into the alternative youth cultures that were springing up all around him as the sixties wore on. James Bond might not have been able to listen to the Beatles without earmuffs, but the actor who had created him was coming round to the idea.

It was in this spirit that, late in 1967, Connery took himself off to Oslo, there to convene with one Dr Ola Raknes, an 80-year-old former pupil of the Freudian Marxist Wilhelm Reich. Like Reich (and somewhat like Laing, though unlike Freud), Raknes was of the opinion that repression is at the heart of the human problem and must be done away with accordingly. (Freud himself knew the damage repression could do – but he believed that that repression was the price we must all pay for living in a civilised society, no matter what its discontents.)

It is to Reich, then, rather than to Freud, that we owe the now surely near universal Western belief that a healthy sex life is the foundation of a healthy life. Such was the thesis of his most famous book, *The Function of the Orgasm* (1927), in which Reich argues not only that all neuroses have their roots in the blocking of the libido, but that since neurosis is so common, very few of us can be getting enough of what the Rolling Stones had recently referred to as 'sssssssssssatisfaction'. This did not, Reich would later argue, mean that he was arguing for a 'free-for-all fucking epidemic'.[11] Alas for him, in the heady days of the late sixties he was taken to have argued for nothing else.

Reich's main claim was that he had discovered the physical basis of libido – in the form of a substance he called orgone energy. This substance, Reich believed, was responsible not only for the sex drive but for everything those of a spiritual bent characterise as love. More than that, this energy could be stored in boxes – and subsequently parcelled out to anyone who spent a little time in what Reich called his 'orgone accumulator'. This last was a six-sided box with an iron interior and a non-metallic exterior; sandwiched between were several alternating layers of steel and glass wool. It all sounds like something out of Ian Fleming, but Connery was sufficiently impressed with whatever happened inside the cabinet of Dr Raknes that when he returned from Oslo to his Putney fastness he had what he called a 'think tank' installed in his study.[12] We can laugh at such mumbo-jumbo – and no scientist has ever granted credence to Reich's claims about orgone energy – but we shall see how such experiences went on influencing Connery for quite a few years.

Not all of Connery's work that year was so fantastical. In January of 1967 he made his debut as a theatrical impresario, subsidising the move of Frank Hauser's Oxford Playhouse production of *Volpone* (starring Connery's old friend Leo McKern) to the Garrick Theatre in London's West End. A couple of months later he put a little money into Cilento's friend Anthony Page's take on Gogol's *Diary of a Madman*, a production starring Nicol Williamson at the Duchess.[13]

No less significantly, he narrated for Scottish Television the script of *Fairfields: Keel of Industry*, a documentary about the imminent closure of Glasgow's largest shipyard. Thanks in part to the show's broadcast, Harold Wilson's government loaned the yard £1 million so that it could buy itself some time for a rescue consortium led by one Iain Stewart. Connery, who had met Stewart on the golf circuit, subsequently suggested they put together another film, this time about the efforts being made to salvage one of Scotland's biggest employers.

The bulk of that effort centred on Stewart's enlightened experiments designed to break down the barriers between Clydeside's putatively 'Red' workers and management* – an aim

---

* Highly enlightened, for the time: we were still the best part of three years away from Barbara Castle's famous White Paper on industrial relations, 'In Place of Strife'.

reflected in the title Connery gave his second take on proceedings at Fairfield: *The Bowler and the Bunnet*. (A bunnet is a flat tweed cap worn by pretty much everyone at the yard below the level of foreman.) Unfortunately, Stewart's experiment came to little. Within months of the broadcast of *The Bowler and the Bunnet*,[14] the government announced that it was nationalising the country's shipyards, consolidating them into larger, geographically centred organisations. Though Stewart stayed on as Deputy Chairman of the Upper Clyde yard, his progressive management techniques were quietly but quickly forgotten.

Given such solidarity with the Scottish workers, the post-Bond Connery made some surprising career decisions. True, he was wise before the fact when he turned down a reputed $600,000 offer from Charles Feldman to appear in the producer's putatively comic take on *Casino Royale* (1967).* But his rejection of a leading role in Tony Richardson's radical retelling of *The Charge of the Light Brigade* (1968) is rather more difficult to account for. Richardson wanted Connery to play Louis Nolan, an Edinburgh-raised, half-Irish, half-Scottish captain highly critical of the deployment of his cavalry division in the Crimean War.[15] The picture, which was shot in the spring of 1967, turned out no masterpiece. But in its insistence on the blundering stupidity of the aristocracy and the eternal nobility of what that aristocracy calls the lower orders, it offered a potent antidote to the fantasies of empire Connery had been guilty of embodying (if not endorsing) in the Bond series.

More mysterious still is why his ambition to play James Hepburn, the fourth Earl of Bothwell, in a projected movie version of Elizabeth Byrd's *The Immortal Queen* was never realised. As of the spring of 1967, *The Hill*'s Ray Rigby was at work on a script, and Connery had hopes that Vanessa Redgrave would play Mary, Queen of Scots.[16] But nothing materialised until a full four years

---

* The film turned out a disaster, though Connery was rumoured to have been up for the job had Feldman been willing to pay him $1 million.

later, when Redgrave ended up playing the same role in a very different picture, Charles Jarrott's *Mary, Queen of Scots* (1971), in which the Bothwell role is taken by the reliably over-the-top – and English through and through – Nigel Davenport.

Davenport's origins matter not because his Scottish accent in the picture is lamentable but because the real Bothwell, though a Protestant, was fervently anti-English. And Connery himself had only recently delivered himself of the opinions that 'the Scots have nothing in common with the English' and 'I don't like the English at all because I'm Scottish'.[17] One needn't go along with such nationalist nonsense to grasp that Connery might have been able to do more for his country's cause by playing Bothwell than by backing any number of SNP election candidates or narrating any number of television documentaries.

Meanwhile, Cilento, more creative than ever, was hard at work writing her first novel, *The Manipulator*. Why the move into literature? 'The trouble with filming,' she said at the time of her book's publication, 'is that it's never really your own work. You don't have much control over what you do; you're in the hands of the director, the lighting expert and the cutter, and they really decide what your performance is like.'[18]

Still, there were, Cilento said, practical as well as aesthetic reasons behind her having picked up her pen. Her husband, she claimed, did not approve of her 'work[ing] away from home'.[19] Hence, she would later say, 'I thought it would appease [Sean] if I turned to writing books. What I failed to grasp was that it wasn't just acting he required me to give up. He did not want me to do any work at all that lay outside the responsibilities of a wife and mother . . . he was just as irritated with the writing as he was with the acting.'[20] And maybe he was, though it should be noted that *The Manipulator*'s dust-jacket image – a Motherwellian red and black scrawl on an orange ground that a more traditional psychiatrist than R. D. Laing might have had a field day with – is credited to one Sean Connery. Moreover, the book, which was published in May 1967 by Hodder

& Stoughton (who paid Connery £30 for his design), bears the dedication 'For Sean'.

Connery took the rest of the year off, finding time for little but golf. Indeed, so relaxed was he that at one point he was contemplating setting up a pro-am tournament as a Scottish rival to Bing Crosby's in Hollywood. But as 1967 clicked over into 1968, Connery was back in the movie saddle – literally so: for the first time in his career he was to star in a western.

An old-fashioned western, you can't help thinking, watching Connery ride the high country as *Shalako*'s opening credits roll. Though the picture was shot in southern Spain (in Almeria, where the trilogy of mould-breaking spaghetti westerns that were making Clint Eastwood's name had just been filmed), the iconography and the typography (a bold, red, shadowed, slab-serif font emblazoned across an arid landscape), not to mention the chorus plainting the virtues of 'the man called Shalako' (the lyrics are by Jim Dale*) – all these contrive to make the picture look like a western from the classic era.

Certainly the man called Shalako turns out to be just the kind of old-fashioned, virtuous westerner Eastwood (and the Vietnam War) had just consigned to the dustbin of cultural history. As played by Connery, Shalako is a man of honour – a man so honourable that, like so many pre-Clint western heroes before him, he cannot function within a society he deems less than honourable. As such, Shalako is one of the pivotal creations on his creator's CV. While James Bond had spent the bulk of his time mocking the very idea of noble courage, Shalako was the first in the long line of uncompromised heroes Connery has ever since been called on to embody.

Admittedly, Shalako's attitude towards the Indians – he calls the Apaches 'dog-killers' with 'an instinct for war' – isn't very 1968. On the other hand, he has no time for the bunch of hapless, effete

* Yes, that Jim Dale.

whiteys the plot makes it his duty to rescue. And at the movie's end, when he is made to fight an Apache to the death, Shalako wins but refuses to kill his opponent.

Perhaps unsurprisingly, punters weren't convinced by Connery's attempt to stretch himself. What's the point in using Jack Hawkins as a washed-up imperialist know-nothing if you're not going to let Connery unleash the insolent wit that made him famous? Why cast Honor Blackman – the only woman who had ever given Connery's Bond a run for his money – and neglect to have her spar with her old oppo? Nor were audiences schooled on 007's devil-may-care seductions impressed when Shalako resolutely refused to put the moves on Brigitte Bardot's Countess Irina Lazaar. What else had they paid their money for if not to see the decade's two great sex symbols get it on? As it is, the two of them don't get together until the movie's closing moment – and then only in distant long shot.

All of which is a way of saying that if *Shalako* was a mistake for Connery, it was a bigger mistake for the people who cast him. Had they given the lead to Steven Boyd (who plays the treacherous but indolent heavy, Bosky Fulton) the movie would have been little duller than it is. But it would have been a lot cheaper – the major expense on *Shalako* was Connery's $1 million salary (plus a share of any profits) – and stood a rather better chance of making its money back. As it is, four decades after its release, the movie is still running at a loss.

Not, it should be said, that *Shalako* is the unredeemable stinker too many critics painted it as. Though Connery never looks quite comfortable in Shalako's Caesar-cut toupee, he sits well on a horse, and works wonders with a severely underwritten character. As Pauline Kael pointed out at the time, Connery had 'more presence and style . . . than this picture deserves'.[21]

Shalako's bigger problem, of course, was that its generic strictures and structures, its notions of noble, heroic individualism, chimed not at all with the public at that time of national breast-beating. Whatever one's take on America's involvement in the war in

Vietnam – and you had to have an Ian Fleming-like devotion to the moral superiority of the West to believe America was right to be there – there was no gainsaying the fact that the losses the country was sustaining there in that *annus horribilis* of 1968 were doing nothing to bolster the myth of the uncompromised, unconquerable American hero that the western was founded upon. Nor, after events like the massacre of Vietnamese women and children by American troops at My Lai,* did the western's essential equation – cowboys good, Indians bad – look any more convincing.

Bluntly, the western – the American movie genre par excellence – was over. By the late sixties, no actor could have starred in an old-fashioned oater and expected to come out smiling. Not even Sean Connery. Especially not Sean Connery. He it was, after all, who in the creation of the screen Bond had worked so hard to pull the rug from under the idea of the untarnishable, irony-free hero. Though events in the real world had done more than enough to kill off the idea of the man of honour, Connery's flip amorality in the 007 cycle had popularised the notion for the mass audience: forget the idea of service to the community, it's an every man for himself world we live in; so do unto the other guy what you wouldn't have him do unto you – which means make sure you do it first – and then crack jokes about how you're doing what you're doing out of loyalty to Queen and country. Whatever else they were, in other words, these were not propitious times for the man called Shalako, much less for a picture named after him.

The *Shalako* shoot wrapped in late March 1968, but Connery, hungry for work after the relaxations of the previous year, was back on location within a matter of weeks for *The Molly Maguires* (1970). There was more than one reason behind Connery's decision to appear in the picture, of course. For starters, its director, Martin Ritt, had only a couple of years earlier made a film with Cilento –

---

* On March 16, 1968, just as the *Shalako* shoot was coming to a finish.

Hombre (1966) – a well-received liberal western that, in its probing of the movies' too pat take on the idea of Wild-West heroism, might be taken as a pre-emptive critique of everything that *Shalako* turned out to be.

For another, the year before *Hombre*, Ritt had directed Richard Burton in a gloomy, monochromatic version of John le Carré's successful espionage novel *The Spy Who Came in from the Cold* (1965). True, the picture did rather less than justice to the le Carré original, but in its dogged dourness, in its devotion to the shades of grey that muddy and mess the frighteningly stark clarity of Oswald Morris's cinematography, in its insistence that far from being a glamorous lifestyle choice spying is a drama-free drudge – a life in which it hardly matters whether you take your Martini shaken or stirred because the only point in drinking is to get numbly drunk: in all this and more *The Spy Who Came in from the Cold* helped prick the Bond balloon.

More than that, *The Molly Maguires* was to be a mainstream companion to *The Bowler and the Bunnet* – another way for a now huge international star to remind the workers that he came from the same place they did, and that no matter what happened he would not be estranged from them. Because *The Molly Maguires* is a picture about working men – about men being paid a pittance for the kind of back-breaking labour that would shock George Orwell in the 1930s. It is a picture about the way such men's pay is docked if they break a shovel or a pick while mining, a picture about the way working men can be angered by such treatment, a picture about the way such men can become disaffected and alienated – a picture about how such men might, in the end, become saboteurs.

The men in question are the émigré Irish that mined the Pennsylvania coalfields in the days when Connery's forebears first fetched up in Scotland. Given a different fork in the road, of course, his own family might have ended up in North America. So Connery had every reason to feel solidarity with the character he was playing. He is called Jack Kehoe, but he might well have been called Connery, as might any of the people in what is essentially a true story. For to a man – and a woman – they are all poor Celts who have taken themselves off to distant places in search of a living.

Connery himself had a living to make too, of course. And even though he took second lead in the picture – the first time he had not been top of the bill since *Marnie* – he was being paid $1 million for the privilege. 'For that,' he quipped, 'they can put a mule ahead of me.'[22] Instead – and rather bafflingly, because Connery was far and away the bigger star – they put Richard Harris ahead of him. He plays James McParlan, an undercover cop charged with bringing the troublesome Molly Maguires to justice.

Now, one does not want to do an injustice to Connery, who puts in some fine work in Ritt's picture. But *The Molly Maguires* might have been yet more intriguing had Connery and Harris swapped roles. Brave as it might seem for the creator of the world's most famous gentleman spy to be taking on the part of an insurrectionary proto-trades unionist, how much braver it would have been of him to have taken the part of the spy who is working undercover to subvert such subversives.

For try as he might, Connery still could not shuffle off Bond's seemingly immortal coil in *The Molly Maguires*. Take the movie's opening sequence, in which we watch Kehoe plant a bomb in the depths of a mine shaft before following him up and out of the pit and into the daylight. The camera stays a step or two ahead of Connery all the way through these long opening minutes, leading him on as he trudges homeward – the mine remaining in shot in the background all the while. The scene goes on and on (to be precise, it is almost fifteen minutes long – fifteen minutes in which not a word is spoken), and we get time to enjoy that look of glassy contempt Connery had perfected for Bond. It almost seems that, like 007 before him, Kehoe is waiting with affectless irony for the explosion that is about to fill the screen. But then, at the last minute, Connery walks out of frame and Ritt cuts – uncomfortably, it should be said, the picture's hitherto loose yet steady rhythm being undone by the edit – back to the interior of the pit for a close-up of the bomb blast. It's as if star and director know that for their movie to have any claim to seriousness it must deny its audiences the destructive pleasures Connery's Bond was designed to deliver. There must, that is, be no wry smiles from Kehoe as another set goes up in smoke. The trouble is that, sound though such iconoclastic thinking is, it means we haven't got a clue what Kehoe thinks he is up to in laying his fiery charges.

As Pauline Kael pointed out at the time of the movie's release, it is never made plain what the Molly Maguires – a secret band of terrorists working within the Ancient Order of Hibernians – hope to achieve by their acts of sabotage.[23] As exploding pit is followed by exploding pit, exploding train line by exploding train line, we're left wondering what – beyond further opportunities for Ritt's director of photography, James Wong Howe, to show off some more of his chiaroscuro lighting – all this is for. How can it possibly benefit mine workers to have the mines they work in put out of service? Is the Maguires' plan actually to wound or kill some of their fellow workers in the hope of discrediting the management who allow such dangerous practices to go on? Devoid of any such explanation, the litany of explosions – for all their historical real-life moral import – ends up having no more impact than those at the end of a Bond movie. Connery himself, it should be said, knew that something was going wrong with the picture. Ritt, he ruefully told one journalist, 'was disinclined to get too close to the sympathies of the character I was playing because he [Ritt] might have been identified with un-American activities: the piece had a very political slant, with its black-faced miners* and trade unions and bosses against workers and all that.'[24]

No less easy to read, though, is the picture's attitude towards Richard Harris's undercover detective. What does McParlan

---

* Pauline Kael wondered whether the picture might be a parable of black power. *New Yorker*, 7 February 1970.

imagine he is doing, for instance, by getting so involved with the Molly Maguires that he actually comes to enjoy the hooliganism and vandalism membership enjoins? What is he about when he becomes so enmeshed in the group's intrigues that he turns killer himself? Who can say? – although no matter how many times you see the picture, you keep expecting McParlan to go fully over to the other side and actively start working against his employers. The fact that he doesn't only makes the movie yet more difficult to read, of course. It's all very well for Ritt to tell us that there really was a James McParlan who really did work for the Pinkerton Detective Agency and really did infiltrate the Molly Maguires and really did provide testimony that sent ten of its members to their death. But you can't make a movie about that man and at the same time turn him into a tortured existentialist (as Richard Harris, in what is far and away his most watchable screen performance, so ably does) – not if you want to tell a story that makes anything like sense.

Nor, suggests *The Molly Maguires*' lamentable US box office take (at $1.1 million a mere $100,000 more than Connery's own pay cheque), can you make a serious, sensitive movie about the travails of the working man and expect a megastar to pull in the punters. Connery, who claims to have told Ritt at the screening of the picture's first cut that 'he'd missed it', thinks the picture's problem is that it lacks humour.[25] Given that *The Molly Maguires* is as dour and smile-free as any picture Connery has starred in, it's fair to say he had a point. But anyone familiar with Ritt's almost self-consciously liberal work ought perhaps have known that he was never going to be the man to look for humour in a drama about troubled trades unionists.

And if it was humour Connery wanted, there was always another Bond movie to be made. For one of the great myths of film history is that Connery washed his hands of Bond immediately upon completion of *You Only Live Twice*. In reality, that film had been merely the last instalment of the five-picture contract he had signed with Broccoli and Saltzman seven years earlier. True, when asked by the Queen Mother at the picture's premiere whether this was 'really your last Bond film', Connery had replied in the affirmative. But that's what he would have said, isn't it? Now a free agent, he wanted to renegotiate his contract for any future Bonds on his own terms.

Seen in this light, the decision to take second billing to Richard Harris in *The Molly Maguires* is easier to understand. What mattered about the picture was not Connery's position in the credits but the fact that he was being paid $1 million – a third more than he had been paid up front for his last Bond and the amount he had held out for on the ill-fated *Casino Royale*.* A precedent had been set, in other words, a point had been made. Been set and made, moreover, by a small-time political melodrama that was certain that it would make all its costs back – and more – simply because among its cast was the biggest star in the world. Now it was time for Broccoli and Saltzman to get real and start paying their million-dollar milch cow what he was worth.

So it was that for several weeks after the wrap on *The Molly Maguires*, Connery went into negotiations for *On Her Majesty's Secret Service*. The talks lasted through September 1968, with Saltzman and Broccoli 'try[ing] to persuade 38-year-old Connery to change his mind about giving up the role. If he refuses, Australian model George Lazenby, 27, the Big Fry man in the TV commercials,† is strongly tipped to take over.'[26] Strongly tipped indeed, because a month later talks broke down and Lazenby was announced as the new Bond.[27] He was paid $50,000 (£20,000).

How much should we regret the loss of Connery to the sixth Bond picture? Given that Lazenby was no actor, and that *On Her Majesty's Secret Service* is by some measure the best *actioner* – the most invigoratingly physical movie – in the whole series, rather a

---

* Though his 25 per cent take on the net merchandising profits for *You Only Live Twice* was said to have taken his final pay cheque close to $1 million.
† The Fry's Turkish Delight ad can still be watched at www.tellyads.com/ show_movie_vintage/php?filename=VA0167.

lot. With Connery in place as Bond it might well have been the series' best movie, the ur-movie, the one that topped them all with such elan that everyone could have cheered, packed up, gone home and got on with their lives safe from the puerile tawdry of the Moore years, the faux realism of the Daniel Craig era . . .

And yet . . . Given Connery's teenage work with horses on that Edinburgh milk round it should not perhaps have surprised us overmuch that he sat so well on a horse in *Shalako*. Still, it is hard to imagine the Connery of the late sixties in the movie's snug-fitting ski-suit. Because there is simply no denying the fact that George Lazenby looks magnificent in *On Her Majesty's Secret Service*'s many action sequences. At a shade over 6ft 2in he's even taller than Connery, and while wonderfully athletic he contrives somehow to be an even more lithe figure than the Connery of *Dr No*. Above and beyond all that, Lazenby looks good on skis in a way that one can never imagine Connery, for all the swaggering impertinence of his gait, managing. And there is no point to *On Her Majesty's Secret Service* if your leading man doesn't look good on skis.

Moreover: can we really imagine Connery having been able to handle the movie's ending, in which his new bride is gunned down mere moments after their wedding? Not, of course, that Connery the actor wasn't up to the task Fleming's storyline set an actor. It's that Connery's Bond, the monolithic construction that he will never entirely disassociate himself from, really couldn't ever have fallen in love. Because that guy was a stud. He didn't do romance. He didn't do this emotional stuff. And that's why he was so adored. In his single-minded, laconic, mocking, self-sufficient vanity, Connery's Bond was the epitome of sixties consumer culture.

You can approve or not, but what you can't do – even if, like Saltzman and Broccoli, you believe the touchy-feely ambience of the Summer of Love played a part in keeping profits down on your last extravaganza – is transport such a figure into a context wherein he simply has to show signs of emotion. And even granting that that long list of impossibles might somehow have been achieved, there was no way Connery's Bond could have been seen to exhibit distress at the fact of his wife's having been blown away. The Connery Bond figure, like the Clint Eastwood of the *Dollars* pictures, would have reached for his gun.

And so, having turned *On Her Majesty's Secret Service* down, Connery spent the next few months doing very little. His biggest achievement of the year was finally persuading his parents that it was time they moved home, buying them a house in the Newington area of Edinburgh. That district is only half a mile east of Fountainbridge, but in outlook, architecture and general atmosphere it might have been half a hundred miles away.

As for work, Connery's only acting endeavours in the summer and autumn of 1968 came in a three-part play for the ITV network with the catch-all title *The Male of the Species.* Connery starred in the first episode of the trilogy (the stars of parts two and three were, respectively, Michael Caine and Paul Scofield) as the titular McNeil, an arrogant master carpenter who treats women as if they were put on earth for no other reason than to pleasure him. No recording of the show exists, alas, so the film historian can but wonder at how what sounds like a critique of the Bond figure turned out.

Written by Alun Owen, the show went out in February 1969,[28] though Connery himself wasn't around to see it. Instead, he was spending three weeks between Moscow and Leningrad, filming *The Red Tent* (1971), a Soviet/Italian co-production that tells the true story of the mission to rescue General Umberto Nobile from his ill-fated expedition – via airship – to the North Pole in 1928.

After the calculated acceptance of second billing on *The Molly Maguires*, Connery was once more the headliner in Mikhail Kalatozov's picture – even though, as that three-week shooting schedule might suggest, his part in the picture is little more than a cameo. In the 121-minute version we have (the picture originally ran longer than two and a half hours), Connery is on screen for not quite ten minutes. Little wonder that Peter Finch, whose role as General Nobile had thus far necessitated a full nine months of shooting, and whose character was the lynch-pin of *The Red Tent*'s narrative structure, was not best pleased to learn he wasn't going to top the bill.[29]

Why had Connery taken this meagre part? Largely, one suspects, to remind Messrs Saltzman and Broccoli that their former star was still a star – a star, indeed, who as well as being able to command $1 million for second-billing appearances can command top billing for virtual walk-ons. Not, it should be said, that *The Red Tent* is entirely without interest. While it is true that Connery's gamesmanship resulted in his taking a role that offered him very little to do, it is also true that his performance as Roald Amundsen was the first of many in which he plays old men. At only just 38 years old, Connery is playing a man almost half his age again – 56 – and playing him very convincingly. Indeed, whatever one's doubts about the wisdom of Connery's choosing to appear in *The Red Tent*, they have nothing to do with the work he put into the picture. There is nothing wrong with his performance, save for the fact that there is nowhere near enough of it.

Now we can call this choice of role many things. We can call it brave – not only because by playing the sensible man, the level-headed man, the man who knows that discretion is the better part of valour, Connery is self-consciously reining in the derring-do heroics that have made his name. We can call it brave, too, because while Connery has never been vain about his looks, rare is the movie star who plays older than his years. Connery, though, will go on doing so for the rest of his career. And it is to the cinema's discredit that it has never really found a properly old character for Connery to play.

But we must also wonder whether playing so diametrically against type wasn't a little foolhardy – another example of Connery wilfully trying to convince the audience who had come to worship him that it was he and not the character they were in fact worshipping.

And we must wonder, too, about how wise it was, in that age when even the most hard-bitten cynic was just a little bowled over by the news that man had landed on the moon, to star in a film that examines the hubris of explorers and their travels. (Once shot and edited, *The Red Tent* was put on the shelf for a couple of years, only finally dribbling into cinemas in mid-1971, a baffling footnote to a career by then seen as deep in the doldrums.)

Meanwhile, Connery had other fish to fry. Having designed that dust jacket for his wife's first novel, having written a ballet that had impressed no less than both Kenneth Macmillan and George Balanchine (Cilento describes it as 'a sort of psychological *Swan Lake*'),[30] and having moved into the role of theatrical impresario with *Volpone*, Connery decided it was time he tried his hand at directing. *I've Seen You Cut Lemons*, by one of the Connerys' Putney neighbours Ted Allan Herman, was the play in question, and though its stars were Diane Cilento and Robert Hardy, still the biggest name on the poster was that of the director – Sean Connery. Not that the production was merely an ego-trip. The lessons he had learned from Laing and Raknes must have stuck with Connery, one thinks as one reads of him telling a reporter a week or so before the show opened that he is 'very disturbed by what society does to people who are insane'.[31]

So the play is a serious-minded one, which is not necessarily the same thing as a serious play. At which point I had better admit that, being eight weeks short of my eighth birthday when the show opened at the Fortune Theatre (and seven weeks short of the same birthday when it closed), I have not seen *I've Seen You Cut Lemons*. But those few people who did see it seem to have been distinctly unimpressed. Herman's drama is a two-hander about incest and child abuse that may or may not be worthy of its subject.* There is rather less doubt, though, that Connery's production – with its strobe

---

* The play was subsequently rewritten by Herman and John Cassavetes, becoming the screeenplay of the latter's *Love Streams* (1984).

lights and shadow effects, its soundtrack of meaningless squawks and squeals – did it no favours. According to the critic John Barber, all Connery's contrivances served to do was 'cheapen the play'.[32] A fellow reviewer picked upon these effects, too, complaining about the play's 'livid lighting' and 'screeching dissonances'.[33] Oh dear. It all sounds eerily predictive of everything that will let down Connery's first movie as a producer, to which we shall turn shortly.

The unavoidable inference is that Connery's overly self-conscious aesthetic, his need to prove to audiences that he was something rather more than Tarzan in a tuxedo (as well, perhaps, as his need to prove to Cilento – who had invited Connery to run the show when the original director dropped out – that he could keep up with her high-flown thespian and literary ambitions), was still in the ascendant. Indeed, what one might call Connery's bipolar approach to his craft and career – a comic thriller followed by a heavy drama – would continue for several more years, until the oil crisis and downturn of the mid-seventies made a mockery of the idea that there was any serious money to be had in a cinema that treated adults as adults.

Nothing daunted by the failure of *I'll See You Cut Lemons*, though, Connery jumped at the chance of working on *The Anderson Tapes* (1971), a meat-and-potatoes heist picture lain over with a Kafkaesque conceit about the paranoia induced by the surveillance society. (In the Lawrence Sanders novel on which the picture is based, the thief Connery plays is an existential individualist whose every crime is seen as a noble challenge to the authority of an overweening state.)

Despite such Nietzschean flummery, what counts most about Connery's performance in *The Anderson Tapes* (which means what counts most about the movie itself) is its essential lightness of heart. While Sidney Lumet's tricksy editing and Quincy Jones's funky, Stockhausen-inspired score conspire to foreground the movie's self-consciously alienated thematic, Connery breezes through the proceedings like a man delighted at the prospect of finally being given the chance to play in a comic drama.

The result is a schizoid picture, with Connery making sport of the world around him while Lumet's sombre, locked-in camera fails to react to his star's joshing tone. Early on in the movie, as Connery's Duke Anderson and his pal Pop (Stan Gottlieb) are released from prison, Pop complains about having been inside for forty years. Anderson says that at least means Pop missed out on the Great Depression, the Second World War and the Korean War. It's a lovely line, and one delivered by Connery with suggestive deadpan, yet Lumet cuts straight away from it the second it's been delivered, denying the audience the beat it needs to smile or even laugh. Indeed, when Anderson draws parallels between organised crime and capitalism,* Lumet's ponderous zoom-in suggests he treats the argument – being put forward by a smirkingly ironic Connery – as a serious political philosophy.

Admittedly, Connery's airiness of tone isn't entirely due to his playing. While *The Anderson Tapes* is the first picture since *You Only Live Twice* in which he wears Bond-style suits and shirts and shiny shoes, it is also the first picture in his career in which he owns up to his baldness and urges us to grasp the fact that he is not the mocking superstud a thousand newspaper features had been asking us to believe he was. Once out of prison, Duke makes straight for the apartment of Ingrid (Dyan Cannon), his former mistress, and before he is through her front door is undressing her, saying 'I haven't been laid in over ten years' – almost precisely the length of time audiences have believed Connery to be the world's greatest swordsman since Errol Flynn.

Because for all that the Connery of *The Anderson Tapes* might dress like 007, for all that the movie's original poster design – with its picture of our suited hero standing hand on hip, a pistol resting nonchalantly against his knee – might be a direct lift from the first

---

* The best part of a year, it is worth pointing out, before the release of Francis Ford Coppola's *The Godfather* (1972).

ads for *Dr No*; for all that, Duke Anderson is so very unlike 007. Open and warm and with a face-cracking grin (there are times in the picture when Duke looks as dumb as the Connery of *No Road Back* or *On the Fiddle*), Duke might be a villain, but despite a comb-over chrome-dome that can occasionally lend him the look of a pub bruiser, he is emphatically not a vicious villain. More than once Connery's Anderson makes it plain that he deplores the kind of casual violence Connery's James Bond had made his own.

Not, it should be said, that Anderson couldn't mete it out if he wanted to. Only months after that victory over *France Soir* and its claims about his waist size, the Connery of *The Anderson Tapes* is plainly in top condition. Look at him in the tight-cut one-piece boiler suit he wears for the movie's big heist scene and you are looking at a man almost as trim as the Bond of *Dr No* and *From Russia with Love*. Watch him cool and collected and draped only in a towel for a sauna scene in which he briefs the gang on the job (everyone else is dripping sweat and complaining about the heat) and you might be looking at a championship fighter.

And yet in his next picture – filmed mere months after the Lumet shoot wrapped – Connery would be a considerably portlier figure. Indeed, given the wrinkled hang of his jackets in *Diamonds Are Forever*, it is tempting to suggest that he is a portlier figure than the one measured up in Savile Row before the shoot ever began. Could it be that Connery's waistline had expanded in line with the contempt for the role that had made his name?

8

You've Had Your Six

As the seventies dawned, how big a star was the biggest star of the sixties? *Shalako* had netted less than $1 million at the US box office, *The Molly Maguires* a disappointing $1.1 million. Perhaps unsurprisingly, the yet to be released *Red Tent* would fare even less well. Only *The Anderson Tapes*, which had taken $5 million in the US, could be said to have performed reasonably well. Connery himself had done very nicely indeed out of these movies, of course. But only a subscriber to the short-term strategies of post-war British management could fail to have been worried by the moneys these pictures were taking.

Compare Clint Eastwood's record over the same period and the Connery box office haul looks yet more sickly. *Coogan's Bluff* (1968), a small-scale cowboy meets the big city thriller directed by Hollywood old pro Don Siegel, took $3.1 million in the US. *Where Eagles Dare* (1968), a big set-piece war movie for which Eastwood was reportedly paid $500,000 (half of what Connery trousered for *The Molly Maguires*), took $7 million Stateside. Granted, neither *Paint Your Wagon* (1969) nor *Kelly's Heroes* (1970) performed particularly well, but neither of those pictures was built solely for the purpose of showing off its leading man.

Now it's true that that triple flop of Connery titles didn't carry quite the negative charge that the *One-Eyed Jacks* (1960), *The Fugitive Kind* (1961) and *Mutiny on the Bounty* (1962) triumvirate had for Marlon Brando a few years earlier. But whichever way you cut it, Connery's years away from Bond, while handsomely burnishing his bank account, had done nothing for his long-term bankability.

Takings aside, of course, several of Connery's non-Bond pictures had been far from disastrous. The trouble was that for all his vaulting aesthetic ambitions, Connery, like the money-men he had so little time for, has always tended to value his work from the bottom-line up. He didn't just want to do better things than Bond. He wanted to do *bigger* things than Bond – and in a market where even Bond's stock seemed to be in decline that wasn't going to be easy. (Worldwide box-off takings for the initial release of *On Her Majesty's Secret Service* were a mere $9.1 million,* less than half of what *You Only Live Twice* took – though nine times and more the earnings of *Shalako*.)

To be fair, Connery didn't only have his eye on the main chance. True, in February 1969, a couple of months after *Shalako* had opened, he was to be found wailing to Lindsay Anderson about the 'irresponsible expenditure' on the picture that was eating away at his investment and therefore profits.[1] But as Pauline Kael was forever pointing out, whatever else he wanted from his career, Connery unquestionably wanted to test himself. Certainly those first three roles of the immediate post-Bond years had been chosen at least partly to prove that he was an actor with stretch as well as bulk. James Bond didn't make me, those movies keep trying to tell us. Rather, they say, it was me – Sean Connery – who made James Bond. Whatever the achievements of the past four years, though, pictures like *The Molly Maguires* and *The Red Tent* had proved that while Connery could indeed act, he could be a *star* only while playing Bond.

* As of February 2008, though, it has taken some $64.6 million worldwide – more than nine times its $7 million budget. True, *Diamonds Are Forever* has taken the best part of sixteen times its estimated $7.2 million budget, but the Lazenby picture's percentage profit isn't much worse than that for Roger Moore's second Bond picture, *The Man with the Golden Gun* (1974), which cost $13 million and has so far taken but $97.6 million. Whisper it soft, but it may be that had Saltzman and Broccoli stuck with Lazenby, Bond would have survived just as well.

And then, in the same week that *I've Seen You Cut Lemons* opened and closed in the West End, George Lazenby announced that he was quitting the Bond beat after just one picture. Connery professed himself not at all surprised by the decision. As he said of his replacement's lacklustre way with dialogue and characterisation, 'Lazenby couldn't do a good job because you have to have technique to get the character right . . . he just didn't have the experience.'[2] It was a fair point, thought that didn't mean Messrs Saltzman and Broccoli were immediately knocking on their first Bond's door. There were, they said, plenty other fish in the sea. Moreover, they were adamant, the fish need not be a big one. As they had proved with Connery, they said, they could make a man-eater out of the merest minnow.

So there was a lot of talk of another new Bond. There was talk of a young actor called Michael Gambon. (Like Connery before him, Gambon's then main claim to fame was a little work in TV versions of Shakespeare.) There was talk that a young RADA dropout called Timothy Dalton – much favoured by Cubby Broccoli at the time of the casting for *On Her Majesty's Secret Service* – was in the frame once more. There was talk of Adam West, TV's calculatedly camp Batman. There was talk of Burt Reynolds, an American a few years younger than Connery and much loved by the ladies. Most of all, there was talk about John Gavin, an actor who was then guesting as Dr Forbes in *The Doris Day Show*, who might have been the model for the garish, cartoony portraits of Bond on Fleming paperbacks of the late fifties, and whose main claim to fame was (as it remains) that he had played Janet Leigh's married lover in Hitchcock's *Psycho* (1960). And in the event there was more than talk about Gavin. In the autumn of 1970, Saltzman and Broccoli announced to the world that he had been given the lead role in what was to be their seventh Bond movie, *Diamonds Are Forever*.

If nothing else, the casting of Gavin was a calculated nod to the American market. Saltzman and Broccoli were always wise to the fact that their movies had to go over big in the States if they were really to be deemed to have done well. In the mid-sixties, with Britain – and specifically London – the most swinging part of the planet, they could get away with having a hard-to-place Scotsman and a harder-to-place Australian play their end-of-empire imperialist. But as the new decade dawned, as the Beatles split up and as the likes of Eastwood and Charles Bronson came to dominate movie-palace hoardings, it was clear that the sun was setting on Britain's cultural sway. An American Bond must have looked like a mighty sane choice.

Then again, maybe not. Certainly the head honchos at United Artists, the studio that had backed the Bond films from day one, were resolutely unconvinced by the new signing. To have replaced the best leading man in the world for your part with one dullard might, as Fleming's original Goldfinger would have argued, be happenstance; to do so again would border on enemy action. And so, for the past year and more, the big chiefs at United Artists had been engaged in hush-hush talks with Connery in the hope of enticing him back into Bondage.[3] And in February 1971, several months after Gavin had been signed up for *Diamonds Are Forever* – and mere weeks before the picture was due to go before the cameras – senior executive David Picker finally succeeded in snaring his man. For the then astonishing upfront pay cheque of $1.25 million, plus a 12.5 per cent share of the gross profits, a further $145,000 for every week that the picture went over its allotted sixteen-week shooting schedule, and a guarantee that he would not have to talk to either Saltzman or Broccoli,[4] Connery agreed to don Bond's shoulder holster once more. 'Nobody,' Picker would later say, 'wanted to take a chance on hurting the franchise.'[5]

Friends and associates of Connery pronounced themselves astounded at the decision, though given that secrecy had been insisted on by both parties they were bound to be surprised. And anyway, given Connery's box-office disappointments of the past few years, the move oughtn't to have come as that much of a shock. Just as Connery had used his time away from Bond to ramp up his earnings, so now he was seeking to boost them some more with the news that he had brokered the highest pay cheque in the history of international stardom. It is true that shortly after *You Only Live Twice* had wrapped, Connery had told a reporter that 'I'll never do anything just for money'.[6] But times change, and few of us fail to change with them. Asked whether, gone 40, he might not be a little old for the part, Connery was heard to say that he didn't 'count age any more – only money'.[7] Little wonder, perhaps, that his producers were less than overjoyed at what United Artists had done. Cubby Broccoli would later admit to having had mixed feelings about Connery's return to the Bond fold,[8] while that sensitive soul Harry Saltzman had long made it clear that he 'wouldn't want anyone working in a film of mine who didn't like what he was doing and his [*sic*] interest was purely financial'.[9]

In truth, while the bulk of Connery's interest in *Diamonds Are Forever* might well have been purely financial, there was a veneer of financial purity about the deal he had structured. He was, he let it be known, donating his upfront salary from the movie to the Scottish International Education Trust, a charity organisation he and Sir Iain Stewart had founded on 4 December 1970 (just a few weeks before the deal with Picker and United Artists was done).* The Trust, which helps fund students and artists, theatres and orchestras, has subsequently gone on to award more than £3 million to thousands of Scottish youngsters. The hope is that such beneficiaries won't, unlike the charity's founder, feel it necessary to leave the country of their birth in order to get on in the world. 'I want the Scots to develop their own pride,' Connery explained. 'Of course they can come down to London and beat the English at their own game. But I'd like them to promote their own future in their own land.'[10]

---

* Since, as I write, in early 2009, *Diamonds Are Forever* has taken $116 million worldwide, Connery's 12.5 per cent share of the gross takings has served him well.

A publicity still for *Another Time, Another Place* (1957) – in which Connery and Glynis Johns are never actually on screen together. Fearsome monobrow aside, Connery already looks very much the matinee idol.

James Bond smoked cigarettes but even puffing on a panatella during a quiet moment on *Woman of Straw* (1964), Connery is the picture of lethal elegance and assurance.

Connery's formal education ended when he was only 13 but since his early twenties, when he decided to become an actor, he has been a relentless autodidact. This is one of many 'Mr Sean Connery at Home' (in Wavel Mews, NW6) type publicity shots from the late 1950s and early 1960s in which books feature prominently.

With Alfred Hitchcock during the *Marnie* (1964) shoot. The light grey suit and thin knitted tie are virtually identical to 007's daywear. Hitchcock, of course, had seen through the glitz of Bond to the barely socialised sexual predator beneath.

With Diane Cilento in 1970, not long before their final separation and divorce. As a writer and translator, an actress and all-round creative fireball, Cilento was a key influence on the man who would become the biggest star in the world.

Connery gave the performance of his career in *The Offence* (1973), but audiences proved unwilling to accept its vision of their tuxedoed sixties hero in a moustache and car-coat.

With Charlotte Rampling in John Boorman's *Zardoz* (1974) – less a dystopic movie of ideas than a study in the physical beauty of its star. The rape scene, Rampling once joked, 'was all over much too quickly'.

With Audrey Hepburn in Richard Lester's *Robin and Marian* (1976). Unlike so many actors, Connery has never sought out work that would emphasise his youth. Here, at 45, the first leading man to proclaim his baldness, he looks ten years and more older.

With Christopher Lambert in *Highlander* (1986), a swords and stallions dud that Connery laughed his way through – all the while inventing the mentor figure, variants of which he has played ever since.

Harrison Ford isn't even twelve years younger than Connery – nonetheless, Steven Spielberg joshingly cast the two men as father and son in *Indiana Jones and the Last Crusade* (1989) in humble acknowledgement of the debt all post-Bond moviemakers have owed Connery.

Released not long after its star was voted *People* magazine's sexiest man of the year, *The Russia House* (1990) centres on a love affair between a man and a woman half his age (Michelle Pfeiffer). Fred Schepisi's picture proved to be Connery's master-work – and a supremely emollient antidote to Bond to boot.

Charity donations aside, of course, Connery was mighty happy with himself at having brokered such a massive deal. For one thing, it went some way towards proving what he had always maintained – that Saltzman and Broccoli needed him at least as much as he needed them. For another, just as filming was about to begin the news broke that he and Cilento had separated once more, with Connery holing up in a flat on London's Embankment that was once the home of Hitler's foreign minister, Joachim von Ribbentrop. Entering middle age, he was starting his life over again.

A year earlier, in March 1970 at a golf tournament in Casablanca, Connery had met Micheline Roquebrune, the woman who would eventually become his second wife. She had taken first prize in the women's competition, he in the men's and, as is customary on such occasions, they had danced the first dance of the evening together. And not only the first. They danced all night, and spent the bulk of the next two days in each other's company, too. Then, the tournament over, they went their separate ways. Roquebrune, who had no interest in the movie business and had little idea who Connery was outside the man she had just met, has said that though they had got along famously she never expected to see him again. Three months later, though, he got back in touch. 'Basically,' he told her, 'I'm very serious. I don't want to play games with you.'[11] After spending a week together, they were agreed that it was time they 'both started working on divorces'.[12]

Confession time. *Diamonds Are Forever* is where I come in. The seventh Bond movie was the first I ever saw. It was the first movie I went to see unaccompanied by an adult, the first movie I can remember actively *wanting* to see. I saw it three times on its initial run, and twice more on re-release as part of a double-bill with *From Russia with Love* a couple of years later. (It alarms me quite as much as it should that I can still remember such things.) But hitherto I'd gone to see pictures my parents thought I'd enjoy, or that my brother (five years and more older, and thus far advanced in realms of taste as well as appetite) fancied seeing. I was just turning ten – just the right age – the age when one's own agency comes up against the world and all its frictions. Certainly, I still see that matinee performance at the Halifax Odeon as one of the hinge-points of my life. Had I not gone to see *Diamonds Are Forever*, I often think, things might have gone rather differently for me. It's laughable, I know, but in some way the movie – specifically, of course, Connery's presence in the movie – offered me a vision of how one could be in the world.

What Connery's Bond afforded worshippers like me was essentially aspirational. Despite Connery's own lowly origins, to want to be him was, for most of the boys in the movie audience, to want to climb a rung or two of the social ladder. It may be that this was but a function of the historical moment – that Connery's Bond existed in the gap between the snobbish certainties of Ian Fleming's England and the meritocratic vanities of Wilsonian white heat. On the other hand, there was something unique about him. Connery's Bond offered you a way of becoming classy while remaining classless. You could go up in the world without having to put on the ponderous airs and graces previous generations had had to affect.

And so, though I have subsequently come to see that *Diamonds Are Forever* is as big a bunch of junk as the Bond producers ever threw together, though I have subsequently come to prize other, very different, movies over the first picture I ever loved, though I have lately come to wonder whether any movie can ever be good enough . . . though all that and more, the picture retains a special place in my memory bank of affections. For all its shabby production values (having been obliged to cough up big-time to get Connery back on the payroll, Saltzman and Broccoli seem to have penny-pinched on pretty much every other aspect of the movie – even Ken Adam is given his head on only a couple of sets), for all its chaotic plotting, for all its clumsy editing, my first Bond movie is still my favourite Bond movie.

I'm not, I'm relieved to say, alone in what the average Bond aficionado would regard as this lunatic loyalty. '*Diamonds*, I think, comes close to being the ideal Bond film,' wrote Margaret Hinxman at the time of the film's release,[13] and though it would be possible to argue that the only Bond movie those words could really apply to is *On Her Majesty's Secret Service*, still, that film didn't have Sean Connery to play with. Or, more accurately, that movie didn't have Sean Connery to *play with it*.

For the Connery of *Diamonds Are Forever* is doing nothing but have a whale of a time at the expense of the improbable hero he has once more been hired to impersonate. As we have seen, Connery was brought into the movie at a late stage of development. Director Guy Hamilton (who had been responsible for the lighter touch on *Goldfinger*) and writer Tom Mankiewicz had been working on a script built around a John Gavin or Burt Reynolds 007. 'It was larger than life,' Hamilton has said, even 'zany'.[14] Yet Connery didn't bat an eyelid when he first got sight of what he was being asked to do, going so far as to tell a TV interviewer that the new picture had the 'best script, construction-wise' of the series so far.[15] Since there is no evidence whatsoever of any thought having been given to the script's construction (to call *Diamonds Are Forever* episodic would be to dignify its litany of vacuous scenes with a purposiveness they do not even pretend to possess), we must assume that Connery saw this as his chance to send the Bond franchise so far up that once it came back to earth it would do so with such velocity that it buried itself.

On the other hand, what was he meant to do with the character? For a man whom we last saw lost and weeping over his gunned-down wife (an incident, though not a heartbreak, the movie's pre-credits sequence makes passing reference to), this new/old Bond seems almost parodically at ease with the world and all it throws at him. If the Connery Bond of *Thunderball* and *You Only Live Twice* had been a bored male model about whom the producers could drape their technological fantasies, the Connery Bond of *Diamonds Are Forever* is a Wildean aesthete who treats with disdain whatever nonsensical contraption the villains think to best him with while holding steadfast to the belief that a tart one-liner will floor even the hardiest of megalomaniacs.

Sometimes he doesn't even have to joke. At one point in the picture Bond rescues Willard Whyte (the Howard Hughes-type figure nominally at the centre of the intrigue and played by country and western singer Jimmy Dean) from an underground lock-up. Within seconds of regaining his freedom, though, Whyte finds himself being shot at. Bond shoots back blindly and as the would-be assassin tumbles to the ground recognises him as Saxby (Bruce Cabot), Whyte's erstwhile right-hand man. 'Bert Saxby?' asks White, momentarily taken aback. 'Tell him he's fired.' No, it's not a great line, though one can imagine Connery doing rather more with it than Mr Dean. But the line isn't his, a fact that allows Connery's Bond the chance to give us a wonderful slow-burn double-take – snarly and quizzical and as tight-eyed as the impassive reaction shots Clint Eastwood had been making a name for himself with over the past four or five years.*

Yet if American tough-guy tastes were being catered to, then so were the more effete English still being granted their pleasures. It's a critical commonplace that *Diamonds Are Forever* is the Bond movie that really lays the ghost of Ian Fleming to rest. And indeed, the movie's plot owes about five minutes of its action to Fleming's original novel (which is, it should be said, no less broken-backed and aimless). Nonetheless, hadn't Fleming suggested to his friend Noël Coward that he would make a perfect Dr No? In the new film he belatedly gets his wish – with Charles Gray turning the sinisterly fascistic Blofeld of the previous three Bond pictures into a camped-up comedian so laid-back about his latest plans for world domination that he can accuse his putative nemesis of harbouring

---

*Though it was only on the next Bond movie, *Live and Let Die*, that the producers went the whole Eastwood hog, equipping Roger Moore's less than macho Bond with a golf-club-sized Magnum pistol.

melodramatic fantasies. Add in David Bauer's turn as phoney funeral director Morton Slumber (an oleaginous creep straight out of late Waugh and by some measure the best cameo in the whole Bond canon), as well as Jill St John as the droll if occasionally dumb drug-smuggling moll Tiffany Case and you have a master class in bedroom comedy on your hands.

Whether you have anything at all thrilling is another question. True, even greying around the temples and somewhat heavier than any self-respecting superspy ought to be, this newly middle-aged Bond still cuts the physical mustard. For a big man, Connery still moves with remarkable compression and grace. In the pre-credits sequence, Hamilton treats us to a close-up of Connery delivering one of those balletic kicks familiar from *Goldfinger*, and though, to be fair, we see only his leg, we could be looking at a man twenty years his junior. To watch Connery run across Willard Whyte's mocked-up moonscape pursued by a gang of uniformed heavies is to see something of the promising footballer Sir Matt Busby's talent scout must have divined in the *South Pacific* chorus boy of almost two decades earlier.

How to explain, though, the fact that Mankiewicz's script gives Connery's Bond so little to do? And how to explain that when it does give him something to do, it invariably has him fluffing the task? This is a Bond who is flummoxed by the elementary-looking controls of a moon-buggy he finds himself having to hijack, a Bond who is unable to work the drop motor on a crane, a Bond who seems happiest when being dressed down for his stupidity either by Tiffany Case or by Blofeld's nuclear boffin Professor Dr Metz (Joseph Furst). 'Nice to see you haven't lost that fine mental edge,' Blofeld tells Bond when at last they meet, and though it is the only line in the picture he utters without irony, which of us could possibly agree with him? Whatever the world's greatest villain is up against here, it is something far removed from the world's greatest hero.

How much of this change in character was forward thinking on the part of Messrs Broccoli and Saltzman, how much Hamilton's influence on the screenplay, how much acceptance of Connery's (and Terence Young's) steadfast insistence that Bond couldn't possibly be taken seriously it is impossible to say. What we can say is that by taking any pretence at seriousness out of the character and the movie, *Diamonds Are Forever* helped invent the emasculated Bond that Roger Moore would play for the next seven pictures in the series. Leftist cultural pundits had long decried the Bond figure as a reactionary throwback. On the evidence of *Diamonds Are Forever* and the subsequent Moore years, though, audiences loved the idea of Bond as a ham-fisted amateur quite as much as they had loved him when he was a mocking imperialist trumpeting the fantasy values of a fast-decaying Britain to the world.

So could Connery have carried on playing this new galumphing Bond? There seems no reason other than his own suspicion that the whole espionage movie game was over to think not. To be sure, Connery was showing signs of ageing in *Diamonds Are Forever*, but good tailoring and a decent haircut can ensure such drawbacks don't become problems. Nor should we forget that, despite Cubby Broccoli's claim that 'Roger brought . . . a younger feel' to the series,[16] Moore was actually two years older than Connery – and at 45 in 1973 a full *fifteen years older* than the Connery of *Dr No*. Since Connery was by nature so much more physically imposing than Moore, there is no cause for thinking he couldn't have gone on as Bond for a few years yet.

Moreover, chafed as Broccoli and Saltzman might have been at the deal United Artists struck with Connery on their behalf, the picture more than recompensed the people who'd gambled on him, eventually taking in a handsome $19 million at the US box office. (If not quite a *Thunderball*-style payout, then one not markedly worse than that for *You Only Live Twice*.)* Indeed, just before *Diamonds Are Forever* was released, Cubby Broccoli told a reporter that he and Saltzman were already hard at work putting together the eighth Bond, *Live and Let Die*, and that 'We've nobody else in mind [for the lead role] at the moment.'[17] A while later, there would be reports that Connery had been offered an astonishing $5.5 million to come back for the picture.[18]

Connery, though, wanted nothing to do with it. Happy at having proved he was the lynch-pin of the operation, he walked off into the sunset. 'Positively, definitely, beyond a shadow of a doubt, this is my last Bond,' he asserted as *Diamonds Are Forever* hit cinemas. 'I won't do another, not even for another million.'[19] 'Of course the films will go on,' he warmed to the theme with another journalist, while purring that they couldn't pretend to be anything like the real thing because 'who'll play me I just don't know'.[20] Blowing away Anthony Dawson's villainous boffin Dent in *Dr No*, Connery's Bond had told the less than good Professor that it was pointless reaching for his gun because 'You've had your six'. Now, James Bond had had his six, too. Sean Connery had other quarry in his sights.

---

* By the end of 1972, Connery was back at the top spot of British cinemas, according to the London bureau of America's *Motion Picture Herald*, beating Clint Eastwood into second place. It's worth noting, though, that *Dirty Harry* (1971), a low-budget Don Siegel cop movie released the same week as *Diamonds Are Forever*, ended up taking an astounding $28 million – almost half as much again as the seventh Bond movie.

9

Bergman in Bracknell

The enormous amount of money Connery was paid for *Diamonds Are Forever* wasn't his only recompense for having returned to the role that had made him. During the deal-making process, he had also strong-armed United Artists into backing two subsequent pictures of his own choosing – to the tune of a million dollars or so each. Now, finally free of Bond, he could, he said, 'make my own mistakes. And I can afford them.'[1] Maybe so, though the question raised by *The Offence* (1973) – the first and, as things would turn out, the last of the movies he made under the deal with United Artists – is for how long he would be able to go on footing any bills. For while there is much to admire about *The Offence*, there isn't much to like about it. A film less like *Diamonds Are Forever* it is difficult to imagine. Audiences delighted by the return of their recalcitrant comic hero to the Bond fold stayed away in droves.

The picture, which began life as a minorly successful play at London's Royal Court back in 1968, was Connery's baby through and through. So impressed was he by that first production that he had for some while been working with the play's author, John Hopkins (who cut his teeth writing episodes of *Z-Cars* for the BBC back in the early sixties, as well as doing some final dialogue adjustments on *Thunderball*), on turning it into a movie. Along the way, the drama lost its original title – *This Story of Yours* – exchanging it first for *Something Like the Truth*, and then for *The Offence*.

For all the wordiness of its predecessors, it's an unsatisfactory title. True, those earlier titles carried *Rashômon*-like suggestions of ambiguity, unsettledness, lability – and mainstream moviegoers are not known for their fondness for floating signifiers. Yet *The Offence*'s great virtue is its insistence on giving us something like the truth – though nothing more. When, after 112 harrowing minutes, the movie ends, with Connery's brutalised Detective Sergeant Johnson having beaten suspected child-molester Kenneth Baxter (Ian Bannen) to death, we have no way of knowing whether Baxter really was guilty of the crime he was being interrogated over.

For the movie is far from your average detective drama. Rather, like Nicholas Ray's *On Dangerous Ground* (1951) or Abel Ferrara's *Bad Lieutenant* (1992), it is an investigation into the workings of a disturbed cop's mind. Where *Diamonds Are Forever* had been a kind of comic riposte to the gung-ho shoot-'em-ups with which Clint Eastwood had knocked Bond from the top of the box office, *The Offence* took a rather more serious tack. In a sense, the movie is an investigation into the real meaning of Dirty Harry Callahan's (and James Bond's) methods of policing.

The key thing to be said about the movie is that Connery is magnificent in it. *The Offence* is the first picture in Connery's career as a star in which we never get to see him strip off and show off his fabulous physique. Yet Gerry Fisher's camera, kept cunningly low whenever Connery is in shot, is the first to really capture the sheer size of the man. Frame after frame of the movie is composed so that Connery's DS Johnson looms in the foreground while – in what, thanks to Fisher's wide-angle lens, seems like the distant background – his colleagues look timidly and minutely on.

More than that, though, Connery's Johnson is on every level a *big* performance. Never before – and rarely since – has Connery been called on to make such a display of histrionics. Writhing his way around John W. Clark's spare set like a bear in a net, he gives us not just a vision of a man possessed but an evocation of what a man who is no longer really a man looks like. Throughout the picture Connery's hands seem to have a life of their own, wandering hither and thither, their putative owner appearing powerless to make them do as he pleases. For all its flaws, one cannot watch *The Offence* without rueing the fact that Connery has never actually got round to giving us his *Macbeth*.

The trouble is that despite the tragic swagger of Connery's performance, its artfully artless grandeur, the movie itself is a trumped-up hunk of pretension. The director, chosen by Connery himself, is his old friend Sidney Lumet – a man drawn instinctively to the liberal and the decent, but drawn, too, to what Andrew Sarris has called 'strained seriousness'.[2] The opening moments of *The Offence* are signal here, as we hear some Moogy, woodwindy noises on the soundtrack, and see, through a foggy halation-effect lens, a slo-mo shot of – well, of what? Heaven? Hell? The murky chaos of Johnson's mind? Elsewhere, Lumet serves up whiteouts and blackouts, cloudy, occluded repetitions of key (and not so key) moments and sundry other visual intrusions. The effect, magnified by the movie's main location – a massive interrogation room empty save for a stack of plastic chairs and loomed over by a mammoth circular light fitting that comes straight out of Ken Adam – is of the stage set for some radical theatre workshop. All these silences, these repetitions, these non-sequiturs, these doomy visuals and grimy soundscapes – they all make sense (which is not the same thing as saying that they work) within the confines of the Dadaist abstractions of post-sixties theatre. But they make no sense amid the rough and tumble of mainstream moviemaking.*

---

* As if to hammer home the point that we are watching a Pinteresque take on the police procedural, the then Mrs Pinter, Vivien Merchant, is cast as Johnson's dully dutiful but otherwise alienated wife. Within the confines of the drama she gives a pitch-perfect performance, raising Connery to new heights in the process. Watch him crumple and sag as the man hitherto known as the cinema's most celebrated sexual Neanderthal sublimates his needs to his wife's no less felt urges. You don't have to buy the Freudian psychology, much less the phallocratic terms the debate is couched in, to acknowledge that you are here watching some miraculous screen acting.

Nor does Hopkins's dialogue help. While Connery gives a physically commanding performance as a man driven to the brink of lunacy by the stresses of his job and the strains of a failing marriage, his Sergeant Johnson has a symbolist eloquence that sits uneasily on his naturalist shoulders. Sean Connery has one of the most distinctive voices in the history of movies, but no film actor could be expected to get away with munching his way through Hopkins's random poetic clusters: 'bodies . . . stinking, swollen, black, putrid, the smell of death . . . chequered, splintered bones . . . filthy, swarming, slimy maggots in my mind, eating in my mind'. Done properly, such Rimbaudesque rhetoric can – one doesn't say will – work on the stage. But the movie screen thrives on the concrete and the real, and does not happily play host to literary afflatus. An actor as attuned to somatic effects as Connery ought perhaps have wondered whether all the words he was having to fight his way through were necessary. The kind of writing he really believed in, he would say some years after *The Offence*, was 'writing where it's not what's said that matters, but what's revealed'.[3] What revelations Connery makes in *The Offence*, though, are made in spite of Hopkins's script, and not because of it.

We should be careful, though, not to put the blame for all *The Offence*'s failings on its writer and director. While its star has subsequently complained about Lumet's having 'gone a bit European on us',[4] the movie we have sounds like nothing so much as that Connery-directed production of *I've Seen You Cut Lemons* of three years earlier. Moreover, Connery had not hitherto been known for being down on those Europeans. Asked not long after the release of *The Offence* who his favourite moviemaker was, Connery said Ingmar Bergman.[5] There is no reason to disbelieve him – and what a fine knight Connery would have made in an English-language version of *The Seventh Seal** – though there is reason to wonder whether Connery's fondness for Bergman might not consist largely in a belief that seriousness is the same thing as significance. Whether encouraged by Lumet's own pretensions

177

or by his own autodidactic belief that importance inheres only in works about putatively important issues, Connery seems unable to understand that any performance, any movie, is susceptible of significance. What counts is not content, but treatment – which does not mean that the treatment need be clever or fussy.

The Offence was shot in and around Bracknell during the dull March and April of 1972. Connery was proud of the fact that under his jurisdiction (or, more precisely, that of Tantallon Films, the production company he had set up with Richard Hatton and the producer Dennis O'Dell) it was brought in ahead of schedule and $80,000 under its $1 million budget. The 'people who make the most sacrifices', he declared, 'will make the most money'.[6]

In point of fact, Connery had long suspected that *The Offence* would struggle to find an audience. 'I will be interested in how the public takes it,' he had said a year before the picture was released (in the spring of 1973). 'It's painful . . . Some people may detest [my] character . . . The British have always been so anti-analysis in every sense of the word, but this film goes into analysis of why this detective became what he is.'[7] Whatever the truth of that, Connery's forewarnings only served to forearm the critics, who were uniformly harsh on what they saw as a pretentious, self-indulgent morass of gloom, and the picture bombed at the box office. Nine long years would have to go by before the picture even earned its costs back. It was a harsh verdict on one of the most fascinatingly flawed movies in the Connery canon, but there is no gainsaying that *The Offence* was always going to cater to a

---

* As a young man, Connery was, like Bergman's knight, a keen chess player. There are photographs of him playing Patrick McGoohan on the set of *Hell Drivers*, and Diane Cilento says her husband thrashed Tony Richardson at the chessboard on the set of *Tom Jones*. Still, it is worth noting that in September 1973, six months before professing his love of Bergman to *Films and Filming* magazine, Connery informed the readers of the rather less rarefied *Sunday Express* that 'The only [films] I never miss are the *Carry On* farces . . . I find they have less boring bits in them than most message films.'

minority – and that that minority was shrinking as the power-cut-suffering, inflation-torn Britain of the early seventies went down the pan. Towards the end of the year, when the massive ramp in oil prices slammed into an already punch-drunk economy, it became easy even for as serious-minded a man as Connery to accept that what movie audiences wanted was reassurance. As he had acknowledged of the Bond phenomenon, 'people will always demand escape'.[8]

And yet, a year or so after *The Offence* had been ushered into an unwelcoming world, a prickly and defensive Connery was to be found arguing that the movie had been released in the wrong way. '*Cries and Whispers*,' he said, returning to his love of Bergman, 'played in London at the Curzon, which caters for a certain kind of audience. So the film has a start – a foothold on its own kind of public . . . [for] *The Offence* . . . the Odeon Leicester Square . . . was just too big.'[9] If, Connery went on to say, you open a small picture in a small cinema, you get crowded houses – and these encourage more crowded houses in their turn. It's a fair point and a logical argument, but it disregards the fact that, at least in May 1973, mere months after *Diamonds Are Forever* had finally come to the end of its near year-long cinema run, films starring Sean Connery simply couldn't be conceived of as opening in small art-house cinemas. Films starring Sean Connery opened at the biggest movie palaces there were. Given the grandiloquent failure of *The Offence*, though, for how much longer would that be true?

At the time, of course, Connery had more to worry about than the future of his career. There was the divorce from Cilento to be sorted out: a painful process – and one made all the more painful by the fact that, days before filming on *The Offence* had begun, Connery's father had died. The news, Connery said later, 'had an absolutely devastating effect on me'.[10] For the bulk of the next year, Connery did little but play golf and court Micheline Roquebrune.

Of work there was no sign. One reason for this may have been the fair-to-middling success of Roman Polanski's blood-spilling take on *Macbeth* (1971). The critical consensus on the movie was that the violence rather got in the way of the poetry, but since Connery had long been hard on those Shakespeare productions that play up the poetic, it is likely that any production he might have masterminded would have been too similar to be bothered with. He would go on talking about the screenplay he had written for his own version of the Scottish Play for another eighteen months, but after October 1973, when the divorce from Cilento finally came through, Connery would talk no more of playing the man goaded into action by a desperately ambitious wife.

And so 1972 drifted by. (Though *The Offence* wrapped in April, United Artists were sufficiently worried by the picture's dour vision that more than twelve months would elapse before its release.) There was talk of Connery starring opposite Rachel Roberts in a movie version of Ibsen's *The Wild Duck*, but talk was all there was.[11] There was talk of the second million-dollar movie of the *Diamonds Are Forever* deal with United Artists being a life of the explorer Sir Richard Burton. Fascinating, of course, to imagine Connery playing the man who admitted to feeling 'quite jolly' whenever he'd killed a man. But given the budgetary strictures, how could the picture ever have come off? No matter how narrow the focus of such a project, given the range and scope of Burton's achievements and life, it could never have been cheap.

Then again, John Boorman managed to cobble a little more money together ($1.4 million, to be precise) to make *Zardoz* (1974), a film that, if it doesn't quite look like a Ken Adam production, certainly looks a lot classier than *The Offence*. Here are kaleidoscopic prisms, here back projections, here splashy colour effects – all of them still, three decades and more on, mighty impressive. Little wonder, perhaps, that Boorman paid his star only $200,000 – a sixth of the money he had been paid for *Diamonds Are Forever*, and – without even taking inflation into account – Connery's lowest pay deal since *Dr No*.[12]

According to Boorman, Connery agreed to do *Zardoz* for so little money because he 'was finding it difficult to get work'. When Connery did agree to the project, though, he cannily asked if he might lodge with Boorman and his wife at their house in Wicklow for the duration of the shoot. For their kindness he paid them a full £7 a week – a sum Boorman believes might just about have passed muster for room rental in the mid-1950s, when Connery was last responsible for such payments. And even then it would have gone little way towards paying for the bottles of single malt whisky Connery insisted he and Boorman worked their way through of an evening. The Boormans' guest did, though, help out in those straitened times – by insisting that all their house lights were turned off at the end of the evening. A day or two into the shoot, meanwhile, Connery had the bright idea of ditching the driver Boorman has been obliged to provide him with. That way, he argued, we can split the £150 a week you'll be saving from your budget.

John Boorman is such an engaging artist and *Zardoz* such an ambitious movie that one feels bad about being disappointed by it. But try as I might, I have never sat through the picture with any pleasure. Boorman seems to have conceived of *Zardoz* as a kind of sci-fi whimsy – a countrified take on Stanley Kubrick's *Clockwork Orange* (1971). But the movie is so full of half-grasped ideas and half-baked confusions that the only real handle you can get on it is that at some level Boorman and Connery have turned it into an analysis of the post-Bond action hero.

Connery plays Zed, a man who works as an Exterminator in Boorman's dystopic vision of a future in which the Eternals (the aristocratic types of 2293) disport themselves diaphanously around a hi-tech country house (the Vortex), while outside Zed and his colleagues (on the orders of the floating godhead Zardoz) go about preventing the Brutals (the wholly redundant lower orders) from procreating. Your standard-issue fascist future, in other words. Boorman himself thought the picture 'an allegory of the haves and have-nots' – a subject always ripe for debate, but in times as ripe as those of seventies Britain why bother with the allegory? Why not just tell your story straight?

And so *Zardoz*'s sole pleasure is that of watching Connery lope and lunge around Boorman's dramatic world with the vicious grace that had made the Bond pictures so watchable. Indeed, as if to foreground its self-conscious, self-reflexive thematics, the movie kicks off with Zed infiltrating Zardoz's giant floating head, working out that the monster's levers are really being pulled by one Arthur Frayn (Niall Buggy) and shooting him dead with the kind of innocent, satisfied glee the Bond of *Diamonds Are Forever* had found trading insults with Blofeld.

Such Bondian parallels can be drawn throughout the picture. At one point Zed, on the run from the Eternals, finds himself surrounded by the Apathetics (Eternals so disenamoured of immortality they are almost dead in life), who feast on his sweat. Quite what aspect of our civilisation's future such behaviour is meant to portend Boorman leaves unclear, but as an unconscious comment on the saltier fan mania Connery had been inspiring for the past decade the scene makes perfect sense. Later, there is a scene in which the Eternals, untroubled as they are by sexual desire, gape agog and aghast at Zed's prodigious erectile function – not unlike the audience of picture houses the world over these past twelve years whenever Connery's Bond had walked on screen. In this imaginary world of eternal, reproduction-free lives, men have been rendered pointless – and yet their most fascinating specimen is embodied by the most potent symbol of masculinity the world has ever known. For above all, *Zardoz* is a study in the sheer physical beauty of its star – a star whose magnificent musculature is the centrepiece of pretty much every one of Geoffrey Unsworth's symmetrically stylised compositions. As Charlotte Rampling (who plays the Eternal Consuella in the picture) joked with Boorman, she was rather disappointed that the scene in which Connery raped her 'was all over much too quickly'.

Nobody could say the same of *Zardoz*. And yet the picture is not an insignificant one on the Connery CV. For all its designer impenetrable psycho-babble, for all its labyrinthine ideating and poetic posturing, *Zardoz* was the movie responsible for discovering the magus figure in Sean Connery – the magus figure hitherto hidden by the glossy veneer of super-heroism, the magus figure he would come to play over and over again throughout the eighties and nineties. Looked at with the advantage of thirty-five years' hindsight, *Zardoz* may just have been the movie that begun to turn round Connery's career in the depths of its post-Bond doldrums.

At the time of its release, though, it looked like just another in the ever-lengthening line of disasters on the Connery CV. After the glum theatrics of *The Offence* and the nervy abstractions of the Boorman picture, Connery found himself back in the position he had been in before *Diamonds Are Forever* – struggling to present and project an identity that had no connection to the world of James Bond. As if to make the point plain, *Zardoz* climaxes in a hall-of-mirrors shootout that was likely inspired by the denouement of Orson Welles's *The Lady From Shanghai* (1948) but ended up, alas, looking just like the one in the closing sequence of Roger Moore's second 007 movie, *The Man with the Golden Gun* (1974).

Perhaps so that he could work with Sidney Lumet again, perhaps so that he would have plenty of down time for golf, perhaps so that he could travel in a rather starrier vehicle than he had done this past couple of years, Connery leapt aboard *Murder on the Orient Express* (1974).* Given its cast (Albert Finney in hair-oil and smoking jacket; Ingrid Bergman in sad rags; Michael York under a Garbo-style wig), given its source (one of Agatha Christie's silliest novels), and given that its screenplay was the work of Paul Dehn (one of the wits from the golden age of British journalism, and the man who had

---

* For all the starriness, Connery and co. were on flat fees of little more than $60,000 each.

gagged-up *Goldfinger*), the picture ought to have been a comic camp classic. But Lumet was never going to be the man for comedy, let alone camp (his having directed a largish cast in *Twelve Angry Men* aside, it is impossible to imagine what Paramount thought they were doing offering this wilfully downbeat director the job), and so Connery's Colonel Arbuthnot becomes not a mocking update of the Charters and Caldicott* the film needs, but a military man of irascible common sense. To be sure, Connery's Arbuthnot is hardly the stiff-backed prig of Christie cliché, but he is a strange creation nonetheless for a man who is adamant that the first thing he looks for in a character is the humour.

Still, the picture was a big hit, though given that stellar cast, who could say who pulled the punters in? That all-star line-up – a forerunner of the mid-seventies vogue for disaster pictures in which everyone who was anyone was knocked over by an earthquake or toasted in a tower block – was a kind of insurance policy: pretty much every moviegoer will go see this movie, the logic ran, because there's a star to appeal to everyone in it. Unlikely, given that his cameo is the smallest of the lot, that Connery's presence kept the picture afloat. On the other hand, appearing even momentarily next to golden-age stars like Lauren Bacall and Ingrid Bergman and Richard Widmark was a clever way of burnishing and bolstering his CV.

Certainly after a couple of years of drift, Connery seemed bent on getting back into the big league. To that end he took on a new agent, Dennis Selinger, long the representative of Peter Sellers and Michael Caine. Selinger, it should be said, was the agent of archetype and comic cliché – a pile 'em high, sell 'em cheap kind of guy whose essential belief was that if you make lots of movies the law of averages will ensure that at least some of them turn out good. It was a strategy that had worked well for Caine over the

---

* The bumptiously superior Englishmen played by Basil Radford and Naunton Wayne in Hitchcock's *The Lady Vanishes* (1938) who were so popular they turned up again in Carol Reed's *Night Train to Munich* (1940) and Launder and Gilliat's *Millions Like Us* (1943).

years, but it was not necessarily a one-size-fits-all philosophy. Caine was (and is) essentially a character actor whose actorly currency was inflated by his emblematic status as figurehead of the swinging sixties. Connery was (and is) a movie star of the old school through and through, and his worth was rather more easily tarnished.

Even in the heyday of the studio system, after all, when actors were simply told what to do, when studios knew just which script was a Gary Cooper project and which a Clark Gable – and would reshape them to suit the actor if required – even then flops were not unknown. How much more difficult to navigate the mainstream when you are in it up to your neck and have no studio to paddle for you. Forget curating a reputation as an actor: even if all you want to be is a movie star, then you had better have a pretty good idea of the kind of movies you should be starring in.

All of which brings us to *Ransom* (1974). The cameraman on Caspar Wrede's picture (shot in the first few weeks of 1974 amid the fogs and sludges of a deeply wintry Norway) was Sven Nykvist – long-time Ingmar Bergman collaborator and the only semi-sensible reason the film historian can come up with for Connery's having agreed to Selinger's suggestion that he star in this low-budget, thrill-free thriller.

Connery plays Colonel Tahlvik, a Finnish security big-shot and a man not afraid of arresting politicians if he has to. So when an aircraft is hijacked at Oslo airport and the British Ambassador is taken hostage, Tahlvik, though instructed otherwise by his superiors, refuses to play ball with the kidnappers no matter who gets killed. In other words, this is 007 rewritten for Dirty Harry. Just as Connery's instinctively insolent Bond had paved the way for Clint Eastwood's succession of moral nihilists, so now Eastwood's core creation was being used as the template for Connery's post-Bond career.* How

---

* Eastwood is a crucial figure in any long-term assessment of Connery. The two men came to fame within a few years of one another in visually iconic roles that would always mark them. Both quickly made it known that they had ambitions grander than being mere matinee idols and action puppets. But Eastwood has

else to explain the movie's redundant bare-torso scene, in which Tahlvik is briefed mid-shower on what Petrie (Ian McShane) and his gang of villains are up to just so that the sixties' greatest sex symbol can prove he is still in shape.

And so he was, though his career was looking increasingly formless. 'Don't you understand,' Tahlvik rasps at a simpering politico, 'there are some orders you must not obey?' True enough, just as there are some films no star should agree to be in. Actors, even actors as big as Sean Connery, have such little responsibility for the overall finish of a movie that they need to know it is worth appearing in in the first place if it is to stand a chance of burnishing their credentials. Ominously early under Dennis Selinger's tutelage, it was beginning to seem as if Connery didn't know what kind of picture he should be starring in – or, worse, didn't care.

---

followed up on his promise, averaging over the decades an actioner every year or so in order to fund something more personal of his own. Connery's own creative record is rather less convincing.

10

Other Times, Other Places

Sean Connery was turning 44 when shooting commenced on *The Wind and the Lion* (1975). The character he was playing in the new picture was a few years older than that – somewhere in his early fifties perhaps – but who could deny that Connery looks older still in the finished movie?

We are not talking about acting here. We are talking of physical reality, of time and its afflictions. Connery had endured a lot over the past few years: the break-up of his first marriage, the death of his father, the abandonment of the part that had made him a star, the realisation that that abandonment meant he was no longer axiomatically a star. And though he continued to look in remarkably good shape, the years will have their way.

True, Connery is still moving spectacularly well. With his urgent stride, his muscular mounting of horses, his swaggering sword-swishing, the Connery of *The Wind and the Lion* often looks as if he might drift off into a dancing reverie. Still, you cannot look at John Milius's historical adventure and seriously believe that its star ought still to be playing James Bond. Indeed, there are moments in the new movie when the man who ten years earlier had claimed that his pockmarked face had made him look 30 when he was only 16 might be on the cusp of his seventh decade.

And yet, while it would be too much to say that *The Wind and the Lion* is the picture that put Connery back on top, there can be no doubt that Milius's grandiloquent epic was the movie that, at least temporarily, put Connery back on track. This was the picture that first breathed life into the promise of the following three and a half decades – the promise that Connery (like John Huston, who stars alongside him in Milius's movie) has it in him to be one of the cinema's grand old men.

If *The Wind and the Lion* (and Connery's next two pictures – Huston's *The Man Who Would Be King* and Richard Lester's *Robin and Marian*) bulk large on the Connery CV it is because they are the first movies since *Dr No* that redefine their leading man, that allow us to read him in radically different ways. Milius's movie is no masterpiece, but it is nonetheless one of the hinges in Connery's career. Just as there is a pre- and a post-Bond Connery, so is there Connery before *The Wind and the Lion* and Connery after it – and they are not the same thing.

He wasn't an obvious choice for the movie. Indeed, not since Howard Keel's turn as the Poet in Vincente Minnelli's *Kismet* (1955) has a less likely Arab than Sean Connery graced the silver screen. *Pace* Milius's jocular suggestion that Connery 'looks not unlike the Ayatollah',[1] few casting directors tasked with finding someone to play a Muslim chieftain would have thought immediately of Sean Connery – especially in the mid-seventies. For the past quarter of a century, ever since Marlon Brando had mumbled his way through *A Streetcar Named Desire*, and especially for the past seven or eight years, since Warren Beatty and Arthur Penn's *Bonnie and Clyde* (1967), the American cinema had prided itself on its devotion to naturalism. The Hollywood pictures we revere from the sixties and first half of the seventies – movies like *The Graduate* (1967), *Five Easy Pieces* (1970), *The Last Picture Show* (1971), *The Godfather* (1972), *Mean Streets* (1973) and *One Flew Over the Cuckoo's Nest* (1976) – are all obsessed with the desire to show us 'real' people in 'real' situations.

The Bond movies were one of the first ripostes to this cinematic emphasis on the natural. Almost character-free and non-stop in their pulsing action, the Bonds took the movies back a generation and more, to the derring-do nonsense of the thirties serials. You loved them or you hated them, but there was no gainsaying the fact that if you did hate them you were in the minority.

So it was Connery's misfortune that when he jumped off the Bondwagon and tried to stake out some territory for himself as a serious actor audiences weren't terribly interested – even when the critics suggested they'd benefit by being so. When Connery tried to score himself some counter-cultural Brownie points, by playing the tormented beat poet of *A Fine Madness*, audiences stayed away in droves. Where was the deadpan cynic they had worshipped this past half-decade? By the time of Connery's next non-Bond, *Shalako*, even the most fanatical of moviegoers was coming to question the idea of the unquestionable superman. As far as heroes were concerned, the times were out of joint. Nobody wanted to see an old-fashioned good guys against the bad guys western when the morally dubious horrors of Vietnam were being brought home to them each evening on TV. The seemingly mindless violence of Clint Eastwood's westerns spoke far more eloquently to such times. And if nostalgia for putatively simpler times was what you wanted, you could always go and see the 62-year-old John Wayne teach youth about right and wrong in *True Grit* (1969).

By the mid-seventies, though, things were changing. The war in Vietnam was over – and America had come out the loser. It was a national humiliation, and one only compounded by the discovery that even as his troops floundered, President Nixon had been attempting to subvert his country's Constitution in a desperate bid for re-election. The American dream was over, and moviegoers, one of whose prime reasons for going to the movies has always been to dream, wanted it back. They were about to get it – in spades. Moviemakers like Steven Spielberg and George Lucas were convinced that what the cinema needed – more than that, what that great wounded beast America needed – was defiantly non-cynical family entertainment. What Vietnam and Watergate had prompted, these men believed, was a great loss of faith in the idea of the

American father-figure. And without father-figures, the country would continue to go downhill. It would fall to the movies, then, to rehabilitate them.

The first task was to reinvent the family film. Sixties Hollywood, frightened of losing its audiences to television, had increasingly made its products for – and marketed them at – the teenage audience. The only exceptions to the rule had been the musical (thanks largely to the efforts of Rodgers and Hammerstein, no longer a genre concerned with the search for a sexual partner but the search for a woman to look after children already born to a departed – or simply gone away – wife) and, of course, the Bond pictures.

It would be over-egging things to claim *The Wind and the Lion* as the first picture to cock a snook at what the American cinema had been up to these past ten years and more.* Nonetheless, this is emphatically not a movie of existential angst and urban deprivation. This isn't a picture in which it's hard to figure out whom to side with in the sympathy stakes. This isn't a movie where the good guys seem as morally compromised as the bad guys. Rather, this is the movie which will establish Milius – who has always been on the right of the political divide, whose ideas of American politics and history had been formed by little more than movies, and who had little time for what he saw as the dopey do-gooding of the Hollywood new wave – as one of the minor architects of Hollywood's pre-Reaganite retrenchment. And the first thing he was doing by casting Connery as *The Wind and the Lion*'s Muslim warrior chief was announcing that he was making an old-fashioned picture.

The movie was inspired by a genuine historic incident, though

---

* That honour goes to Spielberg's *Jaws* (1975). Milius rewrote a justly famous scene in the picture: Robert Shaw's Melvillesque soliloquy has its hammy moments, but its damning verdict on both counter-cultural mores and enlightenment values – both represented in the movie by Richard Dreyfuss's Hooper – has the virtue of emblematising a historical moment.

as the casting of Connery might suggest, it was also inspired by a generous measure of dramatic licence. For instance, while it is true that in 1904 a certain Mr Ion Pedecaris was taken hostage by a Moroccan Muslim bandit chieftain, in the movie we see a *Mrs* Eden Pedecaris, played with lustrous high-spirits by Candice Bergen, who is kidnapped by Connery's Raisuli. Furthermore, while Mr Pedecaris's stepson was kidnapped alongside him, Milius's screenplay has Mrs Pedecaris being held hostage with both a young son, William (Simon Harrison), and a younger daughter, Jennifer (Polly Gottesman). Within seconds of being captured, William is goggle-eyed with joy at the spectacular example of manhood fate has dealt him to mature with, saying of Connery's Raisuli, 'He has the way about him, doesn't he?' We might be in Disney territory, were it not for the fact that the joshingly abrasive relations between the Raisuli and Mrs Pedecaris – never once sexual, always mutually respectful – recall nothing so much as those between Christopher Plummer and Julie Andrews in *The Sound of Music* (1965).

But besides being Connery's first picture since *Diamonds Are Forever* to be aimed squarely at the family market, *The Wind and the Lion* was his first picture since *Marnie* – made a full ten years earlier – to trade on his status as an international movie idol. 'Anthony Quinn was too old and Omar Sharif didn't have the gravitas,' Milius would later say of his decision to cast Connery. 'I said, "This is the only man who feels like he has the power of the Raisuli..."'.[2] Hence Milius's first shot of Connery, which is nothing if not a celebration of his iconic status. On horseback, the masked Raisuli and his men have crashed their way into the Pedecarises' ornate garden, seen off the servants and handymen and rounded up Eden and her children. Now, the territory made safe, the Raisuli unmasks himself. He sits down on a low wall and unwraps his keffiyeh, turning his face slowly to the camera as cinematographer Billy Williams moves in for a tight close-up. As if that weren't enough, Milius double-prints the shot and runs it in slow-motion, further fetishising the visage on which we are being invited to gaze. It's the most self-consciously glamorous introduction of Connery into a movie since *Dr No*.

But then, Connery's whole performance is forever announcing its status as performance. We touched on the Howard Keel of *Kismet* a moment ago, and there's something self-consciously musical about Connery's physical grandeur in *The Wind and the Lion*. This is a Raisuli that never just moves. Instead, Connery has him dance through each scene, twirling here, gesticulating there. At the end of the movie the Raisuli is to be seen whirling and whooping his way along the top of a sand dune – for all the world like a child delighted with the movements of its body.

Would that Milius himself had taken his cue from Connery's elegance and lightness of touch. The trouble was, one suspects, that he fell so in love with the sound of Connery's voice – as who has not? – that he gave him line after moralising line, speech after windy speech to labour through. According to Dennis Selinger, Connery had been keen, after *The Offence*, to find himself a comedy project. To a certain extent, he found one here. Or, rather, he *made* one. Certainly Milius hadn't envisaged his movie as in any way comic. And yet, for all the fascistic impulse of his pictures, he couldn't get a grip on his leading man. 'I wasn't sure whether Sean Connery's character was meant to be as funny as he sometimes seemed,' the critic Kenneth Robinson remarked at the time of the movie's release.[3] It's a fair point, because although Connery plays the Raisuli as an irony-free hero of old, he also knows that no man who takes himself so seriously is to be taken wholly seriously.

Seen in that light, Connery's decision to play the Raisuli with a full-on Scots burr – what one critic called his 'mad Sheikh of Aberdeen' mode[4] – makes a kind of sense. To have attempted anything like an Arab intonation would have run the risk of making the character a Peter Sellers-style figure of fun. 'He was worried about doing the accent,' Milius has remembered, 'so a voice coach worked with him for six weeks, but of course his accent didn't change at all. But that's the way Sean works. His genius is that he has this thing that he does where you believe he's an Arab.'[5] All unarguable, though it is fair to point out that, just to cover all bases, Milius made a tiny adjustment to his script once Connery was cast – a line of dialogue from which we learn that the Raisuli was taught English by a Scotsman.

Connery himself has never seen the need for such get-outs. 'My strength as an actor,' he has argued, 'is that I've stayed close to the core of myself, which has something to do with a voice, a music, a tune that's very much tied up with my background experience.'[6] Or, as he put it more basically to John Boorman: 'If I didn't talk the way I talk, I wouldn't know who the fuck I was.'[7] It's a curious admission for an actor (whose job it is to always be in at least two minds about his identity), though not necessarily for a movie star (whose job it is to be utterly certain of his presence in the world). What makes it the more curious in Connery's case, though, is that it isn't entirely true. While in the lazier moments of the 007 series Connery could revert to his roots with the odd Scots guttural vowel sound, for the most part his Bond spoke with a self-satisfied purr that sifted Burton and Mason over Cary Grant. The Raisuli of *The Wind and the Lion*, by contrast, is nakedly Scottish in speech and intonation.

Hence the comedy that Kenneth Robinson couldn't decide was intentional or not. Because while Milius's script is chock-full of sententious verbiage, Connery himself plainly regards the cod philosophising as nonsense. 'I am Raisuli,' he admonishes a giggling Eden Pedecaris at their first meeting, 'do not laugh at me again.' Nor does she, though she does spend an awful lot of the first half of the picture taking the rise out of his poeticised blather. 'It is the wind that passes,' intones the Raisuli at one point, 'but the sea remains.' 'A stitch in time saves nine,' retorts Bergen's Pedecaris, while simultaneously demolishing the Raisuli's chess strategy. Such repartee had been meat and potatoes to the Connery of *Goldfinger* or *Diamonds Are Forever*, of course: there was nothing Connery's Bond liked better than a verbal sparring match with a pretty girl. No such seductions are on offer in *The Wind and the Lion*, though.

193

While a *King and I*-style warmth blossoms between its two stars, there is never any notion that anything bigger might grow out of it. Indeed, Milius's picture will be the first of many movies in which Connery doesn't get the girl.

Still, for all its confusions, *The Wind and the Lion* pointed far more firmly to Connery's long-term future than had the more intriguingly arty projects he had been involved in over recent years. From now on, Connery would commit to no picture that was self-consciously convinced of its significance, its importance, its seriousness.

At the end of *Diamonds Are Forever*, as he was captured by boiler-suited henchmen at Blofeld's latest operations centre for world domination, James Bond had quipped that he was 'from the Acme Pollution Company. We're cleaning up the world and thought this would be a good place to start.' Not long after the film's release, Connery himself announced that he was quitting Britain because of the 'pollution thing'. The months he had spent in Ireland working on *Zardoz* had, apparently, cleared his head as well as his lungs. Subsequently, time spent in southern Spain – first at the run-down farmhouse he had bought during *The Hill* shoot and had been doing up on and off ever since, later at Casa Malibu, the coastal villa just outside Marbella that would become his base for the next twenty years and more – had, he said, convinced him it was time to go. 'London seemed pretty ropey when I came back,' he said. 'All those car exhausts spewing out muck.'[8]

Hence the Spanish lessons he had been taking in the offices of Dunbar and Co., a private bank of which he had recently become a director. For all that, there was little his new colleagues in the financial sector could do to prevent what Connery called the 'parasites' in Her Majesty's Treasury from getting their hands on his money. 'It got to the point where I anticipated being asked for 98 per cent of my earnings in tax,' he said, 'and I still hadn't paid my agent his 10 per cent.'[9] Connery was hardly alone in voicing such complaints, of course. Starry gripes about the depredations of the taxman were a staple tabloid page-filler in the mid-1970s. It is a myth that Denis Healey, Chancellor of the Exchequer since March 1974, claimed that he was going to 'tax the rich until the pips squeak'. All the same, after a few months of the new Labour government's efforts to deal with the fallout from the previous Conservative regime's pre-election boom, the pips were squeaking anyway.

Spain promised changes in Connery's private life, too. Though he had over the past four years grown ever closer to Micheline Roquebrune, he was adamant that he had 'no desire to marry again'.[10] In fact, even before the divorce from Cilento was finalised in October 1973, the couple had been living as man and wife in everything but the legal sense – and within eighteen months of Connery's divorce they would indeed marry, on 6 May 1975. Once again, Connery chose Gibraltar as the site of his wedding. Once again, he kept the details under wraps – this time by having told reporters that he and Roquebrune had married in secret the previous December, just after the *Wind and the Lion* shoot had ended.

The fact was that Connery had no time for anything but work as 1974 became 1975. No sooner had *The Wind and the Lion* wrapped than, in mid-January of the new year, shooting started on *The Man Who Would Be King* (1975).

The idea for the movie had been kicking around for years. John Huston had written his original script, from a Kipling short story, as long ago as the early fifties. Back then he had envisaged two of his favourite stars from Hollywood's golden age – Clark Gable and Humphrey Bogart – in the picture. Alas, though both actors wanted in on the project, Bogart died before work could commence. Still the idea retained traction for both director and remaining star. A few years later, while they were filming *The Misfits* (1961), Gable suggested to Huston that they dust the script off and find someone else to play opposite him. Huston thought it a fine idea. Then Gable died.

The project resurfaced again a decade or so later. John Foreman, producer on Huston's private-eye thriller *The Mackintosh Man* (1973), came across the director's sketches for the Bogart/Gable production that never was and had an idea. Foreman was the man responsible for that runaway hit of the late sixties *Butch Cassidy and the Sundance Kid* (1969). It was a movie whose success owed much to the marvellous relationship between its two stars: Paul Newman and Robert Redford. Indeed, as soon as *The Mackintosh Man* wrapped, Newman (who was playing Huston's titular detective) was off to shoot another movie with Redford – *The Sting* (1973). How about, suggested Foreman, we cast the two of them again – this time in *The Man Who Would be King*?

Newman took a look at Huston's original script and suggested a few alterations, but was otherwise in broad agreement with the idea. Accordingly, Huston went off with the screenwriter Gladys Hill to cuff a new screenplay into shape. But when Newman saw this later version, he drew in his horns. He had decided, he told Huston, that this movie about Victorian imperialism would make sense only if it starred British actors. 'For Christ's sake, John,' Huston would remember Newman telling him, 'get Connery and Caine'.[11]

So it was that Britain's two biggest stars of the sixties – and the only two to have convincingly sustained their careers into the next decade – were cast in *The Man Who Would Be King*. And what a piece of casting it was. As Huston was to say just months before he died: 'I believe Connery and Caine gave better performances than either Bogart or Gable could have, because they are the real thing. They are those characters.'[12] Indeed, when, a couple of years after the movie's release, Caine and Connery visited Huston in hospital, he greeted them as Danny and Peachy (the names of the characters they play in the picture).[13]

Kipling's plot is simplicity itself. Daniel Dravot (Connery) and Peachy Carnehan (Caine) are a couple of essentially good-hearted rogues hanging about India long after their days with the army are over. They meet up with Rudyard Kipling (Christopher Plummer) and after a run-in with a rebarbative District Commissioner (Jack May) decide to make good their plan to travel to the distant province of Kafiristan, thrash the locals, set themselves up as kings – and loot the place.

The Kafiristanis having been conquered, Peachy and Danny take them in hand and transform a motley crew into something approaching a proper fighting army. But when, during one battle, Danny is hit by an arrow (which actually lands safely in his leather harness) and seems miraculously uninjured, failing even to bleed, he is taken for a god. Danny is about to explain the tribesmen's mistake when the wilier Peachy suggests that they use the Kafiristanis' primitive religious ignorance against them: Danny must play the role of a god for all it is worth. Great riches are theirs, then, but when Danny announces that he plans to take himself a wife, Roxanne (Shakira Caine), she literally bites back – drawing all too human blood from his cheek. At which point the tribe, realising they have been bilked, chase the two men out of their city, scarring Peachy terribly and throwing Danny off a bridge into a deep canyon.

That ending offers a clue to the main reason the Newman and Redford ticket couldn't have been made to work for *The Man Who Would Be King*. *Butch Cassidy and the Sundance Kid* and *The Sting* were built around a spiky sparring competition between their two stars: neither Redford nor Newman was willing to grant the other man top billing. Either both of them would have had to perish at the end of Huston's movie, or neither. The story as we have it would plainly have required the slightly-slow-on-the-uptake character Redford had hitherto played to take the part of Danny while the cannier Newman would be the more cautious Peachy. On the other hand, Newman had a regal air that Redford, for all his beauty, could never pretend to. Which is a way of saying that *The Man Who Would Be King* works because Michael Caine is wise enough and generous enough to know that he is not the man who would be king.

197

Not that Huston's delightfully democratic direction favours one actor over another. The Connery/Caine teaming is one of the most joyous the movies have ever given us, and much of the delight in the picture comes from watching two international stars generously take turns in pointing the key-light at one another. If it's true that Connery's is the character given the big build-up – we have to wait ten minutes or so to meet Danny Dravot – it's equally true that in those ten minutes Caine is given the chance to strut his thespian stuff, limping here, grunting there and generally introducing the narrative drift. Otherwise, they share the dialogue pretty evenly, and between them Caine and Connery work out any number of ways of balancing out the other's more off-the-leash moments. The effect is of watching two men utterly happy to be working as a team, of two men as knowledgeable about what the other is going to do as partners in a trapeze act. They're having as much fun as we are. How one wishes they had worked together again.

One of the many joys on offer is the spectacle of Connery finally being allowed to play the kind of comedy that depends not on deadly repartee but on the gleeful dumbness we have hitherto seen from him only in candid, off-camera moments. Anyone who thinks Connery's clowning and gurning on Ken Adam's home-movie footage from the *You Only Live Twice* shoot looks familiar is likely remembering his performance in *The Man Who Would Be King*. The ludicrous high spirits might be those of Groucho Marx in *Duck Soup* (1933), but where Groucho's Rufus T. Firefly dances purely for comedic effect, Connery's Danny dances for the physical joy of it, the brazen elegance of the moment.

Such elegance is a Connery hallmark, of course, and it is there in Huston's movie from the get-go. When first we meet Danny, sleeping in the first-class carriage of an otherwise crowded train, a panama hat covering his face, Connery uses the moment to play up his extravagant grace. Roused from his slumbers by Kipling, he lifts his trunk from the seat like a gymnast, before gliding across the carriage in a unison of movement that Fred Astaire might have envied.

Beyond Danny's massive physical presence – there are shots of him in his military red coat where he seems bear-like in magnitude – it is this tensile grace that marks him out as naturally regal, as the man other men might come to worship. Throw in a scene in which our soon-to-be king seems to survive being pierced by an arrow and we have a Bond-style superhero on our hands. Obey my orders, he tells the Kafiristanis, who willingly submit to his charge, 'and you'll be able to slaughter your enemies like civilised men'. Just which civilised slaughterer could he have in mind? One does not have to agree with Mark Cousins's suggestion that the scene is 'deeply anti-military' to see that Connery is here relishing the chance Huston's script affords him to poke fun at Bond.[14]

Beyond the delight in seeing Connery happy on screen for the first time since he dispatched the wrong Blofeld in *Diamonds Are Forever*, *The Man Who Would Be King* is a key picture in his oeuvre for its unconscious commentary on his quandary of the past decade and more. This is a movie about hero worship – just the phenomenon Connery had spent the past ten years attempting to extricate himself from. Connery's Daniel Dravot is a star – a godhead worshipped by a tribe of hopelessly admiring subjects. Worse, he comes to give credence to that worship. He's a man who believes his own press, and Connery uses the opportunity this drama offers to investigate his own response to having been the object of so much lauding and fascination in the Bond years.

When Danny learns that the Kafiristanis believe him to be their new king his reaction isn't disbelief or sardonic wit – those staple modes of the first-generation Connery figure – but calm acceptance of the fate he has been dealt. Connery's laconic deadpan has never been more beautifully used than in those scenes of Danny's almost acquiescent hubris – those moments when, in John Huston's words, Danny 'thinks he's Alexander the Great'.[15] Even at his most pompous and obsessive, there's a tranquil aura about Danny – a sense that he has always known his day in the sun would come. Asked, ten years earlier, about how the Bond role came his way, an admirably level-headed Connery had argued simply, 'It was luck . . . And luck only knocks once, and when it knocks you have to grab it quick, and then hang on tight.'[16] Without being remotely self-serving, Connery's Danny would not agree. 'You may call it luck,' he tells the incredulous yet still opportunistic Peachy as he is about to be crowned in front of his adoring subjects. 'I call it destiny.'

Huston films Connery's massive form in this scene first from low down, then, as he parades in front of his subjects, his arms held wide, that big, relaxed grin scything across his face, from on high. Either way – encouraged to take Danny at his own hubristic self-estimation when we see him from below or reminded that Danny is getting above himself – Connery fills the frame. Either way, he seems magical and marvellous: the unvanquishable hero, the mythic creature who really could take an arrow through his heart and survive. Meanwhile, down below, his worshipful fans look on. We're being offered, in other words, a parody of a movie premiere – those glitzy corporate events Connery is famous for dismissing as being among 'the degrading compromises of publicity'.[17] (Indeed, though *The Man Who Would Be King* received a royal premiere at the Odeon Leicester Square in December 1975, Connery himself did not show up.)

All of which means that, regardless of its intrinsic merits – and Huston's picture was pretty much universally well received by the critics, Connery's first such success in several years – *The Man Who Would Be King* is another key movie in the Connery oeuvre. If *The Wind and the Lion* had redefined his on-screen persona, its successor underlined the fact that after a few years of drift Connery was still one of the movies' biggest stars.

And if Connery's $250,000 fee for the picture didn't quite reflect that fact, still, the 5 per cent of the grosses Selinger had negotiated for him (as well as for Caine, who was paid the same fee, too) would do well enough: *The Man Who Would Be King* has so far taken in excess of $11 million in rentals. The trouble was, a couple of years after its release, Connery and his advisors worked out that not all the moneys owing to him from the picture had come his way. By their calculations, Connery was down more than $100,000 on the deal. Alerted to the shortfall, Caine went over his own books and decided Allied Artists (AA) had short-changed him by the same amount.

On 23 January 1978 the two men announced that they were suing AA for residual payments owing. AA countersued for defamation – for $21.5 million from Connery alone. In addition, both men were sued for a separate $10 million each in punitive damages. The two stars had launched a potentially catastrophic action.

In the event, Connery and Caine won the case – though by the time they had done so AA had gone bust. Had it been worth it? Would Connery have been better to follow John Boorman's advice – to stop wasting his time, to keep his head down and shoot a couple of pictures, safe in the knowledge that by doing so he'd have made far more money than he'd win from any legal suit? Doubtless that would have been the sensible thing to do. But for Connery a point of principle was at stake. Despite his recent carping at the welfare state, Connery still believed in the fundamental leftist principle: a fair day's pay for a fair day's work. Let companies like AA ride roughshod over you, and others will feel free to do the same. Over the next few years, Connery would more than once prove willing to sue even the biggest companies if he thought he had been wronged.

The final part of what we can now call Connery's mid-seventies historical trilogy was Richard Lester's *Robin and Marian* (1976). Reviewing Richard Lester's picture in the *New Yorker*, Pauline Kael described Connery's Robin as 'a heroic warrior force . . . a Ulysses or a Macbeth',[18] and there is no denying that set against his TV Macbeth of fifteen years earlier Connery's achievement here is indeed heroic. Quiet, understated, wryly amused and gently self-mocking, Connery's performance here may just be the best in his career thus far. Certainly *Robin and Marian* was the most distinguished picture he had yet made.

The picture was originally called 'The Death of Robin Hood', a title that shows just how closely Lester's project was linked to one of the movies' mid-seventies mini-genres – the burnished elegy on the death of a once famous old man. As with the Spielberg and Lucas pictures, these were stories that could serve to remind the wayward youth that comprised the bulk of the moviegoing audience that everybody needs an authority figure. Henry Hathaway's *True Grit*, on which we have already touched, was the movement's progenitor; Don Siegel's *The Shootist* (1976), which again starred Wayne as a legendary gunslinger, one of its more recent variations. That last movie was marred, though, by its lack of conviction – neither Wayne's lacklustre J. B. Books nor Siegel's uncharacteristically shapeless direction were sufficiently authoritative. *The Shootist* feels like a put-on – one last Lear-like attempt at imposing on the young the authority of a generation whose time has gone. The great virtue of *Robin and Marian*, on the other hand, is that though it gives us a hero we can celebrate and endorse (merely by dint of his being played by the almost over-determinedly masculine Connery), the movie itself is in two minds as to the need for his latest acts of derring-do.

The movie opens with Robin Hood and Little John (Nicol Williamson) returning to Sherwood Forest after twenty years crusading with Richard the Lionheart. Still in love with Marian (Audrey Hepburn), Robin is told that she is now the abbess at Kirkly Abbey – and therefore due for arrest by the Sheriff of Nottingham (Robert Shaw) on the orders of King John. Robin rescues Marian in the nick of time and from there the picture settles into its long, lyrical middle section – the romance that earlier versions of the Robin Hood myth had either giggled at or skirted around. Not so Lester, Connery and Hepburn, who stage and play their love scenes with beautifully wounded integrity. Not once in this romance are we in any doubt that our hero and heroine are made for one another, not once do we believe they are fated to attain that end.

We are dealing, in other words, with one of those doomed love stories the history of narrative abounds in. For all that Connery himself subsequently name-called the producers for trying 'to sell it as a love story, when it's about the mythology of being a hero, exploring what it's like for him [Robin] to be over the hill',[19] it is impossible to watch *Robin and Marian* and not be heartbroken at the spectacle of that impossible love the movies might have been invented to celebrate.

And yet Connery wasn't wrong to talk about the movie in terms of its ageing hero. Audrey Hepburn had almost made a career out of being seduced by older men – Astaire, Bogart, Grant. And though Hepburn was actually born more than a year earlier than Connery, there is no denying that the Robin Hood we have here looks significantly older than the picture's Marian. As he filmed *Robin and Marian*, Connery was turning 45. That's a couple of years younger than Harrison Ford would be when he starred opposite Connery in *Indiana Jones and the Last Crusade* (1989) and a full seven years younger than the Bruce Willis of the fourth *Die Hard* (2007). Yet Connery's Robin looks at least ten years older than either of those two stars do in those pictures. By the mid-seventies, that is, the man who had shot to fame as the eternal superstud was acting rather more than his age.

Hence the ache and grind of Connery's Robin, the sense he gives us of a man who wakes each day preparing himself for death. Given the average life expectancy during the Middle Ages, of course, such preparations would have been par for the course, but Connery's big achievement in the picture is to find wondrously objective correlatives for Robin's sense of sag and wheeze. Standing tall seems an effort for him, and scaling a castle wall – the kind of feat Errol Flynn's Robin pulled off with insouciant bravado – takes him many long minutes, Lester's camera pointing up the sweat and strain in Robin's every tug and pull. Actors had aged on screen before, of course – Orson Welles practically made a career out of pretending to be five times older than whatever age he was – but movie stars are usually bent on work that will emphasise their youth. Whichever way you cut it, then, *Robin and Marian* was another brave move for Connery. Unfortunately, the public weren't buying it.

And so while Connery pronounced himself pleased at the way Richard Lester had chivvied the production along, bringing the ship into harbour in under six weeks, he subsequently declared himself upset at the way *Robin and Marian* all but sank at the box office. Having cost around $5 million, the movie took just $4 million in ticket sales. This, despite fairly unanimous good reviews (the movie is far and away Lester's most distinguished work, largely because it eschews the grab-bag of misunderstood *nouvelle vague* aesthetics that had marred most of his previous work). This, despite the fact of Hepburn's return to the screen after the best part of a decade away. This, despite the fact that in Hepburn, Connery was finally going up against a woman of similar star wattage. The moment when Connery socks Hepburn on the jaw, the better to ensure she should not fall into the villain's clutches, ought to be one of the cinema's most famous moments.

But like Robin himself in the movie, *Robin and Marian* sorted ill with its times. An increasingly infantilised moviegoing audience had no truck with films that embodied and spoke to the new age of anxiety. With the Western economy in tatters, they wanted fantasies, they wanted escape – and these past ten years no actor had served up more delicious fantasies of escape than Sean Connery. What on earth was he doing appearing in these sombre hymns to the death of love and the end of the heroic ideal?

Connery himself began to wonder something similar. On the one hand he was drawn to parts that he believed would help distance him from the Bond image. On the other, he wanted to retain the top-billing megabucks parts that he believed Bond had earned him the right to. His next picture would be his weirdest attempt yet to yoke together these incompatible aims.

11

Cast Adrift

Whether it was the economic crisis of the period or the stabilising influence of his new marriage, Sean Connery's actorly ambitions began to change as the seventies wore on. Micheline, who had barely known who her future husband was when she had met him on that Moroccan golf course, had little interest in the movies, and though she was herself a painter and designer, she was not given to romantic notions of the artist's responsibility to society. As far as she was concerned, the artist's job was to amuse and entertain and move an audience. Sententious, hectoring statements about the human condition and the body politic were for the birds. Connery, still smarting from the failure of *The Offence*, took notice.

A propitious time, then, for one Kevin McClory to come knocking. Two decades earlier, McClory had been a protégé of John Huston, working with him as an assistant on *The African Queen* (1951) and as assistant director on *Moby Dick* (1956). A few years later, in 1959, a mutual friend introduced him to Ian Fleming, then seven books into his Bond series and keen to have them turned into movies. McClory told Fleming that although he thought his novels enjoyable, they were not, as written, at all suited to the demands of popular moviemaking. He found Fleming, that great archivist of detail and design, wanting on the visual front. Moreover, he counselled that the sadism that underpinned Fleming's fantasies would never make it into the cinema.

For all that, the Old Etonian prig and the rambunctious Irishman got on, and when McClory suggested that the easiest way to get a Bond movie idea going would be to ditch all Fleming's extant stories and start a new one from scratch the writer was happy to give it a try. The resultant script was never made into a film, although Fleming himself deemed it good enough to borrow its plot and locations for what became his next novel, *Thunderball*. Subsequently, McClory sued for copyright, Fleming settled out of court, and McClory was listed as 'Producer' on the eventual film version of *Thunderball* (with Broccoli and Saltzman down as 'Executive Producers'). Most importantly, though, McClory was deemed to retain ownership of all script materials. Provided he waited ten years from the release of *Thunderball*, he was licensed to film its story as often as he wanted.

He wanted to now. With the novelist Len Deighton (who had written the novels on which Michael Caine's Harry Palmer trilogy had been based) he was at work on a script called 'James Bond of the Secret Service'. Would Connery, he wanted to know, fancy the titular role? At first, Connery was unsure. True, *Dr No* had just been broadcast for the first time on British television – and garnered more publicity for itself thirteen years on than it had when first unleashed on an unsuspecting and unwaiting world. On the other hand, the second Roger Moore Bond, *The Man with the Golden Gun*, had just performed very disappointingly at the box office, adding weight to Connery's long-held belief that the spy genre was a sixties phenomenon and nothing else. On yet another hand, though he had proved to Saltzman and Broccoli that they needed him as much as he needed them with *Diamonds Are Forever*, wouldn't it be nice to prove that he didn't need them at all? To prove that it was he – and he alone – who had been responsible for the success of the Bond movies.

It wasn't to be. When Broccoli (who had bought Saltzman out of Eon Productions earlier that year) and United Artists got wind of what was afoot they quickly called in the lawyers and scuppered McClory's plans. If McClory wanted to embark on a remake of *Thunderball*, the lawyers said, then he was free to do just that. But that was all he could do. In other words, 'James Bond of the Secret Service' could use every character, line of dialogue, situation and scene from the original screenplay – but it could not include any new material. Given that *Thunderball* was the dullest of Connery's six Bonds, this hardly augured well, and nobody can have been surprised when he chose to 'walk away from it'.[1]

Instead, Connery elected to appear in *The Next Man* (1976). It was an intriguing choice, because although the movie casts him as his second Muslim hero in two years, Connery plays the role in apparel that suggests Bond rather more than it does the Barbary coast. For the first time since *Diamonds Are Forever*, we are offered a nattily dressed Connery (some of the suits costume designer Anna Hill Johnstone fitted Connery out with are as exquisitely tailored as anything he wore in *Dr No* or *Goldfinger*). True, in one scene Connery's Khalil Abdul-Muhsen takes a stroll through New York's Central Park while wearing a flat cap; true, during off-duty moments Khalil is given to donning suede shirts whose collars are as pointed and sharp-looking as the Raisuli's sabre. But otherwise, Connery looks as good as he has ever done in Richard C. Sarafian's fine thriller.

And he needs to, because the casting is ludicrous. Somewhere in Sarafian's script Khalil is given a line explaining that he studied for his degree in Edinburgh – hence the wry Scots burr with which this Arab speaks English. The line cuts no mustard, of course. How could it? Still, once we're past such incidental nonsense there are many pleasures to be had from Connery's appearance in *The Next Man*.

It is nice, for instance, that the part of Khalil requires more of the orotund rhetoric Connery had had such fun with in *The Wind and the Lion*. Khalil, an Arab diplomat who wants to make peace with Israel and admit the country into OPEC, has a way of speaking poetically about even the most mundane matters, and Connery backs up this habitual versifying with one of his more elegantly gesticulatory performances. 'My hands reach out to you,' Khalil tells an audience at the United Nations, 'which of you will take them?' And as he speaks, his hands do indeed reach out with a symmetrical grandiloquence that would appear hammy and operatic coming from any movie star less replete with meaning.

But given that *The Next Man* is a picture about a *Day of the Jackal*-style assassin – Sarafian kick-starts the movie with an impressively eventful double murder – what the movie can't help invoking is the spectre of all things Bondian. 'I do know where they serve an excellent Martini,' Connery's Khalil rhapsodises to a girl he has just met, and later, as gunmen surround the hotel room in which he has just seduced Nicole Scott (Cornelia Sharpe), he starts barking orders at her – 'Get dressed!' 'Give me the gun!' – in the gloriously unreconstructed chauvinist manner Bond audiences had been missing ever since Roger Moore took over the role. And with its globetrotting scenario – from Morocco to New York City and on to the Bahamas – the picture offered viewers the travelogue-style satisfactions of the Bond franchise, too. Indeed, Adolfo Celi, last seen hiding behind an eye-patch in *Thunderball*, even turns up as Al Sharif, a victim of Nicole's seductively murderous charms.

More important than all that, though, is the fact that *The Next Man* gives us a convincing romance. When Khalil tells Nicole that he loves her, it's the first non-ironic declaration of such passion Connery has ever made on screen. (Even the Robin Hood of *Robin and Marian* had been obliged by his incurable self-mythologising to josh with his pals that he had never thought about Marian when he was away on the crusades.) Khalil, though, is more of an old-fashioned gentleman than Connery had ever been asked to play – a man of dignity and honour, and just the kind of innocent romantic the scathing Bond might have been thought to have put paid to. Perhaps unsurprisingly, then, Khalil (like Robin and Daniel Dravot before him) dies at the end of the movie. And whatever else these deaths stood for, they made for an intriguing development in the career of a man whose CV had hitherto been built around the idea of his ur-character's invincibility.

All of which is a way of saying that *The Next Man* is one of Connery's richest pictures, a movie dense with intertextual asides, plush with the bloody passions one of the world's supreme ironists was now confident of bodying forth, alert to the politics of the real world, eager to tell a ripping yarn. And yet, the movie flopped so badly at the US box office (performing no better than *Ransom*) that it never even earned itself a UK opening, finally limping into view in Connery's home country in 1982 (on late-night TV). Quite why the picture did so disastrously it is hard to say, though Connery and Sarafian's highly positive portrayal of an Arab leader likely did them no favours in an America increasingly worried by developments in the Middle East.

What we can be sure of is that, though Connery had long believed that 'there are some pretty good movies made [which] get an audience of 25 people', he himself was beginning to get worried by such numbers being attached to his own output.[2] For all the plaudits he had won for the historical trilogy, for all the efforts he and Sarafian had made to create an intelligent thriller, his reputation as a money-spinner was suffering badly in the mid-seventies.

In a bid to prove he was still an international star, Connery signed up to play in Richard Attenborough's *A Bridge Too Far* (1977). Twice he had turned down Attenborough and his producer Joe Levine's offer, arguing that he didn't want to appear in a film about one of the Allied forces' greatest disasters of the Second World War. After *The Offence*, after *Ransom*, after *The Next Man*, Connery had had a bellyful of failure. Only when he learned that Attenborough's movie was going to be an international co-production – like *Murder on the Orient Express* – did he agree to take part. Now Connery would be up against some of the biggest hitters of the day: *The Godfather*'s James Caan; *The French Connection*'s Gene Hackman; *M*A*S*H*'s Elliot Gould; *Love Story*'s Ryan O'Neal.

Some of them turned out to be hitting rather too big for his tastes. Robert Redford, for instance, was being paid $2 million for his efforts, though he had no bigger a part to play in the movie than anyone else. (*A Bridge Too Far* has many, many faults, but chief among them is the dramatic diffusion that results from Attenborough's wrongheaded decision to cast every remotely famous movie actor and then give them way too little to do with one another.) The trouble was, it was only after Connery had signed on the dotted line that he discovered how much Redford was getting. Quaintly, it was Micheline who read about Redford's salary in a newspaper and informed her husband of the disparity. True, Laurence Olivier was being paid a mere $200,000 for his efforts, and Dirk Bogarde only half that, but at a rate of $250,000, Connery himself was doing little better.

But it wasn't just that he was being paid an eighth of what Redford was on that irked Connery. It was that he was doing significantly more work for his smaller cheque. Not only is Connery's character, Major General Robert Urquhart, in the picture more than anyone else – he is also the lynch-pin of the action as well as the movie's moral centre. 'It's not my fault you got a fucking lousy agent,' Levine barked when Connery let his fury be known.[3] Nonetheless, a few days later, the producer upped Connery's salary to an altogether more handsome $750,000. (Dennis Selinger, it should be pointed out, did not get his percentage cut on the pay-hike Connery had engineered – the beginning of the end of a less than beautiful friendship.)

Granted such grumbles, Connery acquits himself surpassingly well in this misconceived epic. Richard Attenborough was never much of a movie director, but what talents he had were for the small-scale and intimate. Put him in charge of a chamber-piece thriller like *Séance on a Wet Afternoon* (1964) and he could occasionally come up with the goods. Put him in charge of a $25 million epic and he wouldn't know where to look, let alone whom to turn to. Certainly he fails utterly to realise that Connery's Urquhart is the only character in the movie who is acting out of recognisable human motives (rather than the stock clichés of a thousand war pictures that characterise pretty much everyone else's appearance here).

The best way of making sense of the picture is to see Connery's Urquhart as a prototype Bond surrounded by a mass of Qs – jobsworthy bureaucrats with no experience in the field. Unlike the gadgets Q is forever offering 007, though, Urquhart's kit is singularly unfitted for purpose; the weapons he has been promised are dropped by parachute into German-controlled territory; the roads he wants to drive his men down are blocked by people desperate to be liberated; even the crystals HQ has supplied won't fit the local radio sets.

And yet, for all its faults, *A Bridge Too Far* turned out a hit – in terms of box-office take, Connery's biggest of the decade. Though its profit of almost 100 per cent ($50.8 million in takings for a $26 million budget) was poor compared with that of *Diamonds Are Forever* (which brought in more than six times its $7.2 million costs), Attenborough's picture did quite well enough.

In May 1977 the writer and journalist William McIlvanney published a thriller called *Laidlaw*. The book was well received and won the Crime Writers' Association Macallan Silver Dagger. It won, too, the attentions of Sean Connery who, on the back of a couple of interviews he had granted McIlvanney over the years, contacted the writer and told him he'd be interested in developing *Laidlaw* for the movies. Sad to relate, the project never came to anything,* though it's worth looking at the novel for a moment simply because of the fact that this was the first writerly work since John Hopkins's *This Story of Yours* that Connery had been actively drawn to.

The parallels between the two stories are marked. Like *The Offence*, *Laidlaw* is a police story – its titular character is a Glasgow

---

* As McIlvanney told an audience at the Edinburgh Book Festival in 2007: 'Sean Connery called me up and asked if I would write something for the screen about *Laidlaw*. I had this great idea, so I began writing it. But before you all get yourselves over excited, I never finished it. Connery's still waiting.'

DI. Like *The Offence*, the novel deals with violent rape and murder. Most revealingly, though, Jack Laidlaw is – like Connery's character in *The Offence* – somewhat less than a paragon. If he isn't quite an anti-hero, he is still some kind of antidote to popular fiction's reliance on the heroic. Like the criminals he pursues, Laidlaw is less than perfect – and he knows it. Indeed, that self-knowledge is one of the reasons he's such a good cop – because he is able to acknowledge to himself that he is a less than good man. And like so many of McIlvanney's subjects, he is a man constantly toiling against the wasted energies his nature inspires him to. McIlvanney's novel, in other words, owed rather more to the American hardboiled tradition than it did to the classic English detective puzzle. As such it was a natural for the movies. It might have been a Scots version of *Dirty Harry*, with Connery as the tarnished Tartan hero.

Why does one regret that the picture never got off the ground? Because the best work Connery has ever done on the big screen is his performance in *The Offence*. As we have seen, the jumped-up aesthetics of the rest of Sidney Lumet's picture let Connery down badly, but McIlvanney's thriller, though significantly more than formulaic, was kept in check by the structures and strictures of the genre.

Had Connery got the project together, would it have changed his subsequent career for the better? Impossible to say, though it is likely that even if Connery had pulled off a hit in his homeland, a picture about the seamier side of Glaswegian nightlife might not have gone over big in the States. Nonetheless, *Laidlaw* is one of the great might-have-beens of Connery's career – one of those movies in which the *Macbeth*-style shadows to which he has always been drawn could have been projected on to screens bigger than the one in his head. Had it turned out a success, it might have inaugurated a series in which Connery could have given free rein to his deepest dramatic instincts (rather than, as we shall see, having to return to old territory in a desperate bid to shore up his core vote). But McIlvanney never wrote the script and Connery spent the next year and more looking for suitable work.

It wasn't easy. After the massive success of *Jaws* and *Star Wars* on which we have already touched, the movie money men were growing increasingly wary of backing any picture that could not be guaranteed to pull in the teenage audience. For his part, while Connery had enjoyed the busy schedule of the past couple of years, none of the movies he had made had exactly set the box office on fire. His two biggest hits of the rapidly disappearing seventies had both been ensemble pieces, movies that had done nothing to cement his reputation as a leading man. Worse, having spent the past couple of years admitting how little hair he had (and looking rather more than his age in the process), Connery found himself even further out of step with a movie culture more and more devoted to the young.

So it was not by design that no Sean Connery movie was released between the spring of 1977 (when *A Bridge Too Far* opened) and Christmas 1978 (when *The First Great Train Robbery* opened). As early as the winter of 1976, after all, Connery had been in discussions on whether he'd like to play the lead in a big-budget disaster movie to be directed by Ronald Neame.

Connery, still bent on a post-Bond international hit, wasn't sure. Was Neame, who had cut his teeth working under the young David Lean on post-war stiff-upper-lip melodramas, really the man to helm the kind of blockbusting spectacle the American cinema had returned to over the past few years? Maybe not. On the other hand, hadn't he directed *The Poseidon Adventure* (1972), a pedestrian actioner that had turned an almost twenty-fold profit on its $5 million budget? And in the years since the release of that movie, hadn't the annual Hollywood top tens been dominated by similar 'disaster pictures'? Not until Warner Bros, who were pumping $4 million into the internationally backed project, let it be known that they were putting pressure on the producers to 'get Connery' did he begin to feel secure about what would become *Meteor* (1979).

Bolstering the project's appeal was the fact that its original script had been the work of Edmund H. North. A quarter of a century earlier, North had written the script for *The Day the Earth Stood Still* (1951), by some measure one of the most intelligent science-fiction pictures ever made. Filmed at the height of the Red scare, when Hollywood was churning out thinly disguised anti-Soviet propaganda in the shape of sci-fi melodramas, North's script was instinctively liberal, asking that we at least aim for an understanding between the little folk down here and whatever was out there. Such open-mindedness was central to North's latest screenplay, too. Though the movie boasts no little green men, it does offer plenty of big Red ones – the Russian translators and boffins with whom America must cooperate if it is to defeat its latest enemy – a five-mile-wide meteor which is headed straight for the Eastern Seaboard.

What finally swung the deal for Connery, though, was the moment the powers that be declared themselves not entirely happy with North's script and asked Stanley Mann to help Neame rework it. Mann went back a long way with Connery. Besides his having written the screenplays for *Another Time, Another Place* and *Woman of Straw*, the two men had formed a firm friendship when they had been near neighbours in Putney in the late sixties. Once Mann had delivered his rewrite in July 1977, Connery was quick to announce his happiness with the project. Now it's true that this meant Connery was signing up for *Meteor* just a couple of months after *Star Wars* – against all predictions – had begun taking the US box office by storm. It's true, too, that, as Nicholas Ray once said, if it were all in the script there'd be no point in making the movie. And no words are truer than William Goldman's justly famous claim that 'Nobody knows anything'. All the same, how could Connery have imagined this picture might be in with a chance?

Because *Meteor* may well be the worst movie of his career, a film so bad it reduces that fine Method actor Martin Landau to the striking of attitudes. The story contrives to be somehow both slow and shy on detail, the dialogue – be it by Mann or North – lame-brained, the special effects rather less than special. As for the putative romance between Connery's Dr Paul Bradley and Natalie Wood's Tatiana Nikolaevna Donskaya, the best that can be said of it is that at least both stars have the wit to play up its perfunctory status.

And yet . . . Ronald Neame, who had himself initially fought shy of being involved in the picture, hadn't been wrong when he'd said that North's original idea meant the movie 'said more than most'.[4] For one thing, *Meteor* wasn't biased against the Eastern Bloc, as so many Hollywood pictures were. For another, the movie didn't come down hard on scientists while elevating all things military. As with another disaster clunker made around the same time – Irwin Allen's *The Swarm* (1978) – *Meteor* is in no doubt that the voice of reason must and shall prevail.

More than that, Neame's picture gave Connery his biggest chance yet at playing the kind of maverick (the name, incidentally, of Dr Bradley's boat) hero Clint Eastwood had turned into the dominant movie archetype of the previous ten years. Alas, Connery was never going to come fully into his own until he and the people he worked with realised that his star persona was not best suited to playing such outsiders. That said, the mere fact that he was cast in such an Eastwood-like role meant that Connery still had currency in the Hollywood economy of the late seventies.*

Certainly, while *Meteor*'s visuals were almost uniformly awful, the movie's leading man, burly and irascible in a sheepskin car coat, looked rather good. Connery has one wonderful moment in the picture – a solo turn as he waits in a conference room to be briefed on his mission. He walks around the room glancing at the pictures hanging on the wall while absent-mindedly touching and stroking

---

* Eastwood, it is worth noting, never deigned to appear in a disaster movie. He knew that in a fight with the F/X team even as potent a secular saint as he couldn't come out on top.

the leather chairs that surround the office table. The scene serves as a reminder that few actors have commanded the space around them as well as Connery, that fewer have moved around confined areas as well as he has, and that fewer still have his genius for grounding the fantastical with such nonchalant realism.

Not that he needed to be much of an actor to make the movie's post-meteor-strike scenes look real. For long stretches of this part of the shoot Connery was wading through what he called 'a ton of stuff that . . . looks like chocolate pudding but tastes like shit'. He spoke of what he knew: on more than one occasion gobbets of this substance – Bentonite, a gelatinous fluid used in the oil-drilling business that was standing in for the earth's magma layer – splattered into his mouth as he struggled to say his lines. 'Normal mud dries and takes body temperature,' a none too happy Connery pointed out. 'This stuff has oil in it and stays wet, slimy and colder than hell.'⁵

So Connery was more than usually relieved when the *Meteor* shoot wrapped in the late January of 1978. In fact, though, it was only the actors' part in the picture that had come to a finish. The special effects teams still had plenty of work to do – and it was to be another eighteen months before the movie was released, in the autumn of 1979. By then the space-cycle inaugurated by *Star Wars* was more than two and a half years old: everyone and his uncle had already made the trip to outer space – including, much to Connery's chagrin, Roger Moore's James Bond in the absurd, though hugely profitable, *Moonraker* (1979). Given that swell of generic inflation, *Meteor* was perhaps always going to have looked a little tired. Given the cack-handed amateurishness of its construction, though, it contrived to look properly worn out.

Back home from his three months in Hollywood, Connery was told he had bigger things to worry about. Micheline had come to suspect that his business manager was ripping him off. Connery had hired Kenneth Richards, a one-time army major turned movie accountant, back in 1973, not long after he and Cilento had divorced. With his fingers in so many pies – 'business ventures' here, 'companies' there – Connery was, he said, 'a kind of one-man empire . . . I found that it's the easiest thing in the world to start companies. It's when you try to wind them down that you realise how naïve you are.'[6] Richards's first suggestion was that Connery give up on the majority of his non-cinematic interests and investments. Connery, determined at the time to carve out a reputation as a serious actor, was happy to take such advice. It had taken, he said, 'more than two years to free myself from all the business affairs that I built up – but I'm feeling better already. I'll still keep the Scottish Educational Trust and my bank directorship . . . but that's all. From now on I just want to make films – and feel free.'[7]

But had putting all his trust in Richards been so wise? Micheline thought not. Her suspicions began with a mundane domestic incident. When she and Connery had made the move to Marbella a new washing machine had gone missing. Asked if he knew of its whereabouts, Richards admitted to having given it to his son for a wedding present. The Spanish power supply, he told Micheline, meant that a machine purchased elsewhere would have been no use to her. Her suspicions understandably aroused, Micheline told Richards that she wanted to look over the books on her husband's income and investments. She was dumbfounded when Richards told her no such books were being kept.

It emerged that Richards had siphoned off more than $3.25 million – the bulk of the moneys Connery had entrusted him with – and injected it into property deals in southern France. Connery sued Richards in Switzerland (where the accountant worked). Richards disappeared, then reappeared in his home country where he launched a counter-suit against Connery for a 2 per cent share of his former employer's retrospective earnings on thirteen movies – among them his last four Bonds. The case eventually came to court in 1981, when, after eight days of hearings and four days of cross-examination, Richards abandoned his claim and conceded Connery his. Subsequently, Connery petitioned for the recovery of all moneys Richards had taken from him. Another four years went by, and in October 1985 Richards was made bankrupt. Connery never got a penny back.

The long delay between the *Meteor* wrap and the movie's eventual release meant that Connery's subsequent picture ended up in cinemas first. Since the movie in question – Michael Crichton's *The First Great Train Robbery* (1978) – turned out to be one of Connery's sweetest light comedies it ought to have stamped his cinematic authority on the tail-end of the seventies with all the gusto and prowess that *Diamonds Are Forever* had brought to bear on the start of the decade. Mysteriously, though, the picture bombed, taking less than $5 million at the box office.

On paper, Crichton's film – a Victorian caper in which Connery is required to be as devastatingly attractive as the James Bond of *Goldfinger* – must have looked like a sure-fire hit. The robbery is worked out with painstaking cunning and performed with gleeful aplomb. (Connery did his own stunts, hanging by a rope from the side of a steam train as it sped through tunnels and curved round bends.) The costumes look a treat, the location work is stunning (the movie was shot in Ireland in the early summer of 1978), and cinematographer Geoffrey Unsworth, who died only a couple of months after the picture wrapped, gives everything a toasty Dickensian glow. It's impossible to watch the picture, which still airs regularly on television, without realising that everyone around you is having fun. Opening just in time for the Christmas holidays, *The First Great Train Robbery* ought to have cleaned up.

Certainly this is the most Bondian of Connery's post-Bond movies. His gentleman thief Edward Pierce is a kind of prototype 007 – a stove-piped dandy with a suave eye for the ladies and a self-conscious fondness for double entendres. For humour is the driving force of Crichton's script. (The same is emphatically not true of his original novel, which is based on a historical incident that Crichton pulls out all the narrative stops to replicate.) While Crichton's previous two movies, *Westworld* (1973) and *Coma* (1978), had been satisfying genre pieces, *The First Great Train Robbery* is an amusement from its opening moments in which Connery voiceovers his way through the back story to the escapades that are about to unfold.

Velvety smooth, self-satisfied without sounding smug, Connery's richly voiced narration strikes just the right note of amused contempt. It's the perfect back-up to the insouciant comedy act he puts on throughout much of the action. Connery's trick in dealing with the likes of Lesley-Anne Down's seductive but dangerous Miriam – as it was in his dealings with so many of Bond's adversaries – is to let the audience do his character's thinking for him. Hence that dumb, bored look, the slightly quizzical deadpan his face slides into whenever he's letting somebody imagine they're getting the better of him. It's a visual stand-in for the 'oh no he isn't' moment familiar from a thousand pantomimes – that slip in time when the audience is put one up on the villain.

The trouble is that Crichton rather lets Connery's sardonic joshing derail his great train robbery. For Edward Pierce isn't the movie's only mocking ironist perpetually amused by all around him. Crichton grants pretty much every member of the cast their moment of archly delivered double entendre. It is all very well for Connery's Pierce to inform the lady he must seduce if he is to gain access to a bank vault about the massive erections he has seen on his travels. But when Malcolm Terris's unctuous yet randy bank manager starts going on about how Lesley-Anne Down's Miriam inspires him to thoughts of making deposits and hasty withdrawals we are entering *Carry On* territory. Indeed, at one point, *Carry On*'s Peter Butterworth turns up to wobble his chin in saucy panic.

Fortunately, the picture ends magnificently with Connery's Pierce arraigned in court, having been none too convincingly arrested. (The evidence against him isn't even circumstantial.) Why, the judge wants to know, did he engineer such a wicked crime? Crichton's camera closes in on Connery and he stares it and the court out for a long few seconds with a look of baffled disdain before announcing, 'I wanted the money.' At which point the courtroom erupts with cheery working-class types patting their hero on the back and slipping him a key so he can make good his escape – for all the world as if he's James Bond and this is only the end of the pre-credits sequence.

Despite the period fustian, the silken top hats, the frilled shirts, the brocade waistcoats, the frock coats, the Connery of *The First Great Train Robbery* looked younger than he had done for years. Gone was the heavy grey goatee of the *Robin and Marian* period, gone too the openly bald head. In their place was a full, neatly trimmed dark beard and a head of hair lighter than Connery had ever affected before. It would be stretching it to call Edward Pierce a matinee idol. Nonetheless, he was the most brazenly sexy creation of Connery's post-Bond career. As such, he looked forward to what ought to have been Connery's most openly romantic creation – the Major Robert Dapes of *Cuba* (1979).

Richard Lester's movie is set in 1959, and Dapes has been hired to train the Batistas to fight Castro's revolutionary army. But the government troops are hopelessly disorganised, and Dapes realises their cause is lost. Meanwhile, he has been catching repeated sight of Alexandra (Brooke Adams), a former lover who has settled for a comfortable if faithless marriage.

Given that Lester had taken Connery to new heights in *Robin and Marian*, hopes were high for *Cuba*. Moreover, Connery was getting to play an old-fashioned hero: a man who knows what to do and, just as important, when to do it. Or would, if his head hadn't years ago been turned by a girl who just happens to be linked to the intrigue he now finds himself locked into.

But what kind of a romantic hero is Dapes meant to be? Dressed in tweedy, almost teacherly clothes and sporting the narrowest of moustaches, Connery has never looked more like Clark Gable than he does here. But the machinations of the plot Dapes – a hired killer with a tortured romantic past – finds himself involved in recall nothing so much as mid-period Bogart. Even the fat businessman who is forever putting a spoke into Connery's mercenary wheels is called Gutman, as if in homage to the Sydney Greenstreet of *The Maltese Falcon* (1941).

Once again, audiences who had arrived primed for an international intrigue built around the figure of Connery's all-competent superkiller were disappointed to find themselves watching a picture in which their hero was given desperately little to do. The movie's most exciting scenes turn out to be rehashes of the travelogue-style moments in a Bond picture. Yes, there are pleasures to be had from watching Connery's Major Robert Dapes arrive at the Havana airport with a grip in his hand and a snazzy, snap-brimmed fedora on his head. And to see Connery pad around the airport lounge and customs offices is to be reminded that he is the only British actor to have ever really commanded a set in the way the great Hollywood stars once did.

But an hour and a half of the movie are over before we finally get to see Connery become the utilitarian soldier the dialogue has kept insisting he is. All the way through the picture, Lester has been tempting Connery into action, but letting him off the hook at the last moment. It's a trick borrowed from Clint Eastwood's pictures – goad and taunt the hero until he finally explodes into the lethal action we know him capable of. Even now, though, all we get is Connery – and it does look very much like Connery, once more doing his own stunts – climbing aboard a moving tank, summarily dispatching its driver and inaugurating the fireworks the movie has been crying out for these ninety minutes and more.

Lester, it should be said, comes into his own here. As the inventor of the pop video, with its rapid shuttle of brightly lit images, he is not half bad at handling the chaos of battle, and the whole scene is cut with such vigour and vim that one half-wishes he had been given a Bond movie to direct. Not once, not even in Peter Hunt's *On Her Majesty's Secret Service*, did the Bond cycle handle the metaphysics of action this well. Elsewhere, though, the Bond parallels are less flattering. So much of *Cuba* feels product-placed – those lengthy shots explaining how cigars are rolled and how rum is bottled – that the movie ends up looking like an anthology of the television commercials Lester had always made most of his money from.

All of which would be surmountable if the movie's romance felt remotely real. But Connery's relationship with Brooke Adams never convinces. True, in the early stages of the picture, where he is forever catching glimpses of her in moving cars, there is an urgent ache about his shoulders that speaks of cheated dreams. But once the two of them are actually together for what are rarely more than expository scenes, there is so little spark between them that the movie sinks under the weight of its own dread of feeling.

True to form, Connery seems to have realised quite early on in the production that he had got himself involved in another disaster. Certainly his Major Dapes is his most uncomfortable performance since the fledgling Bond of *Dr No*. At the start of the picture, where he is grilled by the airport staff on what he is doing in newly communist Cuba, there is a breathy nervousness about his delivery of the lines screenwriter Charles Wood has given him. At times Dapes seems to be gasping for air mid-sentence, as if he cannot bring himself to finish the latest banality he finds himself obliged to utter.

The same kind of nervy anguish recurs in the movie's long memory-of-love flashback with Brooke Adams. Connery's Dapes emphasises every word of this dreamy reverie, as if to make himself believe what he's being asked to say. True, Lester helps things not one jot by having a sixties-style doo-wop combo groan on the soundtrack, but the scene is so half-hearted it is plain nobody thought for a minute that it was playable. Indeed, Lester himself is on record as saying that he never did believe the movie's central love story. 'I think a lot of the surface of the film was rather good,' he would argue later, 'but I think you just came out with surface.'[8] Or, as Roger Angell noted in the *New Yorker*, 'If Fidel Castro ever catches *Cuba*, he will discover a ready-made subject for a three-hour speech about capitalist waste.'[9]

The pity of it is that the movie could have given Connery a wonderful opportunity to analyse and comment upon the soldier-of-fortune character that had made his name. Major Robert Dapes was, after all, a kind of footloose 007, a man who would take his money wherever he found it. With a better script – the picture is crying out for a Graham Greene or an Eric Ambler or a Nigel Balchin – and a director in control of his material, he might have exposed the shallow machinations of Bond and had love humanise the character. What he ended up making, though, was a kind of parody Bond – a parody fatally short on jokes at that.

Though Lester remained charitable to his star (he gives any film he's in his all, Lester told the BBC's Donny Macleod, because he is always conscious of the fact that without his input there would likely be no movie[10]), Connery himself was withering on the picture and its director. Lester, he said, simply hadn't done his homework. A couple of years later he was to be found arguing that though he hadn't made many mistakes, *Cuba* was one of them. More than a decade on he was still adamant that 'I'd *never* work with [Richard Lester] again.'[11] Nor has he.

12

No Time for Heroics

Richard Lester wasn't the only victim of the post-*Cuba* fallout. Even before the movie was released to its universal drubbing (only weeks after *Meteor* had finally been allowed to meet a similar fate), Connery took it upon himself to dispense with Dennis Selinger's services. Though Connery had done some good work in the seventies, he had come to the decision that too many of the movies Selinger had involved him in had ended up looking less than lustrous.

Selinger's supermarket-style marketing strategy worked well enough for Michael Caine, because Caine was that most unusual of phenomena: a character actor whom the audience were occasionally willing to take for a leading man. There were, though, no such ambiguities about Connery. Almost a decade after *Diamonds Are Forever*, he was still famous the world over as the man who breathed life into Ian Fleming's fantasy spy. Despite the magnificence of his performances in very different roles and movies over the past few years, the Bond image stuck to him – in part because every Christmas saw the much-trumpeted premiere broadcast of a Connery 007 movie on television. Somehow, Connery had to capitalise on the kudos Bond had given him without capitulating to the idea that Bond was all he was capable of. After the disasters of recent times, this was going to be tough. 'It wasn't that easy to sell me,' Connery would remember. 'At the time . . . They weren't breaking the door down for my services.'[1]

Still, on 23 February 1979 he signed with a new agent – 32-year-old Michael Ovitz, a co-founder of the Creative Artists

224

Agency (CAA). It was, Terence Young would later say, 'The best decision Sean ever made . . . Ovitz is the most important man in Sean's life.'[2] At the time, though, the move to CAA didn't look like the major breakthrough it does today. The agency was, after all, less than four years old, and though it was the baby of five big-hitters formerly with the William Morris Agency, it wasn't in a position to call any major shots. Those five agents shared the use of just a couple of cars, and at the reception area of their small, rented office space it was not uncommon to be greeted by one or other of their wives.

What did Ovitz see in Connery? What we all had, of course: the mocking macho monolith we had worshipped at the movies as adolescents. Even now, looking somewhat past its sell-by date as the seventies got ready to cede to the eighties, Connery's was the kind of name a new agency could use to lever open a few doors. Connery gave CAA legitimacy, Ovitz believed, even as the agency gave Connery clout. Once Ovitz could tell people he represented Sean Connery, they'd either want to work for him or be represented by him themselves. Indeed, within a few years of signing Connery, Ovitz famously tempted rival agents to join him at CAA because 'I have a Picasso and you don't.'[3]

Not that Ovitz was just a money man. He had a deserved reputation as one of Hollywood's great trend-spotters. Having kept a weather-eye on the movie climate of the past few years, he had noticed how pictures were increasingly being sold not as stories but as high-concept marketing strategies – display units for spin-off toys and games, rather like the Bond movies of old. Indeed, Ovitz believed that the template for Hollywood's new mainstream entertainment vision (go light on the plot and heavy on the spectacle) had been the biggest Bond pictures – the triumvirate from *Goldfinger* to *You Only Live Twice*. Whether he liked it or not, the fact remained that Connery was a visual and aural synecdoche for those movies. All that remained for Ovitz to do was to build new pictures around what remained the essential Connery figure.

Connery, meanwhile, was won over by what might be called the modesty of Ovitz's megalomania. 'He wasn't making any great, monumental claims,' Connery would remember. 'He said that he wanted an office that would have the best writers and directors, with the best actors and actresses. He foresaw the idea of packaging. Putting together creative and talented people was very much in his game plan.'[4] Moreover, for a man determined not to be tethered to his past, Connery was touched by the way Ovitz emphasised future glories and not earlier achievements. 'Nobody talked that way to me,' he said. 'They all talked about how good they had done in the past.'[5]

Still, how good Connery had done in the past was the reason Terry Gilliam had him in mind all the while he was writing the screenplay for *Time Bandits* (1983). 'The script said, "At this point the swordsman takes off his mask to reveal underneath that he is Sean Connery – or someone like Sean Connery if we can't afford him,"' Gilliam told a television interviewer much later.[6] In the event he did get Connery to play his Agamemnon. It was a role that would inaugurate a key aspect of Connery's post-fiftieth-birthday career: his ability to make a tiny cameo the dominant feature of even the most spectacular picture. Though his work on Gilliam's time-travelling comedy took up only a few days of his time, the finished movie is unimaginable without Connery's presence.

Certainly without Connery *Time Bandits* would make a lot less sense. Above all, this is a picture about our need for heroes. Its central character is a young boy, Kevin (Craig Warnock), the product of a dull, suburban, consumerist family – his parents (David Daker and Sheila Fearn) spend their time debating the relative merits of the latest kitchen gadgets – who is desperate for a little action in his life. He gets it in spades in the shape of a pack of time-travelling dwarves who, *Wizard of Oz*-style, take him off on a journey through the ages towards something approaching manhood.

A balletic swordfight aside, Connery has little to do in the picture, but what counts about his cameo in *Time Bandits* is that he is playing a mentor figure – the first of many to come over the following years. The picture, which ends with Kevin's mother and father dead and Connery (whose dreamy Agamemnon has now become a warm-hearted fireman) winking at the boy as if to say, 'This is it, son, you're going to have to be a man now,' was as far removed from Bond as anything Connery had done. But what Gilliam had seen and had deliberately constructed his jokey story around was the depth of hero-worship Connery had inspired and went on inspiring. For the rest of his career, initially under Ovitz's guidance, Connery would play variants on this character – the sage old man who had been there, done that, and was now passing on his lessons to the youngsters following him.

Time Bandits did wonderful business, taking over $20 million – far more money than anything Connery had been involved in since *A Bridge Too Far*. In neither picture, of course, had he been anything like the star. Still, Ovitz used the success to trumpet his new client – and given the list of projects Connery turned down over the next couple of years, there can be no doubt that the shot-callers were listening. Lew Grade was adamant he wanted Connery to be the hero of *Saturn 3* (1980) – with Michael Caine as the villainous android. Not even the prospect of a script by Martin Amis (then the *Observer*'s science-fiction critic) could tempt Connery, and the part he was earmarked for went to Kirk Douglas. (Harvey Keitel stood in for Caine.)

Coincidentally, Connery was also mooted for the part of the cross-dressing killer that Caine took in Brian de Palma's *Dressed To Kill* (1980). Appreciate as one does the joyous conceit of casting one of the cinema's key emblems of masculinity in this *hommage* to *Psycho*, still it's a stretch to believe that Connery could have evoked the vulnerability the part required. Nor, one suspects, could he have risen to the challenge of playing Daddy Warbucks in John Huston's *Annie* (1982). Still, Connery was sufficiently intrigued by the notion of playing in his first musical since *Darby O'Gill and the Little People* a quarter of a century earlier that he signed up for singing lessons. 'I didn't want to do it and then find I was going to be dubbed,' Connery explained as he finally turned down producer Ray Stark.[7] (Albert Finney took the role.)

What one most regrets about this period is that the barrister Rupert Massey's idea of making a film about Archibald Hall, a real-life Scottish con man who set himself up as a butler and murdered his way round some of Britain's wealthiest households, never came to anything. Connery's class-consciousness and nationalistic chippiness might have come into its own here. Yet though he was interested in the project, nothing ever came of it.[8]

Of movies that did come off in the early eighties, it's a shame that Connery was not involved in *Excalibur* (1981) – in which he had agreed to play King Arthur as early as 1975. It's possible a Connery Arthur might have given the latter part of the film weight and heft, though he would, of course, have been far too old for the earlier, adolescent-centred sections of the movie. So all things considered, we should give thanks that Connery and Ovitz played safe when they signed up for *Outland* (1981). For an outer-space saga attempting to drift in on the *Star Wars* wave, this was a determinedly old-fashioned venture. Peter Hyams's picture, the follow-up to his terrific first-men-on-Mars conspiracy thriller *Capricorn One* (1979), was about the very Hawksian virtues of honour, integrity, professionalism – virtues it found embodied in the persona of its leading man, Sean Connery.

Connery plays O'Niel, the newly arrived marshal at a mining space station on the planet Io. As a workplace, the station is a model of productivity. Still, O'Niel is worried by the occasional miner's tendency to go violently off the rails. When he discovers that such unpredictable behaviour is a by-product of the drug the head honcho Sheppard (Peter Boyle) routinely supplies to his men in order to make them work harder, O'Niel vows to take action. And so, in best western style, Sheppard hires a lynch-mob to put an end to O'Niel's do-gooding ways.

At the time of its release, *Outland* was routinely referred to as

'*High Noon* in space' – one good man taking on the massed forces of evil. And in terms of its storyline and the conception of Connery's O'Niel there is something to this parallel. But beyond that the analogies break down. In Fred Zinnemann's 1952 Oscar-winning western, for instance, it is taken for granted that the majority of people are good, if weak. No such philanthropic reading obtains in *Outland*. Moreover, Zinnemann was able to convince his audience that, in good western style, the gun battle that ends *High Noon* also ends the need for any and all subsequent gun battles. Evil has been eradicated as the credits roll. By contrast, whatever Connery's O'Niel achieves in *Outland*, it is heavily circumscribed. He has emerged victorious from a minor skirmish in a battle that will be never-ending and that will in all likelihood be finally won by the bad guys. Unlike Zinnemann's, in other words, this is not a movie that posits civilisation as the manifest destiny of American capitalism. Instead, it argues that American capitalism is the surest route there is to uncivilised chaos.

What the movie lacks, though, is the courage to argue that such strictures apply no less to its hero than they do to its villains. For in Connery's conception, O'Niel is a somewhat less than ideal hero. He's a family man, we learn in the movie's opening moments, but we also learn that Carol O'Niel (Kika Markham) is unhappy at the succession of ever less civilised outposts her husband's job takes them to. The O'Niel marriage is not, in other words, a union of Quakerish Eden – as that between Cooper and Grace Kelly in *High Noon* was. Carol sees that the work her husband is doing is brutalising – and that he is becoming harder to deal with as a result of it.

All of which is a way of saying that Connery's O'Niel owes far more to the Clint Eastwood of *Dirty Harry* than he does to the Gary Cooper of *High Noon* – a debt that is paid in full in the fine moment when, at the end of a breathless chase-cum-fight scene, O'Niel finally corners his prey who is reaching for another makeshift weapon, and fires his gun in the air saying, 'Think it over.' Yet while

Hyams plainly conceives of the scene in uncomplicatedly heroic terms, Connery has other ideas, playing O'Niel not as the white-hatted goodie but as the compromised obsessive. When Sheppard calls O'Niel 'dumber than he looks', we don't feel goaded for our hero (as we would for Harry Callahan); instead, we wonder for a moment whether Sheppard, for all his shabby pragmatics, might not have a point.

For a man always keen to remind us that the first thing he looks for in a role is comedy, Connery makes O'Niel singularly humourless. There is a moment very early on in the movie when O'Niel's son Paul (Nicholas Barnes) jokes about not having done his homework, and O'Niel jokes him back about how, if he carries on like that, he'll soon be missing his teeth. It's the kind of joke any father might make, of course, yet there is something in the flatness of Connery's delivery that suggests O'Niel actually means what he says.

Later, he will have a similarly jokey set-to with Lazarus (Frances Sternhagen), the abrasive yet affectionate ship's doctor who will eventually team up with him, which concludes with O'Niel telling her that she had better do as he has requested or he'll 'kick her nasty ass all over this room'. It is a moment that recalls Connery's performance in *The Offence* – a moment that reminds you that what is so attractive about this leading man is also what makes him such a fearsome sight. If *Outland* had risen to the challenge Connery sets it – of having a hero who is also a grade-A shit – it could have been Hyams's masterpiece (as well as one of Connery's). As things are, the picture never quite decides whether it is a conventional thriller or a moral fable about the Kafkaesque implications of modern capitalism.

Shot in the oily darkness of film noir, *Outland* is far closer in spirit to the sombre gloom of Ridley Scott's *Alien* (1979) than it is to the stolid hi-jinks of *Star Wars* or, indeed, the most recent Bond, *Moonraker* (1979). Like that last movie, the picture was shot at Pinewood Studios (Hyams had intended to make the picture in

Hollywood, but Connery insisted he would work only in the UK*),
and there are times when we might be watching the Mr Hyde to
Bond's Dr Jekyll. What, after all, are Philip Harrison's sets – all
perforated steel and wheezing hydraulic doors – if not Ken Adam
done over for the age of post-industrial gloom?

The problem is, Hyams never really makes geographical sense
of these magnificent sets: no matter how many times you've seen
the picture, you have no idea what the relationships between all
those different rooms and corridors and gantries are. There's no
sense of a coherent, navigable space. Had Hyams been out to make
a modernist thriller in which all action is seen as senseless and
pointless this aesthetic might have made a kind of sense. But in
what is a largely conventional melodramatic thriller, much tension
is thrown away by our not knowing our way around the old dark
house.

On the plus side, the movie's several fight scenes are Connery's
most physically inventive and involving since those of *Diamonds Are
Forever*. Whatever else *Outland* did, it put an end to the series of
movies Connery had been making about men facing up to the fact
that they were no longer as young as they once were. Hyams treats
us to repeated sequences in which O'Niel chases round the space
station on the hunt for one villain or another. Shooting always from
a low angle, he gives us a vision of Connery as the magnificent
animal refusing to be tamed by the diktats of the Orwellian trap
he finds himself in. Though the stunt work on *The First Great Train
Robbery* had asked for and received much from Connery's burly
charms, those Victorian frock-coats and frills had done little to show
off the magnificence of his stature. Here, though, in his marshal's
uniform of chinos and rolled-up-sleeve shirt he looks every inch
the blue-collar hero – like a steelworker coming off shift in Michael

* A mysterious insistence, because in the seventies and eighties, Connery, like
so many other movie stars and rockers, spent most of his time out of his home
country in order to avoid paying what he saw as exorbitant taxes.

Cimino's masterly investigation of the meaning of heroism in an anti-heroic age, *The Deer Hunter* (1979).

Impressed though he was by Colin Welland's screenplay for *Chariots of Fire* (1981) – 'A film script that I read and made me cry,' he later said[9] – Connery turned down director Hugh Hudson's offer of the part of Lord Birkenhead* because he suspected the project would turn out just another minor homegrown picture. A good call. Academy Award winner though it turned out to be, this Thatcherite tribute to the indomitable spirit of dear old Blighty was no harbinger of a national movie renaissance. 'The British are coming, the British are coming,' Welland declaimed as he picked up the Best Script Oscar in 1982. Well, maybe. As far as the American cinema was concerned the British already had come – or, at least, one Briton had, and his name was Sean Connery.

Certainly Richard Brooks, the director of Connery's next picture, *Wrong Is Right* (1982), suggested as much when he said he 'need[ed] an international star, someone known all over the world . . . Sean Connery came to mind.'[10] The part was that of a roving investigative television journalist who, no matter how big the story, always remained the centre of attention. Why did Connery take on the role? A number of reasons suggest themselves, chief among them Brooks's habit of making movies of highly respected novels. He it was who had written and directed adaptations of Dostoevsky (*The Brothers Karamazov* (1958)), Sinclair Lewis (*Elmer Gantry* (1960)), Tennessee Williams (*Cat on a Hot Tin Roof* (1958) and *Sweet Bird of Youth* (1962)), Joseph Conrad (*Lord Jim* (1965)) and Truman Capote (*In Cold Blood* (1967)): just the kind of faithful, earnest, intellectualised material that the Connery of the Diane Cilento years had felt himself drawn to.

For *Wrong Is Right*, Brooks had found his source material in the

---

* A fervent opponent of Irish nationalism, we might recall . . .

novel *The Better Angels* by Charles McCarry, a Somerset Maugham fan whose work had been compared with that of John le Carré. McCarry's tale, a congested nightmare involving Middle Eastern terrorists, the sale of a pair of suitcases packed with nuclear warheads, and a tottering right-wing US president bent on re-election, seems timelier now than it did a quarter of a century ago. But the plotting of Brooks and McCarry's screenplay is so loose that the movie feels like a news show that is constantly being wrong-footed by the sheer number of breaking stories.

How much of the blame for this chaotic picture attaches to Connery? More than might otherwise have done, since having insisted (as he had with Hitchcock on *Marnie*) that he have sight of the script long before the cameras rolled, Connery subsequently found himself agreeing to work on the rewrites with Brooks. Since the draft of the script Connery was sent would have made for a movie of about three and a half hours, it will be appreciated that writer/director and actor had their work cut out for them.

The finished picture, though, suggests that cut out is all they did. *Wrong Is Right* is one of those movies in which you're constantly asking questions like 'How did we get here?' or 'Did I miss something?' The film proceeds with the kind of unexplained leaps and bounds that even mid-period Connery/Bond pictures would have thought cack-handed. Given that nobody ever went to a Bond picture to follow the story, of course, the unconscious *nouvelle vague* technique hardly mattered. On a movie as putatively serious and moralistic as *Wrong Is Right*, though, logic counts for a great deal. Brooks might have thought himself the engineer of a *Dr Strangelove* for the eighties, but perhaps thanks to those radical cuts to the script his picture lacks the appalling, remorseless logic of Stanley Kubrick's cold-hearted epic. Nonetheless, while Connery has always been happy to blame directors and writers for any flops he has found himself involved in, he went on defending *Wrong Is Right* long after it had bombed at the box office.

Connery plays Patrick Hale, a globetrotting journalist who is to his trade what James Bond is to his: a contradiction in terms. Just as secret agents ought to be anonymous and forgettable, so reporters work best when appearing to be inconsequential figures shambling through events they are not best placed to understand. Hale, though, comes across as a movie star, a man who makes the news as often as he breaks it, and Connery plays him as if he is perpetually auditioning for a part in *Macbeth*. Hale's monologues are not, therefore, the opinion-free drones of your average newscaster, but impassioned speeches and hectoring rants about the moral implications of some story or other.

There are times, watching *Wrong Is Right*, when you get an idea of the kind of theatre actor Sean Connery could have been – grandiloquent, majestic, rhetorical, committed, cawing. The movie's big problem – its clumsy story structure aside – is that its star has nobody of anything like the same magnitude to rub up against. One can see the logic in casting as anodyne a presence as George Grizzard in the role of a puppet president forever being pulled this way and that by his machinating staff. But it has to be seen, too, that nobody so essentially anonymous was going to be able to cut it against a star as fiery as Connery. For the same reason, the death of Katharine Ross's Sally Blake in the first act is rather less surprising than Brooks intended: who could have believed that so lifeless an actress could have held her own up against as looming a presence as that of the leading man?

For all Connery's earthy wit and warmth, though, the picture is signally short on the heart it accuses the media age of lacking. Confusingly, Brooks never really constructs an attitude towards Patrick Hale. Is Connery playing the voice of integrity in a world ever more crazed by the PR game, or is he playing a ham actor on the make? Nobody seems to know. All of which said, there is much that is good about *Wrong Is Right*. The Connery of this movie is as penetratingly ironic as the Connery of the lightest Bond moments, with the added virtue that what is here being satirised actually merits satire. For all its flaws, the picture is one of Connery's best from the eighties, the movie in which he found a new way of interrogating his own starry status and finding it wanting.*

Still, given the populist orientation of Michael Ovitz, one can easily understand the faith he and his main man had placed in Brooks's tale of international intrigue and espionage. Rather harder to grasp is what Ovitz saw in Connery's next picture – Fred Zinnemann's *Five Days One Summer*. Not, it should be said, that the movie is a disaster; in fact, it is one of the most interesting Connery put his name to in the eighties. But there is no denying that Zinnemann's picture is a textbook example of the kind of project Ovitz and his minions came into the business to do away with.

The movie, which tells the story of a brief Alpine holiday undertaken by a young girl Kate (Betsy Brantley) and her older lover Douglas Meredith (Connery), is designed as an investigation of the nature of passion. Douglas, we eventually learn, is Kate's uncle – and his niece has been obsessed with him since she was ten years old. Such adoring fantasies, of course, are fitting Connery country. By 1981, when, hot on the heels of the *Wrong Is Right* wrap, *Five Days One Summer* was shot, two generations of young girls had been fantasising about the movies' ur-sexual sadist having his way with them. If only Zinnemann hadn't fought shy of the suggestive layers Connery couldn't help but bring to his picture. Though Zinnemann was adamant that 'Sean was my first and only choice of actor' for the role of, let us admit it, Humbert Humbert-style lover, there is no evidence that he saw in Connery anything more than a man who looked like he could handle ropes and climb mountains.[11] (Indeed, Connery did many of his own stunts on the

---

* The picture flopped so badly in America that the powers that be decided to rename it *The Man with the Deadly Lens* when it opened in Britain in November 1982. A new poster was designed, showing Connery down on one knee, pointing his titular lens at the onlooker, like 007 did his Walther PPK in the pop-art openings of the Bonds. The public weren't fooled.

picture, which boasts what has rightly been called some of the most impressive mountain footage ever shot.)

And so, rather than wonder what kind of uncle takes advantage of a young niece's crush on him, Zinnemann's picture merely takes Douglas's actions at face value. To compound the problem, Connery, bowled over at the fact of working with the man who had directed *High Noon*, gives in to Zinnemann's pat moral schema. Instead of playing Douglas as either a sexual predator out for whatever he can get or a middle-aged man blown away by the rebirth of the passion he had thought marriage and career and life had long since put paid to, he portrays him as the gentlest of gentlemen, an ingenuous self-deceiver unable or unwilling to face up to the consequences of his *grand amour*.

It's not that Connery isn't up to this kind of repression. Watch him dance the black bottom with Kate – a shy, embarrassed smile playing across his lips as he contrives to look at once ungainly and graceful – and marvel at his controlled innocence. Watch him in the movie's opening scene, in a carriage en route to the Alpine hotel he has booked, and he looks just a second too long at Kate before turning his face away from the camera with wounding self-reproach. By any measure, these are miraculous moments of screen acting, of a star player subjugating his aesthetic essence to the confines of a narrative his presence might have been brought into existence in order to subvert.

And so Connery's best chance since *The Offence* to investigate the predatory pressures of Bond was fudged by Zinnemann's decision to play what Edmund Wilson called the 'feminised Hemingway' of Kay Boyle's original short story 'Maiden, Maiden' as a heavily symbolised yarn about doomed love.[12] Hence we get a scene wherein the couple's walking guide Johann (Lambert Wilson) insists that Kate take an apple on their walk, a scene wherein Johann points at a mountain stream gushing and tumbling and tells his frosty young charge that 'every year the glacier melts a little more'. Such clumsy symbolism comes to a head with the melodramatic discovery of a frozen corpse – the body of a man who died more than thirty years earlier on the day before his wedding. His wife-to-be, Johann tells us as the body is hacked from its icy tomb, has spent the rest of her life alone.

The metaphoric build-up over, Johann finally declares his love for Kate, telling her she is wasting her life on an older man. Given that Kate has shown no sign of thinking her life wasted, Johann's tactlessness might be thought presumptuous – but to the viewer it is doubly presumptuous simply because the older man in question is being incarnated by Sean Connery. The idea that any woman might be wasting herself on this Adonis is risible. Still, the machinations of the melodrama mean Kate must now go through the motions of wondering whether Johann has a point – wondering that comes to a head the day the two men go off walking on their own and, following a mini-avalanche, only one of them is sighted coming back. Which one of them will it be? Cue much soul-searching on Kate's part as she tries desperately to espy the man's identity through her telescope.

To be fair, the picture does succeed in stoking a little tension here, though this is less down to Zinnemann's touch than it is to Connery's curriculum vitae: rare had been the movies of his past decade in which he had either got the girl and/or lived to see another day. On the other hand, Lambert Wilson's Johann is so anaemic a creation that no movie could hope to end resoundingly with him taking the girl into his arms. In short, it isn't really any surprise when it turns out to be Connery's Douglas who has survived the rock fall.

Even here, though, Zinnemann misses a trick. The question is never raised as to whether Douglas might have quietly killed Johann. How much more fun might *Five Days One Summer* have been, after all, had Douglas been toying with the competition, been allowing the young pup to think he had a chance with the older man's girl before being roundly and shamefacedly slapped down? But to have pulled off something like that Zinnemann would have had to have been Joseph Losey, Kay Boyle have been Henry James, and Betsy Brantley and Lambert Wilson able to do more than just moue at one another.

What we have here, then, is a textbook example of a director not knowing what he has on his hands. Because movies are not just their stories. Movies are about their stars, too, and if one of your stars shines as brightly as Sean Connery you had better take care lest you find your celluloid catching fire. Zinnemann, a mountaineer himself in his youth, had apparently been intending to film 'Maiden Maiden' for more than three decades – three decades in which his filmmaker's penchant for tame passion and calm ardour had been roundly overturned, in part by the example of the man he chose to be the lead in his now very old-fashioned picture.

In other words, while Zinnemann may well have wanted Connery for his leading man, he had not begun to work out how his casting would change the terms of Boyle's short story. Connery has likened the part of Douglas to someone out of Ibsen – 'ostensibly a pillar of the community, but ruled by his darker emotions'[13] – yet none of this troubled passion bubbles up during the movie itself. Instead, actor that he is, Connery attempts to accommodate himself to the strictures of Zinnemann's milksop romance by coming on all avuncular and asexual. Whatever he and Kate are getting from one another, he keeps trying to suggest, it is rather more than what Johann and the rest of the Alpine gossipmongers believe it to be. Valiant as Connery's efforts are in this regard, the final result couldn't help but be confused.

Certainly Connery himself was confounded by the flop that *Five Days One Summer* turned out to be. On the other hand, it clarified for him his position in the movie firmament. Zinnemann's picture was the one that finally made plain to him that, no matter how good an actor he was, he remained first and foremost a movie star – which meant that audiences came to him with needs they expected to be satisfied in exactly the same way he had satisfied them hitherto. In Douglas Meredith, Connery had attempted to create a man forever tamping down his emotions for fear of falling victim to his desires. In large part the attempt succeeded – not that many people were around to see it. Like it or not, *Five Days One Summer* made it clear to Connery that audiences weren't yet ready to accept him as anything other than a version of the self he had become for the James Bond pictures.

13

Never Say *Never Say Never Again* Again

None of the films Connery had made over the past few years had set the world on fire, and since he remained an intensely private man, a star bent on avoiding the PR circuit, his appearances in the newspapers were few and far between. But in the early eighties a story did begin to circulate in the press to the effect that upon being told Cubby Broccoli had suffered a stroke which left him half paralysed, Connery had reportedly said 'Fucking good. I hope he's paralysed down the other side tomorrow.'[1] Suitably streamlined and sanitised, that quip wouldn't look amiss in an early Bond script – one of those darkly deadpan moments in which our hero dispatches another nemesis to an early grave. But was Connery joking?

Well, yes, of course he was. Such a gag might have been made by anyone about a boss they had never seen eye to eye with. Nonetheless, as with so much joking, there was a serious undertow to Connery's quip. Because there can be no doubt that Connery saw Broccoli (and Harry Saltzman even more) as the grasping monster of Marxist cliché. To Connery, Broccoli was the guy for whom he had worked his fingers to the bone while being paid peanuts, the guy whose fortune he had made while shackled to a workload that prevented him engaging in more potentially satisfying endeavours. To Connery, Broccoli was still the 'fat slob producer' he had so charmingly christened him in the run-up to the *You Only Live Twice* shoot. Broccoli, at least in public an old-school smoothie, remained resolutely baffled by such name-calling. Over the years he took to telling reporters that all he had ever done for Sean Connery was make him rich and famous.

Despite the depredations of Kenneth Richards, Connery was still a wealthy man, of course. And he remained famous, too, though not for anything he had done over the past few years. True, *Outland* had had respectable notices, and *Time Bandits* had done very well at the box office. But Connery's last big *starring* hit was the now seven-year-old *The Man Who Would Be King* – and his last mega-hit, *Diamonds Are Forever*, now more than a decade in the past. In between times, though, the flops had been stacking up.

It wasn't, it bears saying again, that Connery himself had been doing bad work. Even in the debacle that turned out to be *Meteor* he had proved himself one of the movies' most relaxedly accomplished leading men. Whatever picture he had been in, Connery had quickly stamped his authority on it. The trouble was, too many of the films were unworthy of his commanding presence. Looking back, there was simply no denying that Connery's past few years had been years of drift, years in which he had seemed unsure where to direct his efforts. Was he a character actor best suited to historical roles? Was he a leading man whose uncompromised morality made him seem increasingly anachronistic in an age of romantic cynicism? Or was he simply a very wealthy chap happy to coast on his reputation with a sexily smirking cameo here and an appearance on the pro-celeb golf tour there?

Re-enter Kevin McClory, the man who had helped in the construction of the *Thunderball* storyline and who had the legal right to remake the film as many times as he fancied. A year or so earlier, Philip Mengel, McClory's New York-based financial advisor, had suggested he might like to meet his friend Jack Schwartzman. A tax and entertainment lawyer and former executive vice-president of Lorimar Pictures, Schwartzman (who was married to Francis Ford Coppola's sister Talia Shire) now ran his own movie production company, Taliafilm. He had become, he said, intrigued by the problems McClory had had when trying to get 'James Bond of the Secret Service' off the ground in the mid-seventies. And having done the legal spadework, he told McClory he was confident that a rival Bond picture *could* be made. Provided they had sufficiently deep pockets, he said, they could see off any legal challenge the Bond camp proper might bring. Time, then, to talk to the man they both knew needed to be their star if they were to pull the project off.

Over the years since they had last spoken, Connery had kept a weather eye on developments in the McClory project. More than that, he had been similarly keen-eyed when it came to the moneys that were going the way of his successor as Bond. What he saw there didn't make him happy. True, taking inflation into account, Roger Moore had never bested that record-breaking deal Connery struck for *Diamonds Are Forever*. On the other hand, there was no denying that Moore, an also-ran in the acting stakes, was being paid more for his Bond work than Connery was for his non-Bond work. Connery might have long ago sacked Dennis Selinger, but he still believed that part of being an international star was acting like one – and it was difficult to act like one when your pay was going down rather than up.

More than a decade had passed, of course, since Connery had sworn off all things Bond – and who could deny that he had stuck to his guns? The stuntish hi-jinks of *The First Great Train Robbery* aside, nothing Connery had worked on over the past ten years had so much as tried to send up the idea of Bond. On the other hand, nobody had ever stopped talking about Connery as anything other than the ex-007. No review of the Roger Moore Bond movies was complete without a line about no matter how entertaining the latest batch of secret agent shenanigans, it would all have been so much better with Connery in the lead role.

Connery was also helped in his decision-making by the relative failure of *Outland*, a movie he had had many reasons – genre, director, co-stars – to believe might put him back on the terra firma of stardom. Helped, moreover, by the fact that he was past 50 now – an old man as far as his father's generation was concerned. Even the most beautiful actresses had over the years grown accustomed to having their careers written off once they hit 40. In the old Hollywood (and in the British cinema, too) men had survived a little longer, largely by playing character types. But now, thanks in the main to Bond (and to *Star Wars* and the various creations of Steven Spielberg), the movies were emphatically an arena for young people. What if Connery could revive not only his own flagging career by reinventing the character who had invented him, but revive, too, the idea of the middle-aged man as fodder fit for the mass audience to feast its eyes on?

Still, when Connery did eventually open talks with McClory and Schwartzman, his first insistence was that were he to sign up to the project he be personally indemnified against any lawsuits it might engender. Moreover, he demanded right of veto over script, director and cast.* 'I knew I wanted Edward Fox for M,' he told a reporter after what was to become *Never Say Never Again* had wrapped, 'and I wanted Klaus Maria Brandauer who is one of the ten best actors in Europe to play Largo. I also had control over the director and the lighting cameraman and over the actress who plays the girl.'[2]

And so he did, for Schwartzman agreed to Connery's casting and crew suggestions, and offered him $2 million to become Bond once more. Connery, mindful of the $4 million Moore was being paid for *Octopussy* (1983), said no. Eventually the two men settled on a $3 million pay cheque (almost 10 per cent of the $34 million budget Warners had granted Schwartzman) plus 5 per cent of the net US profits. What would come to be called the battle of the Bonds was on. Given the witless drear of the Moore series, how could *Never Say Never Again* fail?

Answers come there many – several of them within the movie's

---

* 'I got most of my first casting choices,' he told one reporter as the movie opened. George Perry, 'Why Connery Said Yes Again', *Sunday Times Magazine*, 6 November 1983.

opening minutes. First up is the music. Michel Legrand has done more than enough great things in his career to justify his place in any list of top-ten movie composers. But his score for *Never Say Never Again* is not among them. How could the man who wrote the minor-key chromatics of *The Go-Between* (1970) and *The Summer of '42* (1971) have come up with the fuzzy disco three-chorder that heralds Sean Connery's return to the world of James Bond? *Octopussy*, for all its faults, boasted one of John Barry's most succulent scores – a lyrical, string-heavy opus that, though it bore little relation to the putative action it accompanied, was so lovely it quite took your mind off the Sta-Prest antics of Roger Moore and co.

Unfortunately, Legrand's horrific efforts contrive to achieve something similar. No matter how impressive this credits sequence looks – with a fit and agile Connery loping up trees and jumping off roofs – you can't concentrate on it for long because of Legrand's synthesised squeals and Lani Hall's treacly vocals on the soundtrack. How much better it all seems (watching the movie on DVD at least) with the sound turned down. Which is pretty much what the rewrite men had in mind when they conceived the scene. In Dick Clement and Ian La Frenais's conception, this opening sequence (in which Bond must rescue a kidnap victim from the jungle hideaway of a guerrilla army) was to be accompanied on the soundtrack by nothing but an insistent tick-tocking countdown. 'Trust me,' Clement has said, 'when it had a ticking stopwatch over it that sequence had tension.'[3]

Clement and La Frenais, now as then most famous as the writers of TV sitcoms *The Likely Lads*, *Porridge* and *Auf Wiedersehen, Pet*, had been drafted in to *Never Say Never Again* at the last minute. Their brief was to gag up Lorenzo Semple Jr's original script while ironing out any flaws in its structure and logic. On a minor level, this meant inserting a line or two that provided an explanation for Bond's flying to the Bahamas halfway through the picture. Rather more significantly, it meant pointing out that Semple Jr's opening

244

scenes, in which our hero was to have worn a heavy, medieval-style helmet – the better to defend himself in a jousting tournament – might be selling short all those people who had paid good money to see Sean Connery.

So how did the man in question actually look? Better than ever, to hear his wife tell it. 'Don't you think he looks good?' Micheline asked an interviewer during the shoot. 'Better than in *Diamonds*? You know why? It's the eyebrows. I'm a painter. I notice these things. Ten years ago he had these dark overhanging brows. They veiled his eyes. I persuaded him to lighten the brows underneath to show the eyes.'[4] The trouble is, Connery's heavy brow was one of the essential components of the Bond look. Tenebrous and Neanderthal, it spoke to the brooding, romantic violence simmering beneath the character's smoothly tuxedoed surface. Lose that and you lose the air of rapine danger that Moore's bloodlessly ersatz Bond had only succeeded in pointing up.

On top of that – literally – is the toupee. One uses the definite article because this flyaway flop (lighter in colour than any Connery had worn before) remains the movies' *echt* rug, the one everybody remembers. (Though the make-up department had been wise enough to grey his temples a little in *Diamonds Are Forever*, Connery's rugs had hitherto always been as black as his brow.) Once again, the new, lighter look can't help but evoke the sunnier Moore's handsome blandness instead of the ruinous Romany Bond everyone had known and loved back in the sixties. And, like Moore, the Connery of *Never Say Never Again* lacks the gratuitous cruelty, the mocking menace of the original Bond. Even when up against Barbara Carrera's magnificently vampish killer bitch Fatima Blush (by some measure the best Bond girl villain ever) this new 007 is courtly rather than callous.

Physically, it should be said, Connery looked very good in the new movie. Weighing in at around 190lb, he was almost half a stone lighter than he had been for *Diamonds Are Forever* twelve years earlier – and packing a lot more muscle to boot. For the purposes of the movie's gloriously camped-up tango sequence, Connery had engaged the services of Peggy Spencer, a choreographer who had put Rudolf Nureyev through his paces for Ken Russell's *Valentino* (1977). Litheness and a lethal economy of movement had, of course, been central to Connery's conception of Bond two decades before. Spencer's dance classes would, he believed, hone and polish that deadly refinement.

To an extent they did, though much of the hard work Connery put into shaping up for *Never Say Never Again* was thrown away by dint of the get-up Charles Knode elected to have him wear. Give or take a few months, the Connery of the new Bond picture was the same age as the Cary Grant of *An Affair to Remember* (1957) – but he seems older simply because he's been dressed to look younger. With the exception of the black tie outfit he sports for that tango scene, Connery wears nothing in the movie that suggests the Bond of old. Gone are the charcoal grey suits and crisp white shirts of yesteryear. In their place is a whole host of tacky slacks, sickly sports jackets and, at one dread point, a drab-olive windcheater. For the movie's big fight scene, Connery is swaddled in a baggy, pale grey tracksuit – as if he might be about to enrol at a Jane Fonda workout class.

Given such changes, though, one has to wonder why the overall architecture of the picture apes so closely that of the original Connery Bonds. 'I'm approaching it as if there'd never been another Bond film,' director Irvin Kershner said during the shoot.[5] Really? The Michel Legrand number that was bolted clumsily on to Clement and La Frenais's opening sequence, for instance, suggests that the powers that be were fearful of making a Bond movie that lacked a song over the credits. (Since *From Russia with Love*, all bar one of the entries in the series proper had boasted such a number.) By the time the curtains fall, *Never Say Never Again* has jumped through every clichéd hoop in the Broccoli and Saltzman circus – from violently acrobatic opening scene, through tetchy briefing with M (Connery's choice, Edward Fox, going uncharacteristically over the top), scraps with treacherous beauties, and on to another one of those would-be explosive endings.

The mystery is that Kershner (hand-picked by Connery after Richard *Superman* Donner turned the chance down) is on record as saying that he hadn't much cared for the earlier Bond movies. 'From having seen a couple of Bond films,' he once said, 'I knew what the so-called formula was; licence to kill, plenty of women, action, that's about it. There's nothing else to them.'[6] You don't have to believe the early Bond pictures are paragons of visionary cinema to see this for the nonsense it is. Kershner's litany of clichés misses out on everything that genuinely counted about the early Bonds. John Barry's throbbing discords; Ken Adam's timelessly modern design; the pursed yet pornographic title sequences of Maurice Binder; Peter Hunt's Godardian editing: together with Connery's gleefully brutish performance they added up to Britain's key contribution to the pop art movement of the 1960s. Love them or loathe them, those movies had a vision. Kershner (who had recently had a big hit with *The Empire Strikes Back* (1980)) need not – indeed, could not and should not – have been out to replicate it. But he ought to have realised that a spy fantasy without the fantasy would be, well, something very like the last Bond picture proper – John Glen's excitement-free *For Your Eyes Only* (1981).

Worse, despite Connery's offering Kershner a helping hand ('I've done seven Bonds,' he said as the movie opened, 'and this was his first'[7]), actor and director shared mighty similar blind-spots. Though Terence Young would later claim that he had been Connery's first choice to direct *Never Say Never Again* (a choice sagely vetoed by Schwartzman), at some deep level Connery really does seem to have believed that he himself was the only man responsible for the success of the cinematic Bond. While he would subsequently hymn Douglas Slocombe's cinematography[8] and Clement and La Frenais's script-doctoring, Connery gave very little thought to the look and feel and sound of the new picture. The aesthetic/sensuous side of things was all taken care of, he seems to have believed, because he was back as Bond and that was all that counted. The first

Bond script Connery had ever read (months before the screenplay for *Dr No* was written) was for a version of *Thunderball* that was aborted thanks to McClory's legal suit. Now he was at work on a new version of that story: it might almost have been as if those first six Bonds, the Saltzman and Broccoli Bonds, had never happened.

Given the general ballyhoo about his return to the part, Connery could have been forgiven for believing his own press. Back in 1983 there was so much of it – and at least until *Never Say Never Again* opened, it was all laudatory. Throughout that year it was impossible to open a newspaper or magazine without being confronted by a spread on Connery versus Moore – and there was no doubt at all about who came out on top in the tussle. The world and his wife wanted Connery back as Bond. As charming and sensible as it was of Roger Moore to tell a reporter that he wasn't 'going to get hot and bothered [about the competition]. The more the merrier, say I. Does Gielgud complain because Olivier is playing Hamlet at the same time?'[9] there can be little doubt that the men and women working on *Octopussy* were feeling the heat as the man who had made all their fortunes went back in front of a rival set of cameras.

In the event, they needn't have worried. The two Bond movies never actually ended up going head to head. Even as *Octopussy* had its royal premiere, in London in June 1983, the *Never Say Never Again* shoot dragged on – eight long months and more since its commencement. Connery, who had famously bridled at the increasing duration of the original Bond shoots, would doubtless have been chomping at the bit even had the movie been expected to take so long. But it hadn't – which meant he was more furious than ever. The end result, he would later say, 'seemed as long as all the other six I'd made put together'.[10]

The villain of the piece, as far as Connery was concerned, was Schwartzman – a man whose only previous experience as a producer had been in a minor executive role on Peter Sellers's late masterpiece *Being There* (1979) four years earlier. 'He may be a good lawyer,' Connery told one reporter, 'but as a producer he never knew where all the moving parts were.'[11] Schwartzman 'was way out of his depth', Dick Clement concurred. Indeed, had Schwartzman been on top of the situation, Clement went on, he and Ian La Frenais would never have been involved in the picture: 'It's very hard to rewrite movies while they're being shot – it's never a good sign.'[12] Nobody on set knew more about such bad signs than Connery, of course, who was still smarting from the scripting chaos that had been *Cuba*. So it's a measure of the vital part he believed *Never Say Never Again* would play in his future career that he put up with all the bungling and stupidity on the production. Despite the movie's self-consciously jokey title (suggested by Micheline), despite his oft-made protest during production that this was to be positively and absolutely his last outing as Bond, it seems likely that he conceived of the picture as the possible kick-off to a rival series.

So to the key question: Is *Never Say Never Again* as bad as all that? On any objective scale the picture is a stinker – underpowered, tawdry, clumsily structured, uneven in tone, shapeless, arrhythmic . . . the list of censures could go on forever. But in all these regards the picture is no worse than any of the Roger Moore Bonds of the past ten summers. What really lets the picture down, though, is the dour, suety heaviness of Connery's performance. Roger Ebert may have pronounced himself astonished by 'one of those small show-business miracles that never happen. There never was a Beatles reunion. But here, by God, is Sean Connery as James Bond!'[13] Yet for all the rewriting efforts of Clement and La Frenais, the new Bond was a curiously humourless figure. Though the picture's tone is light throughout (astonishing to relate, but there's even less sense of anything being at stake than there was in *Thunderball*), Connery strides through it all looking rather too purposeful, rather too preoccupied. Not even in *Dr No* had he seemed quite so discombobulated, not even in *You Only Live Twice* quite so disenchanted.

And with good reason. Barely had production on the picture begun, he claimed, than he had been forced to all but take control.

'I hate incompetence,' he told a packed National Film Theatre the night before the movie finally opened in London. 'When you get into a situation where somebody who is totally incompetent is in charge, a real ass, then everything is a struggle. There was so much incompetence, ineptitude and dissension during the making of *Never Say Never Again* that the film could have disintegrated. It was a toilet. What I could have done is just let it bury itself. I could have walked away with an enormous amount of money and the film would never have been finished. But once I was in there, I ended up getting in the middle of every decision. The assistant director and myself really produced the picture.'[14] Top marks for candour, if not for salesmanship.

All of which said, *Never Say Never Again* fared well enough at the box office. True, it cost almost a third as much again as *Octopussy* (which cost an estimated $27.5 million), while taking almost $30 million less at the box office.* But these are still mighty healthy figures for an autumn release, and they would likely have been healthier still had the movie been able to open in time for the summer vacation market. Little wonder that despite Connery's protestations that 'I shall never play Bond again – this was just a one-off,'[15] McClory did try to tempt him back once more. In 1985 he offered Connery the then astonishing sum of $15 million to star in 'Warhead'. Given that *A View to a Kill* (1985), Moore's final outing as 007, would end up taking rather less than *Never Say Never Again*, who is to say that Connery and McClory might not actually have won the Battle of the Bonds second time around? Who indeed, because Connery turned the offer down flat.

All through *Never Say Never Again*'s troubled shoot, Connery had been adamant that 'for the first time for many years I've got nothing fixed . . . [and am keen to] . . . think out carefully what I want

---

* As of mid-2009, the actual takings are: *Never Say Never Again*: $160 million; *Octopussy*: $187.5 million (figures from imdb.com).

to do next'.[16] A year later, his cogitations were over. On 20 June 1984 he launched a claim for $225 million against Cubby Broccoli and United Artists (now merged with MGM), charging them with fraud, deceit, breach of contract and inflicting emotional distress. What followed was a legalistic labyrinth, much of it involving the US Securities and Exchange Act of 1934. By January 1985 Connery had had his largest claims dismissed by Los Angeles judge David Kenyon. On the question of Connery's smaller claims, though, he and Broccoli ended up settling out of court – which means we don't know what the terms of the deal were.

What we do know is that, though suggestions of his playing a Bond *villain* would crop up on and off over the next twenty years, Connery would never once publicly air the possibility of his playing 007 proper. After that settlement with Broccoli, he would always say, 'Never again'.

14

Mentor Man

The *Never Say Never Again* shoot was always going to be a tough one. But it was made tougher for its star by a telephone call he received from his brother early on in proceedings to tell him that their mother, by now 74, had suffered a stroke and been hospitalised – condition: critical. In the event, Effie Connery lived on for the best part of another three years, until 2 April 1985, pooh-poohing all her eldest son's suggestions that she might benefit from moving to the warmth and comforts of his home in southern Spain. During that time, Connery visited her as often as UK tax regulations would allow.

That bad news, coupled with the good news that had been *Never Say Never Again*'s box-office success, meant that Connery's work rate slowed for a while. During down time on the Bond shoot he had made space for a walk-on role as the Green Knight in *Sword of the Valiant* (1984), director Stephen Weeks's second take on the legend of Gawain. About the film, the less said the better. Granted, it proved that at 54 Connery could still clank swords with villains half his age while baring an admirably taut torso. Granted, Connery is said to have bagged another $1 million for a mere six days' work[1] – but at this stage in his career weren't such considerations a silliness all their own?

Sword of the Valiant was so bad a movie that it didn't open – and then only briefly (in the autumn of 1984) – for more than eighteen months after its wrap. Not that Connery seems to have been concerned, dividing the year (and much of the next) between visits home to Scotland and the golf course. It would be a full two years after *Never Say Never Again* had wrapped before Connery set foot on another movie set – and even then it was only for a cameo.

Directed by Russell Mulcahy, *Highlander* (1986) is a sci-fi swords and stallions opera set in contemporary New York and the Scottish Highlands of the sixteenth century. Putatively starring was Christopher Lambert, the kind of one-dimensional action hero Connery's Bond might be imagined to have put paid to. Mulcahy, who like so many young new directors of the eighties had cut his teeth making pop videos, spent the bulk of the picture aping the already hackneyed visual codes of Ridley Scott's *Blade Runner* (1982) – all slashing rain and garish flashes. But he had enough about him to know that if his film were to have any bottom it needed something weighty to ground it. Hence the casting of Connery as Juan Sánchez Villa-Lobos Ramírez – an immortal, wordly wise, laughing, velvet-clad tatterdemalion.

After three years away from the screen, in other words, Connery is having a gas. Safe in the knowledge that he has been tasked with the chore of gracing tat, he enjoys himself immensely – as well might a man who was rumoured to be pocketing another $1 million for another week's work. Whether tossing his head back and guffawing at Lambert's every faux pas, or riding at speed across a wave-wet shoreline while parcelling out moralising morsels, Connery used *Highlander* to project his newly sagacious image around the world. Twenty-five years an international star, he was now the older man, the man no longer desperate to hog the limelight but content, instead, to chorus ironically in the background – and all the while trusted implicitly by the audience as the man who knows how to get things done.

Which means that *Highlander* is one of the hinges in Connery's career. Glossy trash though Mulcahy's movie might have been, it pointed the way forward for its only bona fide star. In movie after movie, from now on, Connery would play variants on the mentoring figure *Highlander*'s Ramírez had minted – the man younger men looked up to and wanted to be. This was not, of course, a new route for big stars to take. John Wayne spent the last fifteen years of his career playing one or another ornery oldster whose job it was to inculcate traditional values into young hotheads who had gone off the rails. By contrast, though, Connery's mentor figures are never put in charge of *recalcitrant* youths. These kids *want* to learn from their master. Hence the Connery sage is never exasperated by the inabilities of his young charges, merely wryly amused and warmly distanced.

If ever he doubted that he had vanquished Bond, then, there was no need to. Though the template for Connery's third major series of roles clearly owed its lineaments to his first, in spiritual, moral and emotional terms it couldn't have been more distanced from it. You may, as Ian Fleming had claimed, only live twice. But Connery was now entering his second professional life as an altogether heartier hero, a man gleeful and avaricious for experience, bold, beaming and perpetually amused by the joys the world bestows. Bond had been a man of taste. So many of Connery's new creations would be men of appetite.

Given the geographic implications of its title, *Highlander* might always have had Connery's name floating somewhere in its orbit. Vanishingly few can have been the readers of *The Name of the Rose*, Umberto Eco's smash hit novel of the early eighties, who would have thought Sean Connery the ideal man to play Eco's medieval prototype Sherlock Holmes, the Franciscan friar Sir William of Baskerville. True, Baskerville was an intellectual – and Connery had more than once proved himself capable of summoning a mystic air that in other contexts could pass for ivory-tower abstractedness. But what director Jean-Jacques Annaud had spied in Connery's recent work and thought suitable for his Eco adaptation was the strain of magisterial wisdom on which we have already touched. Whatever else he is, Connery's Baskerville is a mentor figure – the journeyman fondly protective of his young apprentice, Adso of Melk, played with uncharacteristic restraint by the 16-year-old Christian Slater.

Working with Connery, Slater said, 'was great. I grew up watching the Bond movies, and working with him at 16 was like having a master class in acting, life, all sorts of things.'[2] Watching the finished movie, there is no need to doubt the fact, though it is also the case that Slater's performance is terrifyingly assured. Sean Connery wasn't acting this well at 26, let alone 16.[*] Indeed, given that Adso is the narrator of the story, and that it is he who during the course of the movie travels what screenwriting theorists like to call the character arc, there is good reason to suggest that Slater is working a lot harder than Connery for the bulk of the picture. Adso it is who must learn about the evil that men do and the fleshly desires that man is heir to. And yet, in the finished film, Slater barely registers on the screen next to Connery.

Because Connery is the still centre of Annaud's movie, the man of reason who solves crimes not by action but by thought. And Connery is masterly at suggesting the interior workings of a man who, accustomed to reading the signs so many of us miss, is an expert at imperturbable inscrutability. A twitch of his head here, an adjustment of his oversized pince-nez there, the flicker of a raised eyebrow, the momentary adjustment of a set of jaw – such are the minuscule tools at Connery's disposal, and he makes subtly bravura use of them all in the picture.

No doubt about it: Connery is enjoying himself here. If you never quite catch the 'many little vanities' Adso's narration advises us Sir William is guilty of, nor are you ever in doubt that you're dealing with a man who takes a kind of theatrical delight in his continual

---

[*] Intriguingly, it was during the *Name of the Rose* shoot that Connery made a gift of £50,000 to Britain's struggling National Youth Theatre. 'British actors and actresses, writers and directors are among the best in the world,' he said. 'The NYT is one source of this talent, a source that everyone should be proud of. It shouldn't have to go cap in hand for money.' See Brian Glanville, 'Connery Gift of £50,000 to Save NYT', *Sunday Times*, 13 April 1986.

rightness. While in calmer moments Connery's Baskerville disports himself with the flamboyant certainty of Basil Rathbone's Sherlock Holmes, at more excited ones he comes on like the headmistress of St Trinian's. Having finally worked out where the hidden room that will explain everything is located, Baskerville squeals 'I knew it' with the orgasmic breathlessness Alistair Sim was forever bringing to another of life's litany of disappointments. None of which means that Connery's performance is a patchwork quilt. Sir William of Baskerville is among the most unified creations of Connery's career, fully deserving of the many plaudits it won. More surprisingly, given its challenging semiotic origins, the movie itself was a big hit around the world, a moral bolster to a Connery who had been largely absent from cinema screens since his Bond retread.

The Name of the Rose's most important effect, though, was in cementing the idea of its star as the wise old man, the rock-solid sage to whom the callow and the uncertain come for advice. Throughout his subsequent career, Connery would play variants on this role – the exemplary man to whom youth looks up for guidance. If there was something of what Eco's more lame-brained acolytes would call intertextual self-referentiality about this development – the man who in creating James Bond had inculcated whole generations with ideas of manhood now playing men whose job it is to inculcate younger men into manhood – it must thankfully be said that Annaud's picture fools around with it not one jot. Not once does this movie about signs play games with the idea of Sean Connery as signifier. How easy it would have been, given the self-consciously jocular nature of Eco's original novel, to fool around with the idea that Sir William of Baskerville was a kind of prototype Sir James of Bond. But no. Rather, one watches the film certain that, for perhaps the first time in his long career, Connery has finally put the spectre of Bond behind him.

Forget *From Russia with Love*. Forget *Goldfinger*. Sean Connery's best fight scene is to be seen in Brian de Palma's *The Untouchables*

(1987). It comes midway through the picture and pitches a 56-year-old Connery against a 50-year-old Richard Bradford. The scene is a dark alley; neon lights pulse in the background; the rain hisses down. Glamorous it isn't. And there is little glamour about the punches Connery throws or has thrown at him. What we see is the impact of fist on face, flesh on flesh. De Palma is keen to emphasise not just the solidity of the Connery body, but its stolidity, too. Connery's Jim Malone wins this fight with his chief of police Jake La Motta style – not by landing the best punches, but merely by dint of being able to take whatever his opponent throws at him. Malone isn't, the movie will prove, a Bond-style invincible. Nonetheless, he is a strong man – a strong man, moreover, with right as well as might on his side.

Which is to say that de Palma's picture, as scripted by David Mamet, is as cosy, as reassuringly old-fashioned, as so much other mid-eighties Hollywood product. This is a movie about good guys and bad guys, about the innocent joys of finding courage under fire, about the unarguable bliss of marriage and parenthood. You don't have be a fan of de Palma's early work to acknowledge that this is the picture that marks the end of his career as one of the most singular moviemakers the American cinema has ever given us. Gone is the Hitchcock worship that gave us *Carrie* (1976), *Dressed to Kill* (1980), *Blow Out* (1981), *Body Double* (1984). Gone, too, the obsession with what one might call the techno-gothic. What we have here is de Palma's entry into mainstream moviemaking. And as if to hammer the point home, he cast as his picture's locus of uncomplicated rectitude Sean Connery.

But there is another reason Connery was a natural for the part of Jim Malone. Just as he was in *The Name of the Rose*, Connery is cast here as the wise old mentor, the man whose essential task is in bringing youngsters like Kevin Costner's Eliot Ness to maturity. While Connery had shot to fame, that is, as a young maverick exasperated at the petty bureaucracies his seniors insist he suffer, he had now become a maverick oldster – a rebel who might not play by the rules himself but is adamant that everyone else should.

Yet Malone is never a mere martinet. As played by Connery, he's a gentle, kindly soul whose bossy bravura is almost a put-on. 'I like contrast,' Connery said of Malone (recalling Robert Henderson's advice that he look like a truck driver but talk like Dostoevsky). 'I like it when an actor looks one thing and conveys something else. With Malone, I tried to show at the beginning he could be a real pain in the ass, so that you wouldn't think he could be concerned with such things as Ness's feelings or Ness's family, and then show he was someone else underneath, capable of real relationships.'[3]

The movie's problem, its pat moral schema aside, is that the obedience of Malone's underlings is mirrored in the kowtowing attitudes of Connery's co-stars. Try as they might, Charles Martin Smith and Andy Garcia are a little too in thrall to the presence of the main man. 'When you are with Sean,' Costner (the movie's ostensible star) once told a reporter, 'you learn pretty quickly your place in the galaxy.'[4] Certainly on the evidence of his performance in *The Untouchables* Costner did. This is as colourless and characterless a turn as his CV of colourless and characterless turns has given us – and the blame can be only partially ascribed to Mamet's attitudinal, one-dimensional script. Costner's Eliot Ness kicks off the movie by declaring that he'll do anything he can to bust Robert de Niro's prohibition-breaking Al Capone 'within the law'. It takes the death of Connery's Malone to convince him that the law just isn't up to the task he's set himself – though we know this only because Ness tells us so, not because Costner makes us feel the man's anguish and anger.

Which means that Connery's death is really the heart of the picture. It's not just that de Palma's movie sags when Malone has been gunned down by Frank Nitti (Billy Drago) in a cowardly set-up. It's that we see the life force drain from Connery so languidly, so purely, in Malone's murder and slow, slow death that nothing else the movie throws at us could hope to compare to it. Bluntly, none of the other characters in the picture has anything like a life we might see drained away. It is true that we don't know what the movie's closing forty or so minutes would have been like had de Palma not run out of money. We don't know that the shootout on the train that he and Mamet had envisaged as their show-stopping denouement might not indeed have stopped us in our tracks. But it is unlikely, simply because Connery's bloody death – in many ways the scene seems as neon-lit as his earlier fight with his chief of police – really does feel like a heartbeat being stopped.

Seen in that light, *The Untouchables* might be the populist brother of *The Offence*. What stays with you about Malone's death, after all, is both its cold-blooded immorality – of all characters, Jimmy is the least deserving of an early grave – and its warm-blooded immensity: this is a death that lasts longer than the famous gassing of the Russian agent in Hitchcock's *Torn Curtain* (1966). But it is not, as Hitchcock believed his murder scene to be, any kind of an attempt at realism. With its blaring, pounding Ennio Morricone score, its operatic turn from de Niro, its opulent art-deco sets and its references to Eisenstein's *Battleship Potemkin*, de Palma's picture is a piece of pulpy pop art – as hard-edged, as stylised, as abstract as the early Bonds.

Shot over fourteen weeks in the autumn of 1986, *The Untouchables* did more than any other film of the preceding ten years to make Connery a bankable star once more.* Why so? Largely because Jimmy Malone's no-nonsense heroics chimed with the 'Morning in America' vision of President Ronald Reagan. Just as Reagan came to power promising to banish what he saw as the lily-livered America of the past two decades, Malone believed the job of toughening up the youngsters who were following in his footsteps was no more than his duty.

Which shouldn't detract from the unifying depth of Connery's performance, the tics and twitches and turns of head he uses to humanise Mamet's abstract, conceptualised vision of the

---

* And how the presence of Kevin Costner reminds us that stardom need not be for ever.

unimpeachable hero. Certainly the performance got the plaudits it deserved – right up to an Academy Award. (Pauline Kael compared Connery's 'impudent authority' in the picture to that of Olivier.)[5] No real lover of acting (or, indeed, the movies) sets any store by the Oscars, of course, and there was something of the monkey that types *Hamlet* about Connery's winning the Best Supporting Actor award for *The Untouchables*. Still, it was nice to see him finally honoured.

Connery himself seemed less than bowled over. Admitting that he had not 'experience[d] any great elation' when given the Oscar, he later told an NBC reporter he was convinced the award had been made more 'for a body of work' than for one particular performance.[6] Just as momentous, as far as he was concerned, was the fact that he had decided to take a small upfront salary of $50,000 for de Palma's movie (the producers couldn't have afforded him otherwise), with a 10 per cent share of the takings. To date, *The Untouchables* has earned more than $186 million worldwide. Such moneys are not to be sniffed at, of course, least of all by Sean Connery. Still, the bigger reward the movie and the Oscar offered him was the chance to re-establish some control over his future career.

The offers came pouring in almost immediately. Connery accepted and later rejected the part of the King in Terry Jones's *The Adventures of Baron Munchausen* (1988). A good call. Neil Jordan, who had wanted Connery for the part that eventually went to Bob Hoskins in *Mona Lisa* (1986), offered him the part of the struggling oldster whose castle turns out to be haunted in *High Spirits* (1988). The role went to Peter O'Toole, the picture down the pan. Another good call. Not that Connery could be too gleeful. He had turned down another part that ended up being taken by O'Toole – that of the Scottish tutor to the titular character of Bernardo Bertolucci's *The Last Emperor* (1987). This time the results were rather happier. Meanwhile, anyone who has seen *Warlock* (1988) cannot but wonder how weirdly different a picture it would have been had Connery taken the Richard E. Grant Witchfinder role (as director Steve Miner had wanted).

But the big disappointments of this period are, first, that Connery rejected the lead role in Barbet Schroeder's *Reversal of Fortune* (1990). What sadistic frissons he would have brought to this account of Claus von Bülow's arrest and trial for the murder of his wife. Second, and more distressing still, a planned movie of Hemingway's novel *Across the River and into the Trees*, starring Connery as Hemingway's ageing, cashiered Colonel Cantwell preparing for death (in Venice), never came off.[7] What might Hollywood's new mentor man have made of the colonel's love affair with a Venetian girl of 19? Over the past twenty years of Connery's career we have had hints – but hints, as we shall see, are all we have had.

All of which means that Connery's next picture came as something of a shock. And yet while with the benefit of hindsight Connery's acceptance of the lead role in *The Presidio* (written originally for Marlon Brando) seems hard to account for, there was in fact no mystery about his choice. For one thing, the movie was being directed by Peter Hyams, whom Connery had enjoyed working with on *Outland*. More importantly, the picture was a typically Hyams-like nod to a classical Hollywood predecessor – in this case Howard Hawks's *Red River* (1948). What Connery saw in Hyams's script was a self-consciously Oedipal narrative in which his grizzly old patriarch would be taught that youth must have its day. Had the picture come off, it might have served as a record of the moment when all those men around the world who had grown up believing Connery to be the embodiment of masculinity could begin to move on.

The problem was that Jay Austin, the picture's Oedipus, was played by Mark Harmon. A few months before *The Presidio* shoot commenced, in the late autumn of 1987, Harmon had been voted *People* magazine's sexiest man of the year. (Two years later, on the cusp of 60, Connery himself would ascend to that dizzy throne.) But despite Harmon's undoubted good looks and athleticism, all his work in *The Presidio* ended up proving was that actors can't get by with merely surface charms. Though Connery's Lieutenant Colonel Alan Caldwell ends the movie apparently resigned both to the young pretender's having usurped his authority *and* run off with his daughter Donna (Meg Ryan), the movie itself never makes you feel that resignation – and how could it, given Harmon's exsanguinated performance? Look like the Montgomery Clift of *Red River* Harmon may do; come on like Clift he does not. 'I suppose,' a more than usually diplomatic Connery would argue after the movie had bombed, 'Harmon could have been stronger.'[8] Hence we are left with a picture wrenched out of shape less by Connery's tensile way with even the clumsiest expository dialogue than by his monumentality. If you're going to make a picture that challenges this man's masculinity, you better have a challenger who is up to the job.

'Who would be the equal of Indiana Jones,' Steven Spielberg asked himself when settling down to construct the third movie in his hit series of the eighties, 'but James Bond?'[9] Who indeed? It's a critical commonplace to claim that Spielberg's 'Indy' pictures had their roots in the 'B' thriller serials that went out before the main features back in the thirties. But really, it was Bond who owed those series the big debt. The likes of *Dr No* and *Goldfinger* were just *Flash Gordon* with a sheen of ironic consumerist sixties glitz sprayed on. If Spielberg's movies paid obeisance to anything it was to Bond.

For all that, one of the reasons the Indy pictures had been such big hits was that set against latter-day Bond they looked like the height of realism. Indeed, next to the Spielberg series, even the sprightliest of the Connery Bonds looked lame and tired. More happens in the opening ten minutes of *Indiana Jones and the Last Crusade* (1989) than in the whole of *You Only Live Twice*. More happens in the movie's two hours than does in the whole of the Roger Moore Bond saga. The level of invention to be found in each and every one of Spielberg's set pieces – and like the Bonds, the Indys are no more than set piece after set piece – has no rival within the cinema up to that date. Childish and relevance-free and the death knell for a certain kind of cinema the Indiana Jones series might be. Lazy and incompetent they are not.

But the movies were refreshingly different in the context of their director's own previous work, too. Here, for once, were Spielberg pictures not weighed down with mawkish sentimentality, nor by that obsession with the dysfunctional joy of the nuclear family Spielberg had mooned over since *Jaws*. After the gloopy patriarchal fantasies of *E. T. The Extra-Terrestrial* (1982), *Raiders* seemed joyously free of family ties, not to say significance: good guys, bad guys, big guns, bigger guns, such were the ingredients of Spielberg's fizziest pictures yet. The only paternalist in sight was Adolf Hitler – whose dreams of setting up a fatherland were to be dealt a heavy blow by the picture's knockabout heroics.

Still, it was always likely that the amoral hi-jinks of the Indiana Jones series would at some point find themselves thickened by the folding in of Spielberg's core thematic. It happened in *Indiana Jones and the Last Crusade* (1989), in which we finally get to meet our hero's father – played by Sean Connery. As in-jokes go, this is a nice one. Whether it's enough of a joke to sustain an entire movie is more moot, but there is a bigger joke to come: as played by Connery, Jones senior is far from being the priapic action hero who might conceivably have given birth to Harrison Ford's whip-cracking gymnast. For all that Spielberg introduces Connery in cod *Dr No* fashion – a close-up of a wrist here, a curl of a mouth there, a voiceover throughout – there is little about Professor Henry Jones that recalls the part that made his maker. Tweedy and fishing-hatted, Connery's professor looks more like a refugee from P. G. Wodehouse than the inaugurator of a whole cinematic genre.

Before signing up for the part, Connery was keen to tell Spielberg and producer George Lucas that their conception of Professor Jones 'didn't add up'. Indeed, according to Harrison Ford, the original Jones senior was rather more of a Sir William Baskerville-style figure – 'a more elderly, gnomish, Yoda-like father'. Connery, though, had other ideas. He 'was after something a bit more Victorian and flamboyant, like one of the old expeditioners, Sir Richard Burton and Mungo Park . . . and that's what we got'.[10] Well, up to a point. A better way of understanding Connery's work in *Indiana Jones and the Last Crusade* is to see him as a wry parody of the ur-Walter Brennan figure – jittery, irritable, gleefully incompetent and with an excitable lift in his voice at times of high-pressure action. No James Bond with a walking-stick this.

Certainly, Jones senior seems unaccustomed to the fantastical action sequences the movie is forever contriving to throw at him. Bombs don't go off without his being startled, the workings of machine guns are a mystery to him. Tied back to back with his son by the Nazis, Connery manages to extract a cigarette lighter from Indy's pocket – before setting the whole room on fire and nearly burning the two of them to death. Connery's Jones isn't quite as much a hindrance to the hero as the Tiffany Case of *Diamonds Are Forever*, but it isn't for want of trying. If his James Bond was from the off a send-up of the British stiff upper lip, then his Indiana Jones senior is an out and out mickey-take of all that Bond stood for. Because what Connery – at last certain of his place in the starriest pantheon – is playing for in *Indiana Jones and the Last Crusade* are the biggest laughs of his career.

And indeed, the picture was more fun than *Family Business* (1989), a slight Sidney Lumet comedy in which rather more than the centrepiece cack-handed robbery fails to come off. Connery plays Jessie McMullen, a rough and ready gypsy type who claims Cherokee blood along with his Scots ancestry but who married a Sicilian woman in the Hell's Kitchen area of post-war New York. The result of that union was Dustin Hoffman's Vito, a man who has sworn off his father's clumsy criminal ways and set himself up nicely in the meat-packing business the better to send his own son, Matthew Broderick's Adam, through college.

This is, then, an American parable – a lesson in how in the land of the free each generation, as Adam jokes to his grandfather, 'does slightly better than its predecessor'. Except that Adam, for all his exam-passing achievements in school, wants to revert to type. He's been given the low-down on a can't-fail robbery and wants Jessie and Vito to ride shotgun for him. Cue familial tensions, arguments about class, education, breeding – along with some high-spirited japery for the heist.

Such, at least, was the idea. And no movie with Connery and Hoffman in it could be entirely without its moments. But Lumet's picture never makes any kind of overall sense. True, Hoffman works his usual miracles in making a one-dimensional part seem fully wrought. But while the tensions between Jessie and Vito are nicely worked out, those between Vito and Adam aren't dramatised at all. Broderick never once convinces as the bright young man who feels he has been forced to study against his will. With his geeky spectacles and wimpy sweaters he's too much the preppy kid to be taken seriously as a criminal-in-the-making by his father, let alone his grandfather, who ought to know that what you want for any robbery is a bunch of pros. (Adam's a student, so why not give him a worrisome debt for motivation?)

And yet, for all that, the movie makes a kind of sense simply because Adam's grandfather is played by Sean Connery. Even a Connery with rat-tail hair and sideburns like scimitars, a Connery dressed in dog's-tooth sports coat and bookie's trilby, is, after all, a Connery you can't help looking up to. Literally, because Connery towers over his fictional progeny in this movie. (So much so that Vincent Patrick – whose screenplay was based on his own novel – was obliged to give Jessie an explanatory line about how if he hadn't married a Sicilian woman his son might have been a whole lot taller.) At one point there's a medium close-up shot of Connery and Hoffman at loggerheads in which father raises his fist at son – and the fist is almost the same size as the son's head.

Connery fills every frame he's in – not merely thanks to his size, but by virtue of his greedy rapacity for energy, for whatever is vital and functioning. In one shot Lumet places Broderick and Hoffman in the foreground of Jessie's apartment as they outline the plan to one another while somewhere in the background Connery sings to himself in the bathtub. It takes you almost the whole scene to spot him tucked away at the bottom right of the frame – but spend the scene searching for him you do. Despite Hoffman's bravura subtleties, it's Connery you want to see, it's Connery who's the life force of the picture.

Needless to say, the robbery goes awry, our three heroes are busted, and though Vito and Adam are let off lightly, the judge comes down heavily on Jessie and sends him to jail for what, says his lawyer, could well be the rest of his life. Come off it, you think, as Jessie is led away: men like that go on for ever. But the next thing you know you're being told that he has died in Nassau County jail.

'I have some differences with Sidney Lumet about how he resolved the end,'[11] Connery would say a few months after *Family Business* opened. As well he might, since nobody in the audience believes for a moment that Jessie is really dead. But he is, and the movie ends with a wake at which son and grandson are reunited in grief and a kind of understanding. And not for a moment do you believe it because . . .

. . . because which of us can conceive of a world without Sean Connery in it? A couple of years ago there were pictures of him in the papers, striding around his home city in a kilt and sporran, and he looked like a giant and a giant-killer rolled into one. He looked like he would happily take on all comers. He was then, the papers reminded us, 77.

'I suppose more than anything else,' Connery said more than four decades ago, 'I'd like to be an old man with a good face.'[12] Well, he got his wish. Now 80, he looks 60. Not bad for a man who claimed that at 16 he looked 30. But unless he really is one of those mystical, magus-type figures he has been playing these past two decades, Sean Connery will one day die. And for a while at least, the world will make a little less sense.

15

From Russia with Love

During the *Indiana Jones* and *Family Business* shoots Connery had suffered with an occasional dry throat. Since then things hadn't improved. Having consulted a specialist at UCLA Medical Center, Connery was told there were white spots on the right side of his larynx. If he wanted, the doctors could perform a biopsy, but probably the best advice was a month's resting of the vocal cords and then a second examination. Connery took himself off to his house in Spain and settled down to thirty days' silence.

These could hardly have been other than contemplative days, though the contemplation was ill helped by the British tabloid newspapers' 'Connery in cancer scare'-type headlines. Nor did things improve much when, following his month of rest, Connery was told by his doctors that they were going to have to perform the biopsy anyway. Several bouts of laser treatment followed, and it was not until April 1989 that Connery was given a clean bill of health – with the proviso that the throat be checked twice-yearly.*

The first victim of Connery's troubled throat was Tom Stoppard's *Rozencrantz and Guildenstern Are Dead* (1990). Stoppard, who had doctored a line or two of Connery's dialogue for *Indiana Jones and the Last Crusade*, had persuaded Connery to appear as the Player King in this long-awaited movie version of his first hit play. Filming

---

* Four years later, after another round of radiation treatment on his vocal cords, Connery, sickened by tabloid tittle-tattling about his general health, chose to make his entrance to David Letterman's US TV chat show by means of an army jet-pack such as 007 had once used in the pre-credits sequence of *Thunderball*.

was due to start in just three weeks' time when, on 13 January 1989, it was announced that Connery was pulling out of the movie.

Announced, but not explained. Connery, ever shy of publicity, wanted to keep stories about his health out of the newspapers. But Stoppard, unapprised of the situation, was furious, convinced the man he had helped out with his dialogue was reneging on a friendly deal because he had subsequently had a better offer. Lawyers' letters were soon flying, and it is a measure, perhaps, of how distressed he was by his health problems that the habitually litigious Connery chose to buy himself out of Stoppard's movie. At a cost of $300,000 – more than four times what he would have been paid to be in *Rosencrantz and Guildenstern* – Connery jumped ship. 'Who,' he asked rhetorically, 'needs another lawsuit?'[1]

And so *Rosencrantz*'s Player King is another of the what-might-have-beens in Connery's CV. One of the might-have-beens is that Connery's appearance in a Tom Stoppard picture could have ended with his being taken seriously by the critics – too many of whom still shared his own ill-founded belief that seriousness of intent is the only thing that can possibly ensure seriousness of outcome. Then again, the picture Connery did choose to star in after his health forced him to bail out from *Rosencrantz* was as serious as the modern Hollywood blockbuster is ever likely to get.

For some reason, *The Hunt for Red October* (1990) is the picture that Sean Connery impersonators most frequently quote from. They love to parody Connery's punchy yet slurred, ever so slightly sibilant 'S' sounds, as in *Red October*'s 'Tonight, gentlemen, we shail into hishtory'.* And for some reason, John McTiernan's movie is regarded with great fondness by Connery fans. Why this should be so is something of a mystery. For starters, the picture, which commenced shooting within days of Connery's being given the all-

---

* In technical terms he is transforming a fricative into an affricate consonant; the verbal tic is, I suspect, the result of Connery's – Scottish? – habit of speaking out of the corner of the mouth.

clear on his throat problems,* is a long one – well over two hours long – in which nothing much happens. Moreover, the nothing much that does happen happens within the dark, narrow confines of a submarine. Physical action, that is, is a near impossibility in this movie. Which means that whatever else it is, McTiernan's follow-up to the Arnold Schwarzenegger spectacular *Predator* (1987) and the Bruce Willis spectacular *Die Hard* (1988) is a somewhat less than spectacular Sean Connery movie.

Connery plays Marko Ramius, the Lithuanian captain of the picture's titular vessel, who has chosen to sail said sub into enemy (i.e. American) waters. The enemy, for their part, wants to nuke this up-to-the-minute 'magnet hydro-dynamic drive'-powered *Red October* before it can do anything similar to their boys. But Jack Ryan (Alec Baldwin – the lead character in Tom Clancy's original novel, and theoretically the movie's too) is convinced that Ramius, whose history shows him to be something of a maverick, wants to defect.

Plotwise, that's about it. True, there's a twist here and there, but the bulk of this 134-minute movie turns on whether Ramius really is out to defect or whether he is trying to inveigle his submarine into American waters the better to do the country some harm. Add to this lack of a storyline a forbiddingly tenebrous palette, much didactic speechifying, an almost slothful slowness and an unswerving devotion to stretching scenes way beyond the moment where their point has been made – add all this together and it has to be concluded that *The Hunt for Red October* is as far removed from the blockbuster template as any contemporary Hollywood picture could dare to be. In short, it's a curious movie for even the most diehard *Die Hard* and/or Connery fan to get carried away with.

---

* In April 1989. Connery, it should be pointed out, didn't join the shoot until the end of May. Indeed, even granting his $4 million pay cheque, it 'took very delicate interpersonal negotiations' to get Connery on board, McTiernan later claimed (*Premiere*, April 1992).

How to explain its $23 million and counting success?

Given that dearth of spectacular pleasures, the answer is almost entirely to do with the sombre charms of Connery's matchless stillness. Never before had this most kinetic of actors devoted himself to containing all but his most necessary movements. Think of Connery's Captain Marko Ramius and you think first of his Bernini-like monumentality. And like Bernini, Connery gives his character a sense of dynamism frozen in time: his Ramius moves slowly and precisely so that we might realise he is a man who has nothing left to prove. Rare is the frame in the picture in which McTiernan does not shoot Connery from below, so as to make his already imposing figure loom the more majestically. Watch the movie again and observe that although Connery dominates from first to last, he isn't actually on screen all that much.

Indeed, the nostalgic exchange about fishing with Sam Neill's Vasily Borodin aside, Connery has little to say in the entire movie. Most of his dialogue is taken up with orders to the crew of his submarine. One result of this is that it's left to everyone else to try to fathom Ramius's motivations. Does he really want to defect to the US? Is he a double agent? Nobody knows – least of all the audience. Hence the movie's closing shot, in which the *Red October* cruises above sea level into US waters, resembles nothing so much as the end of Rouben Mamoulian's *Queen Christina* (1933), with Connery's Ramius a Garbo-like blank canvas on which we can all project our interpretations.

This air of impenetrability, of mystery, it needs stressing, is nowhere to be found in Larry Ferguson and Donald Stewart's screenplay (much less in Clancy's original novel). What we have here is Sean Connery taking another one-dimensional part and breathing life into it out of sheer delight at the challenge. Not that he did it alone. After having had first sight of the script, Connery insisted on a rewrite. 'I got them to bring in John Milius to explain things,' he said as the film received a royal premiere in London. 'What would make this guy defect after giving his whole life to the navy? I wanted that made clearer . . . Milius made it all make sense.'[2] You don't have to believe that Milius entirely fulfilled his side of the bargain – nor that as played by Connery Ramius looks like 'a sort of mixture of Stalin and Samuel Beckett'[3] – to accept that Connery succeeded in fleshing out an otherwise enigmatic character.

Rather less assured is Baldwin's Jack Ryan, who spends the bulk of the picture trying to out-Connery Connery. 'Pleasure to be aboard, sir,' Ryan quips at Commander Bart Mancuso (Scott Glenn) after having been winched down from a helicopter being buffeted by rough winds even as Mancuso's submarine is buffeted by rougher waves. The line, a direct lift from the submarine scene in *You Only Live Twice*, is uttered with the same laconic offhandedness Connery gave every one of Bond's – but Baldwin is too intense an actor, and Ryan too much the intellectual, to pull off such self-mockery. The result is that Baldwin only beefs up Connery's presence yet more.

Given this highly uneven competition in the charisma stakes, the picture moves with near inevitability to its final mentoring scene – the two men atop the conning tower of the *Red October*, Ramius the practical empiricist teaching Ryan the bookish intellectual about the pull of tides and the stars in the skies. At once romantic and restrained, it is one of Connery's most heartfelt moments in a film that is perhaps a little too wise for its own good. Thrillers, no matter how intelligent, oughtn't forget to at least occasionally thrill.

Not that it was needed by the time of its release, but *The Russia House* (1990) may have been the best antidote to Bond that Sean Connery has ever worked on. Indeed, there is some reason to think it the best picture Connery has ever worked on – and more reason than that to suggest that Connery's performance in Fred Schepisi's picture is his best ever. Certainly it's his most moving. Enormous movie star that he is, Connery can too often be cast in parts that require little of him but his iconic status. In terms of histrionic range *The Russia House* was Connery's most demanding picture since *The Offence*.

Unlike *The Offence*'s DS Johnson, a character that served to analyse and comment upon the sadistic undertow of the part that had made Connery famous, Barley Blair, the drunken publisher he incarnates for *The Russia House*, is a vision of sensitivity, warmth, kindness and love. Moreover, the picture requires Barley to mature and bloom into full adulthood. For an actor whose chief *raison d'être* had so often been exemplifying machismo norms, this was a radically satisfying departure.

On top of all that, in dramatising and exploring the love of an older man for a woman half his age *The Russia House* might be the movie Connery was born to play in. The sadness is that nobody has since thought to cast Connery in parts that require so much of him. How one wishes that it had been this picture – and not *Highlander* or even *Indiana Jones* – that had been the subject of sequel after sequel. What a Jacques Rivette, what a Luis Buñuel might have done with this ageing mascot of untarnishable sexuality.

The volume of Connery's achievement in *The Russia House* is amplified by the fact that, as played by Michelle Pfeiffer, Katja Orlova, the woman he falls in love with during the movie's two hours, is little more than a cluster of clichés. This is not, it needs saying, because Pfeiffer lacks the equipment to take on Connery's game. Rather, it is simply because her part is woefully underwritten. As conceived in Tom Stoppard's script, Katja is little more than an innocent – though heavily maternal – heart-stopping beauty. Pfeiffer, laden down with a Russian accent, can do little to grant the poor girl the depths the script insists are there. Miraculously, though, Connery's Blair imbues her with the three-dimensional sensibility the rest of the movie works so hard to confound.

The story, true to the John le Carré novel on which it is based, can occasionally be hard to penetrate, but its gist is clear. Blair is a drunken, dissolute and louchely old-fashioned publisher who during a book conference in Moscow is approached by Katja and surreptitiously offered the tell-all memoirs of a disillusioned Russian scientist called Yakov (Klaus Maria Brandauer). In the proposed book, Yakov will blow apart the recent peace deal between America and Russia – by exposing the fact that the latter has no nuclear arsenal to call its own. Can it be true? Or is it part of some fiendish double bluff? Soon enough MI5 and the CIA are involved, and Blair finds himself at the centre of an international trade-off.

A trade-off, alas, in which Blair's allegiances are never in doubt – partly because he has fallen head over heels in love with Katja, but largely because, as he tells Yakov, the pointless warring between East and West means that for enlightened liberals like themselves, treachery is the new loyalty. Fair enough, but why kick off the movie by letting Barley get such sentiments off his chest? How much better a picture this would be had Blair started off with at least a residue of patriotic verve. Given Connery's own Scottish nationalist instincts, and his back catalogue of unswerving allegiance to Queen and Country in the form of Bond, it would have been the easiest thing in the world to have Barley maintain a stiff-upper-lip take on East–West relations. Then, as he warmed to Katja, that old-world mindset could have been found wanting. As things are, the deck is stacked against the West from the off – so much so that one hardly needs the bureaucrats' typical le Carré-style admission that they don't actually want Dante to be telling the truth. If the Russians really haven't got any weapons, James Fox's Ned laments, then the Americans needn't be spending quite so much on their own. And that would never do.

Which makes Connery's achievement in a movie about love versus duty in which the love side of the equation is never in question all the more remarkable. Because to make up for the lame espionage shenanigans, Connery finds ever more ways of showing us a man amazed at his change of fortune and astonished by his newfound capacity for falling in love. The open-hearted warmth of his performance never ceases to amaze. For so much of his career Connery had been obliged to hide the sugary glow of his soft brown eyes behind the cruel mask of Bond. Here, though, as Barley begins to register once more emotions and opportunities he had thought long departed from his life, Connery's eyes look positively doe-like. Never having appeared more vulnerable, more wounded by the prospects of love, Connery makes of Barley Blair an utterly comprehensible everyman, a soul rumpled and roughened by the torments of time. As he tells Katja on the phone before their first meeting, he's easy to recognise because 'I look like an unmade bed with a shopping bag attached.'

He doesn't, of course. Drunken and dissolute Blair might be, but even shambling through Moscow in crumpled suedes the near 60-year-old Connery can't help but cut a dash. As the movie progresses he smartens up his act, abandoning the open-necked, untucked shirt for the kind of trim golfer's sweater he had last sported in *Goldfinger*. For all Barley's hangdog air of failure – his publishing company is only just short of bankruptcy – you never doubt that you'd want him on your side. And so, just this once, a Connery character gets the girl. The movie ends with Barley hunkered down in his Lisbon apartment, preparing for the arrival of Katja, her children and her uncle. In the final shot he walks down to the harbour and hugs each of them as they disembark from the ship that has brought them to their new life – a life that will be overseen by the newly honourable Barley, a man redeemed by love.

A man redeemed by love, moreover, played by a man redeemed by the fact that he is playing a man redeemed by love. Not since *Robin and Marian*, fifteen years earlier, had Connery been able to bring such an open-throated warmth to a performance, not since the Lester picture had his aged beauty seemed such a virtue. (Too many of the pictures he had made in the eighties had been self-conscious and ironic about the fact of Connery's still burgeoning attractiveness.) The Barley Blair of *The Russia House* was Connery's most entrancing creation in years not just because he got into the part, but because the part got into him. Certainly, in the several interviews he granted at the time he seemed more and more at ease with the idea of his blooming middle age.

Any hopes that *The Russia House* might augur a great future for Connery the actor were short-lived, though. For one thing, most critics misunderstood the film, believing that they were watching an espionage movie gone wrong, rather than one of the cinema's great romances. More alarmingly, though, writers and producers failed to take the opportunity the movie had afforded Connery of moving with increasingly serious times. Asked to take the role of the wife-beater brute opposite Kim Basinger in *Sleeping with the Enemy* (1991), he came in too expensive and the part went to Patrick Bergin.* Now it is true that Joseph Rubin's eventual film was not one of the highlights of the decade. And yet one cannot but regret the loss of a Connery version of the movie. Why? Because here would have been a chance for Connery to dramatise, examine and comment upon the charges of male chauvinism that had clung to him these twenty-five years and more. Indeed, just four years earlier, in 1987, on US TV's *Barbara Walters Show*, Connery had bravely stuck to his guns on the question of whether it was ever right for a husband to strike his wife. 'You surely don't think that's good?' Walters asked. 'No, I don't think it's good,' Connery came back, 'but I don't think it's bad. It depends entirely on the circumstances.'⁴ As logical argument this is flawless stuff, suggestive of the Scottish lawyer a better-born Connery might have made. But as the type of utterance designed to have you once more cast into the showbiz version of high dudgeon it is, alas, equally flawless.

And so to what must be the biggest regret in any Connery-lover's list of might-have-beens: the axing of a remake of Joseph Mankiewicz's masterpiece, *The Ghost and Mrs Muir* (1947). Connery had been lined up for the part of the irascible but affectionate ghost of a naval captain (played with incomparable charm in the original

---

* Basinger's role went to Julia Roberts, next to whom Connery had originally been slated for *Pretty Woman* (1990).

picture by Rex Harrison). Michelle Pfeiffer was to play Mrs Muir.*

What went wrong? Twentieth Century Fox got cold feet after the Connery/Pfeiffer pairing of *The Russia House* failed to fire up the box office and the project was pulled. Well, that is how pictures get made and not made. Never kid yourself that we are dealing with an unsullied art here. At the movies, the bottom line, the line that forms outside movie theatres, is the only line that counts. So while you and I might rue the fact that Connery's ghost never got to harass Pfeiffer's young widow, the movie honchos moved on.

So it would not do to be too harsh on our man for what he did end up doing after *The Russia House*. Which was pocket $3.5 million for a couple of weeks' work on *Highlander II* (1991), a tiresome follow-up to a tiresome original. And who can blame him for taking another $250,000 a couple of months later by making (as a favour to Kevin Costner, who was playing the titular lead) an uncredited one-day walk-on as King Richard the Lionheart in *Robin Hood: Prince of Thieves* (1991).†

EXECUTIVE PRODUCER: SEAN CONNERY, it says in the opening credits of *Medicine Man* (1992). Not since *The Offence*, almost twenty years earlier, had Connery been able to exercise such artistic and ideological control over a movie. This, you could say, is Connery's first statement picture – the kind of serious-minded cinema he had long wanted to be involved in. And given what it has to say about the destruction of the South American rainforest, *Medicine Man* is as serious-minded as movies come. Which is not the same thing as saying that it has anything intelligent to say about the fate of human life.

So let us spell it out: *Medicine Man* is an insult to anyone who cares about the state of the world. It is a movie that has as much that is intelligent and relevant to say about what the human race

---

* As, later, was Julia Roberts.
† The money was donated to charities (among them Dundee and Heriot-Watt Universities).

is doing to the planet as it does about a cure for cancer. And yes, Connery's Dr Robert Campbell has come up with just such a cure. Fortunately, at least for the purposes of the plot, he has somehow managed to lose it again – which is where Dr Rae Crane (Lorraine Bracco) comes in. Dr Crane has been dispatched by Campbell's sponsors to find out what he has been doing with his time in the rainforest these past six years. He, meanwhile, has requested that he be sent a research assistant. Cue a screwball-style comic mismatch 'twixt boy and girl.

Except, of course, that at 60-plus, Connery is no boy. But no – this is not the movie wherein the world's sexiest oldster finally gets it on with a girl half his age. *Medicine Man* skirts quite as many sexual issues as it does ecological ones. Even at the end, with Connery and Bracco's characters resigned to the fact that they adore one another, we are never given so much as an embrace, let alone a kiss.

It's a shame because, given *Medicine Man*'s seriousness of intent, how fitting it would have been to have Connery's Campbell bemoaning the despoiling of the earth while he himself is busy despoiling a nubile young beauty who ought to be busy getting herself a family together. Plainly, John McTiernan (who had helped Connery win such plaudits for *The Hunt for Red October*) was never going to be capable of *Chinatown*, but better writers than Tom Schulman and Sally Robinson might have spotted the possibilities here. Instead, we get a rom-com on very traditional lines – all the bicker, all the banter, all the byplay of a thousand pictures from the thirties. But while Connery's readings are as spry and weightless as ever, Lorraine Bracco gives her dialogue neither snap nor sneer. To be fair, the part is woefully undeveloped. And how, even within the confines of a rom-com, can a high-flying young doctor be so dumb? Why not have her run scientific rings around Campbell in the movie's opening scenes, to set up a real sense of competition between them? (Bracco, it should be noted, was personally chosen for the role by Connery, after he had seen her in Martin Scorsese's *Goodfellas* (1990): 'We needed,' he said, 'someone who could be tough, dynamic and had a sense of humour about it.')[5]

It is laudable, of course, that a movie with such serious intent should want to amuse its audience too. But there is such a thing as serious entertainment, and such a thing as seriousness that is not at all entertaining. And judging by the on-location travails of the *Medicine Man* shoot, entertainment was the last thing on the minds of many of its players. Connery and co. spent ten weeks in the Mexican jungle that summer of 1991 enduring temperatures of up to 115 degrees. Watch the film and you can practically taste the humidity – and smell the enmity. Indeed, at one point Connery had the set cleared to tell McTiernan what he thought of what was being allowed to happen. There were, though, those who thought the star himself was at least partly to blame for the picture's difficulties.[6]

Certainly, Connery had a deal of extracurricular stuff on his plate during the *Medicine Man* shoot. While script negotiations were under way on the picture he had been honoured with a BAFTA for his 'Outstanding Contribution to World Cinema'. And then, on 11 June 1991, midway through production, he was made, like Dickens and Disraeli before him, a Freeman of the City of Edinburgh.

It was an award that had been a long time coming. A full quarter of a century earlier, in 1966, the city council had discussed some kind of civic honour for its most famous son. Nothing had been forthcoming then, perhaps because Connery had only just gone on record with his first comments about the rights and wrongs of husbands and wives hitting one another. But in the pre-Christmas rush of 1990, the city's then Lord Provost, Eleanor McLaughlin, was adamant that Connery's 'distinguished contribution to world cinema . . . his largely unpublicised work in founding the Scottish International Education Trust . . . and . . . the respect and high esteem in which he is held by the people of . . . Edinburgh' all made him a natural for the freedom of the city. Of the fifty-seven councillors who voted on the motion, only eight said no to the idea. Moreover, nine out of ten callers to a phone poll organised by the *Edinburgh Evening News* backed the suggestion.*

And the awards kept coming. Six months later Connery was made a Chevalier légion d'honneur – the French equivalent of the knighthood he had never been offered at home. As if accepting a Napoleonic honour wasn't enough of a snook cocked at the English, Connery then finally made the jump he had been rumoured to be pondering for years and became a card-carrying member of the Scottish National Party. 'He adds,' the SNP leader Alex Salmond declared, 'a certain gloss to a powerful message.'[7]

The Sean Connery of *Rising Sun* (1993) has a certain gloss, too. Sheathed from neck to toe in Armani silks and serges, John Connor is the best-dressed Connery character since the Bond of *Never Say Never Again*. And like Bond, Connor is a master of Oriental martial arts – the kind of man who can silence an opponent with little more than a touch of his fingertip. Like Bond, Connor moves with ease through cultures that leave everyone else baffled. Unlike Bond, though, Connor is no elitist. Not for him the certainty that whatever he does is right and proper and good and true. For Connor is a cultural relativist – a man who knows that in order to get results you have to go along with the power structures of whatever it is you're trying to get the bulge on. In other words, he is rather more of a spy than James Bond ever was.

He needs to be, because while the plotting of *Rising Sun* is hardly labyrinthine, its bad guy is rather harder to track down than, say, Auric Goldfinger was. As Terrence Rafferty noted at the time of the movie's release, 'Kaufman's detectives are like characters in an absurdist reworking of *The Big Sleep*: they bear down hard on the problem at hand but there's something faintly silly about their efforts, because, unlike Marlowe, they don't stand heroically apart from the world they're trying to figure out.'[8] Which is a way of

---

* The *Scotsman*, meanwhile, chose to remind its readers that Connery set foot in his homeland only as often and for as long as the tax man would allow. Brian Pendreigh, 'Sealing the Bond of Affection', *Scotsman*, 11 June 1991.

saying that summarising the plot of *Rising Sun* isn't easy. What had been, in Michael Crichton's original novel, a not so thinly disguised attack on Japanese corporate values has been turned by Kaufman and fellow screenwriter Michael Backes into a post-modern whodunnit, part *Basic Instinct*, part *Blow-Up*. Sufficient to say that John Connor is the brilliant detective who can solve a crime at a hundred paces and that Wesley Snipes's Web Smith is the slow-witted, slightly resentful sidekick all convoluted cop stories need.

Rising Sun is so dull and clumsy a movie that it really only comes together as an analysis of the post-*Never Say Never Again* Connery. John Connor was the latest in Connery's lengthening line of mentors. As if to hammer home the point, Kaufman has Connor tell Web Smith that he is 'the senior man who guides the junior man', for all the world as if they're starring in an Oriental version of *The Name of the Rose*. Such intertextual joshing worked a treat in the Bond movies, where Connery's sly ironising was forever pulling the rug from under whatever putative thrills were on display. But it sits uneasy in a movie that purports to alert us to the reality of the Baudrillardian simulacrum – that place where fact and fiction are impossible to tell apart.

Which is a way of saying that *Rising Sun*, as its overly cute character/actor name parallels suggest, is really a movie about acting. Early on in the picture Connor tells Smith that dealing with Japanese people is different from dealing with Americans: the Japanese expect you to talk softly, to bow your head, to make no sudden movements. Later, by means of a little Photoshop-style trickery, video footage of Connor and Smith talking at one another is doctored so that Connery's head is on Snipes's body and vice versa. The result is, of course, comical – but it is also serious in that it points up Connery's stilled solidity next to the wired jitteriness of Snipes. Acting, the picture argues, is intrinsic to simply being.

The trouble is that this self-conscious tomfoolery is far and away the most interesting aspect of Kaufman's botched thriller. Jettisoning what he saw as the calculated racism of Michael Crichton's original novel, Kaufman ended up with an impenetrable but still dull mystery. Signally, Crichton's overarching narrative backdrop – what he saw as the Japanese takeover of the American economy – is of interest to no one other than Harvey Keitel's Lieutenant Tom Graham – a devious racist who is of no importance to the movie's overall trajectory. Movies being corporate efforts themselves, of course, they can't go out on limbs the way novels can. But if the limb your chosen story goes out on is actually the spine of the work, how can you expect to do without it and not end up with a broken-backed film?

For all that, *Rising Sun* did good business at the box office. Much of this success was down to the fun to be had from watching Connery breeze his way through a potboiler with the devil-may-care nonchalance he had once used to humanise Ian Fleming's priggish hero. As conscientious about his performances as he could be uncaring about his choice of roles, Connery seems to have made a policy decision to the effect that no matter what went wrong in any movie he was attached to, he himself would always be blameless.

How else to explain his appearance in Bruce Beresford's *A Good Man in Africa* (1994), another mentor movie in which Connery's titular exemplar does his best to make a less than bad man of Colin Friels's skirt-chaser of an English diplomat?* Or his signing on for Arne Glimcher's *Just Cause* (1995), a legal thriller that derives almost entirely from the lighting scheme of Jonathan Demme's *The Silence of the Lambs* (1991) and the location work in Martin Scorsese's remake of *Cape Fear* (1991)? Once again, Connery acquits himself assuredly, but if a thing isn't worth doing it hardly matters a jot whether it is done well. The question that loomed ever larger as Connery approached his homeland's conventional retirement age was what his talents and skills were for.

---

* The only other possible explanation is that William Boyd's clumsy screenplay gives Connery the chance to indulge in some of those *Carry On*-style double entendres he has always said he loves. 'Do you see anything?' asks Friels's Morgan Leafy, as Connery's Dr Alex Murray examines his manhood for signs of sexual disease. 'Nothing significant,' comes the woefully predictable reply.

16

Loose Ends

Despite the *Carry On*-style antics of *A Good Man in Africa*, Connery has more than once claimed Ingmar Bergman as his favourite director. 'I find I sit through his films absolutely unaware of time,' he told one reporter.[1] There is nothing strange about such wide-ranging tastes. It is unusual, though, whenever anyone of such catholic breadth admits to a preference for the comic over the tragic. Among the factors that have prevented Woody Allen from ever quite making a masterpiece is his adolescent faith in the idea that sadness is intrinsically more serious than smiling. Kenneth Tynan once argued that Uncle Vanya's 'tragedy is that he is capable only of comedy'.[2] Allen's is that he considers it a tragedy to be capable only of comedy. And yet in the movie world, nobody has known that comedy and tragedy are merely moods in which we look at life more than Allen's great hero – that man Bergman again. *Smiles of a Summer Night* (1955), for all its aerated joys, knows that love can sear as well as soothe the heart. What is *The Seventh Seal* (1956), with its tenebrous chess games with a guy who calls himself Death, if not a black comedy?

Love comedy as he does, though, the autodidactic Connery finds it just as hard as Allen does to credit laughter with moral seriousness. Comedies, he believes, are a way of escaping life, tragedies a way of confronting it. In which case, the tragedy of Sean Connery's late career is that he has appeared in little but light comedies and lighter thrillers. Hence, perhaps, his involvement in the London production of *Art*, Yasmina Reza's play about the meaning and validity of abstract painting to probe the workings of friendship.

Micheline had seen this three-handed, all-male drama on its debut run Paris in 1995 and thought Connery, who had long been fascinated by Michael Ovitz's collection of Robert Ryman white-on-white canvases, might be interested in starring in a movie version. Reza, though, was adamant that her play remain a play, at least for a while, and though Connery bought up the film rights, he also had other movie commitments which necessarily took precedence. Still, he was instrumental in having the play translated into English (by Christopher Hampton), and bringing it first to his home country and then on to the USA. The resulting show was a huge success, playing for countless performances in the West End and on Broadway. The critics loved it, too. In London, the production won Evening Standard and Olivier awards; in New York it was the recipient of a Tony.

Meanwhile, in January 1996, at the Golden Globes Awards Ceremony, where he picked up the Cecil B. DeMille award for a lifetime achievement in motion pictures, Connery explained to an audience of movie worthies why art mattered: 'It is the stuff in between the shooting and the punches and the car crashes that really counts. The scenes . . . that try to say something about how we really behave, what we really feel . . . that . . . sends [audiences] into the movie houses.'[3] Noble artistic sentiments indeed. What would Jerry Zucker make of them?

'If you want to do Ingmar Bergman,' Zucker once opined, 'what you end up with is a film where everybody is covered in shit. And who wants that?'[4] Evidently not Sean Connery, who had pledged allegiance to Zucker – hitherto best known for *Airplane!* (1980) and *The Naked Gun* (1988) – and his next picture, a light-toned take on the Arthurian legend by the name of *First Knight* (1995). Strange to relate, this wasn't as ill-advised a move as it at first seemed. Despite Zucker's fatuous curriculum vitae; despite an anachronistic screenplay by William Nicholson; despite Richard Gere as a Lancelot who pouts a lot: despite all this, it is fair to say that nobody comes out of *First Knight* covered in shit.

Certainly, Connery emerged from the picture with rather more laurels than he might have done. As far back as *Adventure Story* and *The Age of Kings*, after all, he had proved he looked good in period costume, and in *First Knight* he strides around John Box's sets draped in a succession of velvety, shoulder-enhancing tunics that make him look every inch the monarchic hero.

Crucially though, what his King Arthur doesn't get to do is wield a sword. *First Knight* is the first picture in Connery's career that genuinely accepts that he has become an old man. Indeed, Connery's age is one of the plot's central motors: the then 29-year-old Julia Ormond's Guinevere has been pledged to marry Arthur for as long as either of them can remember. Whether she loves him is another thing – though granted the protection Arthur can offer her people from Prince Malagant (Ben Cross), she has managed to convince herself as to the depth of her feelings. Add to that the facts that Connery's Arthur is as valiant and unflinching a king as the movies have yet given us and that he still looks and sounds terrific, and what's not to like about this marriage?

Nothing at all, were it not for the arrival of Gere's Lancelot, who in swordfight after swordfight proves himself a handy man to have around. The trouble is that none of that swordplay is evident in his dealings with Arthur, who treats him first like a favourite son and later, after he finds him embracing his wife, like a favourite son who has mucked up his exams. In other words, what *First Knight* lacks is any genuine sense of tension about the fact that its kingly figure is practically of pensionable age. Despite Connery's youthful claim to wanting to be an old man with a good face, that is, and his frequent protestations that wanting to remain young is a joke, he seems unable to commit to a story about the waning of a man's strength. In the movie's big battle scene, Arthur and his men win, but they do so not by dint of strength and integrity, but by hiding in the trees and waiting for the enemy to fall into their trap. And even here, Connery's monarch stands back from the action and lets his minions get on with it.

Indeed, though Connery sits as well atop a horse as he has always done, stories did the rounds during the *First Knight* shoot that he needed a step-ladder to actually get up there. To be fair, Connery declared himself quite happy for Gere to be the picture's swashing hero: 'I looked and thought: "Let him get on with it." I have done plenty of that in my time and it was nice to play the elder statesman for once.'[5] Maybe so, but it is still a shame that Zucker's movie never finds the time for Connery and Gere to fight it out – not to the death, of course, but to the moment when Arthur, having bested Lancelot a couple of times, finds himself on the floor under the younger man's blade and acknowledges that it is time to hand over the reins. But *First Knight* clumsily obviated the need for such dramaturgy, by having Connery play Arthur as an oldster from the start.

What's depressing about this is not that Connery is indeed an old man here. (He doesn't, after all, look all that much older than he did playing Robin Hood almost twenty years earlier.) It's that Connery has it in him to be one of the movies' saltiest old men – a grey-haired goat who gets the girl not because she feels obliged to give herself to the guy who used to be James Bond but because he is both warmer and cooler than the young bucks who might be thought more in her line. Imagine a picture that asked a young girl to really fall for an old Connery without recourse to a May to December love-potion from Merlin the magician. Imagine a picture that asked Connery to really fall for a young girl. Imagine what that picture might tell us about romance, about love, about, yes, sex. *First Knight* could have been that movie – the movie in which Sean Connery finally lives up to what he has always claimed he believes, realises that nothing is for ever and admits that the game of youthful heroics is up.

By the mid-1990s movie screens had paid host to no new Bond movie that decade. The last 007 picture, *Licence To Kill*, had come out in the summer of 1989 and bombed. Timothy Dalton had looked terrific as Bond – the spitting image of the illustrations on the front of a million paperbacks in the pre-Connery fifties. But he was also a classically trained actor who had come up through RADA and the Royal Shakespeare Company, and he was insistent that what had gone wrong with Bond not just post-Moore but pretty much post-*From Russia with Love* was that the franchise hadn't let its leading man take his part seriously enough. What the series needed, he argued, was a strong measure of realism – and promptly proceeded to play Bond as if he were playing Hamlet with a hangover. Top marks for ambition, though the public were having none of it. After just two Bond pictures, it was plain that Dalton had issued himself with a licence to be killed off. Connery's essential insight – that nobody, and least of all the man himself – could take Bond seriously had at last been proven.

Sociocultural factors had been at work in Bond's demise, too. *Licence To Kill* had come out mere months before the Berlin Wall was pulled down, inaugurating a new era in the Eastern Bloc. This is not the place to debate the pluses and minuses of that new era. Sufficient to say that in the post-glasnost epoch the idea of Western spies dodging bullets fired by shady Eastern types looked distinctly old hat. (In *The Living Daylights* (1987), Dalton had actually found himself on the side of the Mujahideen in their fight against the Russian infidel. Quite how this picture now plays on US television I should love to know.)

And then, suddenly, in the mid-nineties, Bond was back. In harness this time was Pierce Brosnan, a TV star who had been unable to take the role a decade earlier because of his commitments to the series *Remington Steele*. True, Brosnan couldn't do much beyond look joshingly self-satisfied, but he had a nice, laid-back Celtic touch, he moved well and he looked good in a suit. Moreover, a new team which might just know what it was about was in charge at United Artists. For the first time in the two and a half decades since *On Her Majesty's Secret Service*, then, Connery's original Bond was about to have something approaching a competitor.

It may have been that Connery would have signed for Don Simpson and Jerry Bruckheimer's latest production without the prospect of Brosnan's debut in *GoldenEye* (1995). It may have been that after a string of cameos and walk-ons and voiceovers Connery and Michael Ovitz thought it was time for another potential blockbuster.* But whatever the reasons, sign up for *The Rock* (1996) Connery did – and in his capacity as executive producer ensured that the movie both praised and parodied the series of movies that had made his name.

First then, just as he had done on *Never Say Never Again*, he hired Dick Clement and Ian La Frenais to gag up his dialogue. Their essential task was to stress – with properly affectionate irony – the similarities between Connery's John Patrick Mason and his James Bond. Mason (even the name puts us in mind of one of the key influences on Connery's 007), it transpires, is the only man to have ever escaped from Alcatraz. Now the FBI are asking him to break back in there and take on a crack team of renegade Marines who have a cache of missiles laden with nerve gas beaded on San Francisco. But where, a senior military man wants to know, did Mason learn his unique espionage skills? 'British Intelligence,' comes the smirking reply.

Still, even the best agents need help, and joining Mason on what director Michael Bay ensures is an action-packed mission is Dr Stanley Goodspeed (Nicolas Cage), a whizz-kid boffin who knows everything there is to know about missile technology and less than nothing about work in the field. Cue the by now standard-issue Connery mentoring dialogue, suitably ironised by Clement and La Frenais. 'Didn't you read my résumé?' Mason chides a dumbfounded Goodspeed after he has put paid to another renegade troop. Why bother, when the movie itself is one long Connery résumé – a

---

* After finishing work on *First Knight*, Connery had voiced the dialogue of a dragon called Draco in *Dragonheart* (1996).

car chase from *Diamonds Are Forever* here, an underwater rescue from *Thunderball* there, a heist from *Goldfinger* thrown in for good measure.

Because more than any of Connery's movies of the previous ten years, *The Rock* is founded on the Oedipal structure that underlies all narratives of mentoring. At its most basic level, Michael Bay's picture tells of how, under the tutelage of John Mason, the frazzled and fearful Stanley Goodspeed at last becomes a man. To hammer the point home, the movie opens with Goodspeed taking receipt of a mail-order purchase – a mint-condition first-pressing of *With The Beatles* that has cost him $600 and that makes plain the fact that his adolescent fantasies are built around the high Bond years of the early sixties.

Connery's problem is that the movie gives him nothing at all to do beyond the puns and the post-modern parodying of the part that had made his name. John Mason is a self-conscious reworking of Bond ('I'm too old for this,' the newly pensionable Connery has to quip after one particularly hairy moment in *The Rock*'s non-stop litany of action), but that's all he is, and not even Connery's best efforts can make him any more. In small part, this is down to Cage's performance, by some measure his most mannered to date. Indeed, the two men's widely differing approaches to their craft – Connery's need for plenty of rehearsal time sorting ill with Cage's more Methodical urge to find whatever was required during the moment itself – engendered both on-set fracas with Bay and an on-screen relationship that never sparks into life.

The bigger drawback is that the movie gives Connery no women to spar with. 'Maybe I'm losing my sex appeal,' Mason ruminates during a lull in Bay's Alcatraz fireworks, but it would have been nice if *The Rock* had given Connery the chance to test the point. The only females there are in the picture are Mason's daughter (written in only to give his retaking of Alcatraz a personal twist) and Goodspeed's fiancée, Carla Pestalozzi (Vanessa Marcil). Mightn't the movie have benefited from a scene in which Stanley introduces her to Mason and she wonders just momentarily whether she might be marrying the wrong guy?

All of which said, *The Rock* turned out to be the huge hit Connery and Ovitz had hoped it would be, earning back a third of its $75 million budget in its opening weekend. In the years since, it has taken another $300 million worldwide – by some measure Connery's biggest hit since *The Hunt for Red October*. Still, put Connery back on top of the heap though it may have done, the movie's emphasis on his back catalogue meant that it offered no pointers for his next move. 'You're caught between a rock and a hard case,' Connery's Mason counsels the villainous Brigadier Hummel (Ed Harris) midway through the movie. That the play on words would have meant little to audiences outside Connery's home country is by the by. What counts about the phrase is that it described with eerie precision Connery's own quandary.

As long ago as 1963, Connery had claimed that he'd 'like to play a bad guy now and then'.[6] Thirty-five years after *Woman of Straw* he got his second chance. No, not as the Macbeth he had for so long been promising, but in Jeremiah Chechik's slow-witted take on the hit sixties British television show *The Avengers* (1998). Mention of Shakespeare is apt, though, because Connery's Sir August de Wynter (named, perhaps, for Lawrence Olivier's Maxim de Winter in Hitchcock's *Rebecca* (1939)) has a habit of referencing the bard. His plot of holding Britain to ransom by hijacking its weather system is to be done by means of some computerised program he calls Prospero. Later we see him brief his minions – all of them dressed in pop-art-coloured teddy bear outfits; Connery, though, removes his mask, and in what remains of the suit, with its black sheen and bulbous shoulders and tiny head, he looks like Olivier's Richard III. And when he explains his dastardly plans to the powers that be he prefaces them by telling these impotent oafs that 'Now is the winter of your discontent'. Alas, poor Connery, *The Avengers* was to afford him rather more than one season of unhappiness. The picture was a disaster.

The worst of it was, though, that try as he might to pin the blame on the producer (Jerry Weintraub) and the director (Chechik), Connery couldn't convincingly exculpate himself. 'If I could get my hands on any of them, I'd kill them,' he said a little while after the movie had opened to universal drubbing.[7] 'If ever there was a licence to kill, I would have used it to kill the director and the producer.'[8] But the gentleman doth protest too much. Underlying this diatribe, mightn't there be an unconscious realisation that Connery himself had screwed up?

For limited though his on-screen time in the movie is (it was so hacked about before release that the whole film doesn't even reach the 90-minute mark), Connery's performance in *The Avengers* is one of the low points of his career. Here he is, the crazed villain, playing the organ as crazed villains do. Here he is strutting in kilt and sporran declaiming, 'Rain or shine, all is mine!' – a line that even the Blofeld of *Diamonds Are Forever* would have sent back for a rewrite. Beyond the undeniable fact that *The Avengers* would afford Connery the opportunity of playing the gleeful villain in a parody sixties spy thriller, the suspicion lingers that he also saw his becoming the bad guy as a way of cocking a snook at the Bond producers.*

Even had Chechik's movie not come out a clunker, *The Avengers* was always going to have problems, if only because the original TV series remains so fondly remembered. Many are the one-time fans that grew out of *The Persuaders* or *Jason King*, but *The Avengers* is a curious show in that one actually finds oneself *growing into* it. Looking back, you realise the series wasn't really meant for the

---

* In November 1996, after all, only a couple of months before he committed to *The Avengers*, Connery had pointedly failed to show up at a tribute to Cubby Broccoli (who had died that June) at the Odeon in London's Leicester Square. Roger Moore was there, Timothy Dalton was there, Pierce Brosnan was there, all of them paying homage to the man who had done more than anyone to ensure their lasting fame.

children of the sixties at all, but for those adults who had grown increasingly mystified by the Beatles' artistic progress and yet admitted that their Edwardian hankerings and borrowings did have a certain charm. Certainly one suspects that the presence of so much talent in the movie – Ralph Fiennes, Jim Broadbent, Eileen Atkins, Fiona Shaw, Eddie Izzard – is down to their love of and loyalty to a show they grew up watching.

And since the original series' debts to the domesticated surrealism of Magritte and Max Ernst meant that no episode ever really made any kind of sense even within its own terms, all those stars can perhaps be excused for having missed the fact that what they are working on plainly had no plot, less dialogue and even less intelligence. Perhaps, they may have imagined, this was how the originals were knocked up. And perhaps they were. The difference was that the original show's makers were liberated into creativity by having a budget of next to nothing, whereas Jeremiah Chechik had an estimated $60 million to play with but no idea what to spend it on. The picture took little more than a third of that sum at the box office.

Connery himself was paid a mere thousandth of *The Avengers'* budget for appearing in his next movie. Even suitably adjusted for inflation, the $60,000 he accepted for Willard Carroll's *Playing by Heart* (1998) was by some measure the smallest pay cheque of his entire career. Still, perhaps shamed into sentience by the disaster of the previous year, Connery had made the right choice. True, Carroll's picture isn't a great one, but it is ambitious and intriguing and pregnant with promise. Most importantly, this was Connery's first movie aimed squarely at the adult market since *The Russia House*: instead of his by now standard-issue father figure, Connery plays a father for real. It's hardly casting against type, but in the context of Connery's recent CV it feels almost as off the wall as Woody Allen's use of Michael Caine in *Hannah and Her Sisters* (1986).

But then, *Playing By Heart* is something of a surrogate Woody Allen movie. (Since Gena Rowlands, who plays Connery's wife, is called what she is, I can't see why Carroll didn't title the picture 'Hannah and her Daughters' and have done with it.) And if the movie isn't distinguished enough to have done for Connery what Allen's picture did for Caine (win him an Oscar nomination), we should still give thanks that it gives us the chance to see Connery refuse the easy satisfactions of the action movie. Because for once he is playing an ordinary adult man who's having to adjust to the compromises of something that – despite the presence of such beauties as Gillian Anderson, Madeleine Stowe, and Angelina Jolie – looks remarkably like the real world.

True, the dialogue he is given feels forced and phoney next to the stream-of-consciousness ranting Allen gave Caine in *Hannah and Her Sisters*. 'I never slept with Wendy,' Connery's Paul tells Rowlands's Hannah in another of their rows about a long-ago love affair, 'because I was too much in love with her.' You don't have to share the offhand cynicism of the original 007 to see such talk for the rot it is. A better movie would have made a properly adulterous adulterer of Connery's here near-perfect husband, have had him finally confess to a sexual secret now long past and have him wonder out loud and in front of his family how it figured on the scale of his past conquests.

But then, a better movie could have done so much more with its leading man. If you're going to cast Connery as a father to three variously beautiful daughters, after all, shouldn't you act on those Learish implications and make more of the world's oldest sexiest man than a generous, good-natured father? More than once in the picture Paul points out that his daughter Gracie (Stowe) isn't wearing a bra. It's done out of irritation – 'If I have to wear a tux,' Paul gripes, 'she has to wear a bra' – but it would have been nice if there'd been just a hint of something covetous in the complaint. That tuxedo can't help, after all, putting us in mind of the sexual predator that was Bond, and it would have been nice if some of that beastliness had found its way into Connery's conception of Paul. All that was needed, surely, was for Gracie or one of her sisters to make reference to their father's dangerous beauty. Would the rather lustier Catherine Zeta-Jones be up to the task in Connery's next picture?

How do movies come about? Orson Welles described a film director as a man who presides over accidents. Howard Hawks talked about how he just loved 'doing some scenes'. Certainly movies aren't organic wholes that emerge fully formed from one consciousness – even a consciousness as fully formed as, say, that of Welles. So it doesn't make much sense to say that if *The Rock* was Connery's riposte to *GoldenEye*, then *Entrapment* (1999) was his reply to Pierce Brosnan's non-Bond blockbuster of the period, *The Thomas Crown Affair* (1999). Movies, especially movies as mucked up and messed about as *Entrapment*, don't come into the world like that. And yet who is to say that somewhere down the long line from what we must call original idea to finished movie there wasn't at least one voice somewhere saying, 'If this new Bond guy can be in an old-fashioned caper picture, then what's to stop the old Bond doing the same?'

Not that *Entrapment* is in any way mystifying. The picture makes sense both within its own carefully plotted terms and on the CV of its star. The story is simplicity itself: Robert 'Mac' MacDougal (Connery) is a mastermind burglar with a long list of majestic robberies to his credit. Virginia Baker (Catherine Zeta-Jones) is the insurance agent on his trail. Except that when she catches up with him she doesn't arrest him. Rather, she suggests that they team up for what will be the biggest robbery of his career. Cue the 'but you're not ready for that big a job'-type debates that such movies are built on. Follow it up with the feisty young pup showing her mettle and earning her spurs and you have a pleasant enough way of killing a couple of hours provided you enjoy telling yourself over and over that you don't for a minute believe what you're being asked to believe.

And there we might conclude our discussion, were it not for the presence of Catherine Zeta-Jones. One way of understanding how *Entrapment* fits into the Connery oeuvre would be to see it as another of his mentor movies. *The Name of the Rose* or *Rising Sun* all over again, save for the fact that the protégée is here a girl – a girl, moreover, whose dialogue makes it plain that Mac is her kind of man. One stresses that it's the dialogue doing the work, because Zeta-Jones just isn't up to the job the movie needs her to pull off – the job of coming on to Mac while suggesting to us that she might be doing so merely to rip him off.

What a movie that might have been – a movie in which the world's oldest sexiest man finds himself falling slavishly for a beauty half his age.* A movie in which one of the cinema's great sexual beasts falls victim to the machinations of a raven-haired vixen who takes him for every last penny – and he still looks pleased at the end of the picture because he's been allowed to be near her for just a few moments! Too excitable? But surely we can still imagine a movie in which the Hawksian tensions between wise old can-do guy and feisty young chick are worked out through dialogue with zip and snap and the kind of ironic snarl Connery was made for – *His Girl Friday* with a heist thrown in.

That last idea is pretty much the one *Entrapment* aimed at – and missed by a long mile. To be fair, I suppose I can understand why somebody – Connery, the producers (which means at least in part Connery again), the director Jon Amiel – said that you don't choose Sean Connery as your leading man only to have him led on by a girl young enough to be his daughter. This is a mainstream movie, after all, and in the corporatised world of mainstream moviemaking you are held to fool around with audience expectations at your peril.

All of which said, nobody is ever going to be able to excuse the

---

* Though Connery was 68 when he was shooting *Entrapment*, and Zeta-Jones not quite 30, Mac himself is said to be 60.

ham-fisted job *Entrapment* makes of its far more traditional take on sex and violence. Good as it would have been to see the man who once described the pictures that made him as 'sadism for the family' play a slave to passion,[9] it would have been good, too, to see him, approaching 70, once more commit to the sexual savagery he had bodied forth in *Marnie* or *The Offence*. But no. As things stand, Mac dresses Virginia, he dresses her down, he orders her about, he puts her through her paces, he puts her in a matching leotard and blindfold and has her bend and shimmy her way through a web of security system laser beams as Amiel's camera gazes helplessly upon the bend of her waist, the swell of her butt, the thrust of her crotch. Of the desires underlying such diktats, however, we get no clue. Instead, the movie takes its cue from Mac's barked order 'Knees together!' midway through one of Virginia's more entrancing arabesques.

At one point Mac and Virginia lie down together on their sides, she shoving her rear into his groin. Amiel moves in tight for a close-up of one of Connery's massive hands wrapping itself round Zeta-Jones's *two* tiny wrists, the better to prevent them setting an alarm off – and still there isn't a twinge of sexual tension on Mac's part, mere cool professionalism as he gets on with the job in hand. True, we twice *hear* the Connery purr as we in the audience are treated to fetishistic close-ups of Zeta-Jones's body – but we don't get to *see* him *watch* her, so that in the context of the plot he could merely be hymning his assent to her gymnastic abilities.

It would be easy to argue that *Entrapment*'s problems begin and end with Catherine Zeta-Jones's inability to be any more than a slinky sex kitten. Still, I'm not sure that all the film's problems would have been solved had, say, Nicole Kidman been its leading lady. While it is true to say that Zeta-Jones so lacks suggestiveness that when Mac at first rebuffs Virginia's advances it almost seems like presumptuousness on her part, it is equally true that Connery can't or won't commit to the notion that a man of 60 might genuinely be attracted to a girl thirty years his junior. And yet the idea of such a girl dragging the aged Sean Connery off to bed is far more believable than what passes for the rest of *Entrapment*'s narrative.

And so to watch Connery's last picture of the twentieth century is to think of what might have been. And what might have been, I think, is something along the lines of *La belle noiseuse* (1991), Jacques Rivette's psycho-sexual power-play drama about a magus-like older man and a near-naked young beauty. The Michel Piccoli of that movie bears more than a passing resemblance to the 60-plus Sean Connery, after all, and the way his martinet of a painter stretches and bends Emmanuelle Béart into one uncomfortable position after another was surely an inspiration for the maze of lasers Mac has Virginia bend and squeeze her way through. But Connery fights shy of giving the movie what it needs – the man he once called 'the proper sadist . . . never completely passionate . . . always aware of what he's doing',[10] while Zeta-Jones can't begin to live up to Béart's capricious, competitive candour.

Granted such candour, *Entrapment* could have been the movie that laid to rest the bestial ghost of Bond. Given the ludicrously cosy, chaste yet putatively charged way the movie ends – Connery and Zeta-Jones going off together in love – that chance was likely lost long before the cameras got rolling. But a braver Connery, who as a producer on the film had more than a little say in its construction, might have seen the parallels between Mac's repressed fetishism and Bond's brute imperialism and used the movie to throw light on them. If anyone seems trapped in this picture, it's not Virginia Baker (in thrall to Mac's unavoidable smoulder though she may be), nor Robert MacDougal (enraptured by the silky flesh and generous curves of his young charge as he is), but Sean Connery – still in hock to a vision of himself as an old-fashioned leading man who believes in honour and decency. Entrapment indeed.

Entrapment's Robert MacDougal had been Connery's most emphatically Scottish creation since the stuttering Spike of *No Road Back* forty years earlier. Not only did Mac speak with an unashamed Scots burr, he spent his down time in a castle (Eilean Donan in the Kyle of Lochalsh) in the Scottish Highlands. And during the making of the movie, Connery, who admitted that filming in Scotland was 'a bonus',[11] began making noises about quitting his home in Spain and finding somewhere to live in his home country. For a while, in fact, he had his eye on a mansion in North Berwick, a beach-town book-ended by golf courses a few miles east of the city he had been born and raised in. That move wasn't to be, but Connery's restless urge kept him and Micheline looking. As he told his old friend the writer William McIlvanney, everywhere pales eventually.[12]

Certainly the delights of the Casa Malibu were beginning to fade. The Andalusian coast had been a quiet place when Connery first fetched up there more than three decades earlier. Since then, though, the Costa del Sol had burgeoned into one of the biggest holiday traps in Europe. Millions of sun-worshippers beat a path to its beaches every year – and quite a few of them turned out to be Connery-worshippers, too, eager to cop a bead on their man.

Not all of the fans were female, either – a fact that Micheline at least found alarming. 'The women, I guess, is okay,' she remarked of this fan mania. 'But the men – well that can be not so good for Sean, of course.'[13] Back in the sixties, Connery had always said he envied the Beatles because there had been four of them to handle the flak from press and fans. John Lennon had been flying solo, though, the night he was gunned down outside his Manhattan apartment block. And Lennon was a peacenik. Connery, for all his efforts to persuade people he had only been playing a part, was still most famous as the man with the Walther PPK. Who knew what fantasies his worshippers cherished?

But Connery had positive reasons for seeking a Scottish bolthole, too. In May 1997, Tony Blair's New Labour government had come to power, promising, among other things, a referendum on Scottish devolution. Working across party lines with the likes of Labour's Scottish Secretary Donald Dewar, the Scottish Liberal Democrat leader Jim Wallace and, of course, SNP leader Alex Salmond, Connery spent the next few months campaigning for a Yes vote. Come September a majority of those Scots who turned out did so to endorse the idea that they should have their own parliament with its own tax-raising powers. Finally, in May 1999, a Scottish parliament met for the first time in 292 years. Disappointingly for Connery, the new Scottish government was made up of a coalition between Labour and the Liberal Democrats.

More disappointing still had been his missing out on the knighthood he had been nominated for by the outgoing Tory government in the previous New Year's Honours list. The reason for the snub, anonymous sources in the now governing Labour party claimed, were those by now 35-year-old remarks Connery had made about hitting women on the set of *Thunderball*. Connery himself had other ideas. He was convinced he'd been knocked back because of his support for the SNP.[14] Probably the real reason was what the Charles Gray of *Diamonds Are Forever* would have called 'nothing so melodramatic'. The likelihood is that internecine politicking between standard-issue apparatchik mediocrities had done for Connery that year. Certainly, as the new millennium dawned, mere months after the inauguration of the new Scottish Parliament, he was offered a knighthood. 'Alas,' a similarly laconic fellow nationalist quipped, 'he felt he had to accept.'[15]

In reality there was nothing at all turncoated – let alone surprising – about Connery's decision. Unlike certain showbusiness knights and ladies before him, he had never knocked the honours system until the day he was invited to become a part of it. Indeed, having always proudly accepted whatever honours came his way, Connery had admitted to being 'rather depress[ed]' by that snubbing of two years earlier.[16] Just as in his professional life, where he had talked a rather more ambitious game than the one he had most of the time played, so in his political life it had long been clear that he was as pragmatic as he was principled. As he said at the time his first nomination fell through, a Sean Connery knighthood 'certainly would be helpful in terms of the Scottish Nationalists'.[17] That he said so from the home he now called his main residence – on New Providence Island, west of Nassau in the Bahamas – was duly noted in reports on the fracas.

Back in the late fifties and early sixties Sean Connery could hardly be photographed without a book in his hand and a stack of others figuring elsewhere in the composition. Look closely at those books and you will see on their spines the names of Shakespeare and Proust and Stanislavsky and others from that pantheon Robert Henderson had urged on his young charge during down time on the *South Pacific* tour. Many of the same authors appear on the yards of groaning shelves in the apartment of Connery's titular lead in *Finding Forrester* (2000). Asked by troubled young literary hopeful Jamal Wallace (Rob Brown) whether he has 'read them all', a tetchy Forrester says, 'No. I just keep them there to impress my visitors.' Over the next two hours, though, William Forrester will do what so many Sean Connery characters of the past fifteen years have done – turn into a Henderson-style mentor figure for the troubled Wallace and coax him into existential self-definition.

Movies being movies, of course, Forrester himself must open up a little, too. He has, after all, been holed up in his Bronx apartment for the best part of half a century (since about the time that Sean Connery moved to London in the hope of finding himself). Back then, at the dawn of the fifties, Forrester had hit the big time with his first – and thus far only – novel. Rich enough to quit, he did so, distraught at the distorted readings critics were making of his masterpiece. Now, though, even as this terse-bordering-on-taciturn mystery-man introduces the basketball-loving Jamal to the world of books and *Bildung*, Jamal will return the compliment by introducing his Salinger-style recluse to the world outside his window.

Even for a wilfully lonesome writer, though, Forrester's apartment is heavily tricked out with the trappings of the gothic. Its fusty books and dusty shelves, its low-wattage bulbs and creaking doors locate it firmly in the landscape of Hawthorne and Poe (who gets name-checked by one of Jamal's English teachers). Does this mean *Finding Forrester* is a kind of closet horror movie? Not at all, but the generic confusion can't help but make you realise how much more satisfying a picture it would have been had there been some sense of friction between its two leads. But the movie fights shy of dramatising any interracial enmity, and this putatively ill-matched twosome become friends far too quickly and easily. Hence the piling on of unnecessary conflicts at school, where F. Murray Abraham's Professor Robert Crawford has it in for Jamal for no discernible reason save the needs of twisting the plot. Without that mini-battle the picture would be as mushy and warm as the Robin Williams movies it so shamelessly apes. It is true that the Connery persona is too instinctively irascible to allow such a movie to come into being around him, but that is not to say that *Finding Forrester* couldn't do with rather more by way of abrasiveness. The odd snap at Jamal about his not working hard enough aside, the movie is well short of the kind of histrionics it needs if its volte face denouement is to have any torque. Why not sharpen things up by making Forrester a kneejerk racist?

The director, Gus Van Sant, would once have been the man to help things along here. Van Sant it was, after all, who filmed a kind of queer version of *Henry V* in *My Own Private Idaho* (1991), and who in *Drugstore Cowboy* (1989) had made the American cinema's most understanding treatment of the drug problem (by for once admitting that not all addicts think they have a problem) since Nicholas Ray's *Bigger Than Life* (1956). Above all, he had seen through to the sordid foundations of stardom in *To Die For* (1995) – at that time probably his most conventionally structured picture, but also his most daring. The move, in just five years, from such ornery-minded troublemaking to the conventional mores of *Finding Forrester* – which took more than $15 million in rentals – would be inexplicable in any arena other than contemporary Hollywood.

300

It would be nice if we could end it there. But though after
Finding Forrester there were three years of silence from Connery,
he did eventually return to the screen – with the worst picture
of his forty-seven-year career. What to say about *The League of
Extraordinary Gentlemen* (2003) other than that Connery's Allan
Quartermain kills off a villain called M (Richard Roxburgh)? Even
in a winningly jokey picture that moment would have looked post-
modern cute. In Stephen Norrington's humourless, ham-fisted
take on Alan Moore and Kevin O'Neill's comic book series it looks
almost suicidally self-referential: Sean Connery murdering the man
who got him into this action hero lark in the first place.

But then, *The League of Extraordinary Gentlemen* was a pretty
murderous movie to make. Relations between Connery and
Norrington were strained throughout shooting. At one point
Norrington is said to have asked his star to punch him in the face –
so that he'd have an excuse to punch him back.[18] When the movie
premiered, in Las Vegas, Norrington failed to show up, prompting
questions from reporters as to his whereabouts. 'Ask me about
someone I like, will you,' Connery rasped, before suggesting that if
they really wanted to find the director they should 'check the local
asylum'.[19]

Not everyone blamed Norrington for what had gone wrong on
the movie, though. Alan Moore, for instance, has mockingly argued
that Connery's insistence on having 'a bigger explosion than the
one he's had in his last film' was among the reasons the picture
ended up making a loss. 'It's in his contract that he has to have a
bigger explosion with every film he's in,' Moore claimed. 'In *The
Rock* he'd blown up an island, and he was demanding in *The League*
that he blow up, was it Venice or something like that? It would have
been the moon in his next movie.'[20]

There has been, though, no next movie. A year after the release
of *The League of Extraordinary Gentlemen* Connery quit what would
have been his follow-up picture even before the get-go. The

project in question was 'Josiah's Canon', a heist extravaganza that was to have been directed by Brett Ratner, in which Connery and whatever gang had been assembled for him were to have bust into a Swiss bank vault to retake gold deposited there by Jews on the run from the Nazis. Impossible to pronounce judgement on a picture that was never made, of course, but given Ratner's past form – *Red Dragon* (2002) – and subsequent form – *X-Men: The Last Stand* (2006) – it seems unlikely Connery or we missed out on much.

What we have missed out on are the Connery memoirs. These last, indeed, were the reason he gave for having quit Ratner's project in the autumn of 2004. Although for years Connery had maintained that he would never write his life story, a couple of months earlier he had accepted a £1 million advance for the British and Commonwealth rights to the projected book. With American and European rights still to be sold, Connery was set to bank around £2 million for his story.* Thus far at least, the book has not been written, and Connery has returned his initial advance to the publisher HarperCollins.

Along the way, he asked first one then another ghost-writer to help him cuff his thoughts and memories into shape. The first of these was Meg Henderson, a Glasgow-born journalist and novelist whom Connery had befriended in the mid-eighties through charitable connections – but who was less than charitable about him after claiming that 'the deal he offered me wasn't viable'.[21] Nor, one suspects, was it meant to be. Given the money on the table, neither Connery nor his publisher could afford to take any chances on the project. Accordingly, Hunter Davies – who was having a big success that year with *Gazza*, the pull-no-punches 'autobiography' of the troubled footballer Paul Gascoigne – was hired for the project. Davies wanted, he said, to write a 'warts and all' life story.[22]

---

* A tidy sum for a writer, though peanuts next to the $17.5 million Connery would have got for 'Josiah's Canon'.

It wasn't to be. Six months later Connery pulled the plug on the project, a decision that cost him what he later called 'a stonking amount of money'.[23] The Fleet Street rumour mill, never kind to Connery because of his unwillingness to grant lengthy interviews, whirred into life. Soon enough, journalistic innuendo would have had you believe that the book had foundered because of Connery's refusal to talk about Diane Cilento's by then forty-year-old – though oft-repeated – claim that their marriage had been a violent one. Now that innuendo might, of course, have been bang on target. But even allowing that it was, even allowing that Connery did not want to write about his first marriage (he had, after all, always refused to talk about it), it does not follow that he had done what Cilento claimed.

Which doesn't mean that Connery, as so often in his life, couldn't have made things easier for himself. A denial of Cilento's claims would be in no way actionable. No court in the land could settle a case that came down to one person's word against the other. Connery would have done better, in other words, to go into print with his side of the story. The fact that he chose not to surely means there is no reason to doubt his own claim – that he abandoned the memoir simply because he 'can't be bothered'.[24]

Nor, despite all the rumours, could he be bothered to play father to Harrison Ford once again in *Indiana Jones and the Kingdom of the Crystal Skull* (2008). Which is a shame, not because Spielberg's fourth Indy picture turned out a masterpiece but simply because as things stand *The League of Extraordinary Gentlemen* is the last entry on the Connery CV.

But only in movies and books must you quit while you're ahead. In life proper there are always plenty of reasons for quitting while things aren't going your way. And it would take a more fanciful storyteller than this one to suggest that things haven't generally gone Sean Connery's way. Yes, over the past couple of years he has finally begun to look like a man approaching 80. But despite an operation in 2006 for what turned out to be a benign kidney tumour and those throat problems of the early nineties, Connery continues to look in rude health.

So too his finances. According to the 2009 Sunday Times Rich List, Connery remains the wealthiest British actor in his own right. It is true that at £80 million his fortune shrunk by £5 million during the preceding year, but his ranking rose by 230 places.[*] Given what happened on world stock markets during 2008, I think we can conclude that Connery is a pretty canny investor. Otherwise, what strikes you most about Connery is his sheer down-to-earth ordinariness. Unlike so many movie stars, he is not a man who thinks of his private life in dramatic terms, he is not a man permanently 'on' for some imaginary camera or other.

Essentially, he is a man who has sought the freedom – for which read the money – to be able to play golf whenever he chooses. After what became an unhappy first marriage, he found contentment with a second wife who has never conceived of herself as in competition with him. Amen to that, though given the lumpy disappointments of so much of his subsequent work, it may be that Connery – like so many men entering middle age – ceased to be in competition with himself, too. *The Offence*, for all its faults, was a bold attempt at finding a new direction, and it is a shame that Connery let its failure at the box office hurry him into silence.

'There was a time when I had to prostitute myself to pay the bills,' he once said. 'The Bond films ended that.'[25] Alas, they ended other things too, chief among them the idea that the movies might be a suitable vehicle for properly adult entertainment. Because love Connery in the Bonds though we do, there is no gainsaying the fact that that series has been an entirely malign influence on popular cinema. History isn't made up of straight lines, and the confluences of those lines are never entirely clear. But at least part of the blame for the post-seventies infantilisation of the cinema can be lain at the door of the Bond series. And since, as I have argued, there would

[*] From 924th to 694th.

have been no series without him, it follows that Connery is, if not entirely culpable, then at least partly responsible for the premature death of the movies. Impossible in these twilight years not to see Connery as an actor destroyed by the tradition he himself created. What a Baron Frankenstein he might have made . . .

All of which said, and beyond the deathly yet undying impact of his Bonds (several of which are on digitally doctored cinematic re-release as I write), Connery has his name on four indisputably great pictures – *Marnie*, *The Man Who Would Be King*, *Robin and Marian* and *The Russia House*. Not many, you say? Maybe so, but Humphrey Bogart (a similarly exemplary role model for generations of men) had only one more – *The Maltese Falcon* (1941), *To Have and Have Not* (1944), *The Big Sleep* (1946), *The Treasure of the Sierra Madre** (1948) and *In a Lonely Place* (1950) – and John Wayne one less – *Red River* (1948), *The Searchers* (1956) and *Rio Bravo* (1959). Movie careers are tough to get going, but they are tougher to sustain – and tougher still when, like Sean Connery, you are working outside the tutelary confines of the studio system.

All popular artists are on the hunt for two audiences – the faithful followers (who need to be kept sweet) and the easy-come, easy-go hangers-on (who need to be kept on their toes). The popular artist must keep faith with the first group while breaking new ground for the second. Occasionally, he or she can do both – Sinatra with *Songs for Swingin' Lovers* or *Only the Lonely*, Clint Eastwood with *Unforgiven* (1992) or *Thunderbolt and Lightfoot* (1974) – but mostly it is an either/or situation. Certainly Sean Connery has never found an easy passage between that particular Scylla and Charybdis. Trying to please the faithful, he has served up the likes of *Never Say Never Again* and *The League of Extraordinary Gentlemen*. Trying to please the hangers-on, he has given us pictures like *Zardoz* and *The Offence*. Much to his chagrin, the twain met and

---

* How one would love to see Connery in the Walter Huston role in a remake of that movie.

meet only at screenings of the early Bonds.

Thankfully, Connery – whom Steven Spielberg once thought of casting as Aristotle in a movie about Alexander the Great[26] – is philosophical about the shape his career has taken. 'I can honestly never tell what any film is really going to be like,' he has said. 'I look at the script, the director and the circumstances, and hope people will like what I do. But beyond that, so many things can happen. So many things can go wrong. I have found that this entire business has been a very tough university for me.'[27] It is hard to argue with that description of the chaotic matrix that is the world of movie making. The miracle of the movies is that any actor, any director, ever manages to make anything meaningful.

'I have no illusions,' Connery told a more than usually probing interviewer, 'that anything I'm going to do will give me this completeness that you're implying I'm in search of.'[28] But we are all in search of such completeness – and at least occasionally and momentarily we find it by gazing at certain movie stars. For the essential function of the movie star is to body forth to the world a (doubtless chimerical) vision of a unified self on to which can be projected a million and one atomised fantasies. Not since the days of Bogart and Cary Grant, of Bette Davis and Katharine Hepburn has anyone fulfilled that function as frequently and as potently as Sean Connery. Maybe he really does have no illusions. We should be thankful, though, that for almost half a century now, he has granted us so many of our own.

Acknowledgements

This book was the brainchild of Walter Donohue at Faber and Faber, a man who has seen more movies than anyone I know and somehow kept a level head. I want to thank him for the basic idea, for toning down some of my more empurpled prose, and for helping me steer the book to somewhere near the port we'd agreed on. Thanks also to Anne Owen at Faber and Faber and my copy-editor, Trevor Horwood, for piloting me through the final stretch.

I can't say I was surprised that few people were willing to talk about having worked or dealt with Connery, but I am grateful that many of the people who did agree to meet me were around in the important early years. Requests for anonymity have been respected, but I can still give a big thank you to Alvin Rakoff, Michael Foot, John Boorman and Julie Hamilton.

My friend Sinclair McKay, the author of a book on the Bond movie phenomenon with whose every opinion I pretty much disagree, was a constant source of inspiration and humour. Andrew Rissik, the author of a now quarter-century-old study of Connery's work, helped out with ideas, memories, tape recordings of interviews and a faith in the idea that people are not necessarily slumming it when they talk about the movies. David Thomson, the finest critic the cinema has yet had, was an example and mentor throughout.

The staffs of the London Library, the British Film Institute Library, the Victoria and Albert Museum's Theatre and Performance archives and Kensington Central Library were all unfailingly helpful.

For affording me research facilities and opportunities well beyond the call of duty, I owe a special thanks to my friend Andrew Davies.

Sharon Kemp sat through more screenings of *Diamonds Are Forever* than anyone remotely sane should have to. My parents helped out with recordings of several movies unavailable to those of us who won't pay for more television than is available through the licence fee.

The book is dedicated to the memory of my father, David Bray, who died as I was cuffing the final edit into shape. The reader may remember that we began in 1971 with my father telling my nine-year-old self that Sean Connery was a 'has-been'. I am glad to say that, like so many people, he modified that opinion over the years.

Christopher Bray
Blackheath, May 2010

Notes

Introduction

1. *New Yorker*, 12 June 1989. Reprinted in Pauline Kael, *Movie Love* (Plume, 1991), p. 145.
2. Zoë Heller, 'Great Scot', *Vanity Fair*, June 1993.
3. Kael, op. cit.
4. See the *Radio Times*, 19–25 July 2008, and the *Guardian*'s G2 section, 16 July 2008.

1 On the Road

1. George Perry, 'Why Connery Said Yes Again', *Sunday Times*, 8 November 1983.
2. William McIlvanney, 'The Big Man', *Sunday Times*, 11 August 1996.
3. *Sean Connery: A Profile*, Channel 4, 30 December 1994.
4. J. D. Salinger, *The Catcher in the Rye* (Penguin, 1958), p. 5.
5. Lineages are hard to trace in Ireland, alas, because so many records were lost in the civil war.
6. Sean Connery (with Murray Grigor), *Being a Scot* (Weidenfeld & Nicolson, 2008), p. 14.
7. Edwin Muir, *Scottish Journey* (Mainstream, 1979 (originally published in 1935)), p. 9.
8. Diane Cilento, *My Nine Lives* (Viking, 2006), p. 161.
9. Speech of 22 November 1932, quoted in Richard J. Finlay, *Modern Scotland 1914–2000* (Profile, 2004), p. 73.
10. Connery, op. cit., p. 13.
11. David Lewin, *Playboy*, November 1965.
12. Ibid.
13. Connery, op. cit., p. 14.

14. 'The Other World of James Bond', *Sunday Express*, 8 August 1965.

15. *Sean Connery: Close-Up*, ITV, 1 January 1999.

16. Cilento, op. cit., p. 235.

17. Philip Thomas, 'Bad Medicine', *Empire*, June 1992.

18. Quoted in John Hunter, *Great Scot* (Bloomsbury, 1993), p. 25.

19. *Daily Mail*, 22 November 2005.

20. 'The Other World of James Bond', *Sunday Express*, 8 August 1965.

21. Michael Feeney Callan, *Sean Connery*, revised edition (Virgin, 2002), p. 39.

22. Henry Gris and Sheldon Lane, 'The Man Who's Got 007's Number', in Sheldon Lane (ed.), *For Bond Lovers Only* (Dell, 1965), pp. 138–9.

23. Cilento, op. cit., pp. 137–8.

24. 'The Other World of James Bond', *Sunday Express*, 8 August 1965.

25. Gordon Gow, 'A Secretive Person', *Films and Filming*, March 1974.

26. Kenneth Passingham, *Sean Connery* (Sidgwick & Jackson, 1983), p. 21.

27. Leonard Mosley, 'Mr Kisskiss Bangbang', *New York Times*, 22 November 1964.

28. Former art student Hilary Buchanan, quoted in the *Scotsman*, 22 August 2003.

29. David Lewin, 'Sean Connery', in Peter Tipthorp (ed.), *James Bond in Thunderball* (Sackville, 1965), unpaginated.

30. Colin Dangaard, 'Connery', *Photoplay*, January 1984.

31. Connery, op. cit., p. 8.

32. Muir, op. cit., p. 30.

33. Robert Sellers, *Sean Connery: A Celebration* (Robert Hale, 1999), p. 27.

34. *Health and Strength*, vol. 82, no. 5 (5 March 1953).

35. Clive James, *Flying Visits* (Jonathan Cape, 1984), p. 94.

36. Ethan Morden, *Rodgers and Hammerstein* (Abrams, 1992), p. 117.

37. Callan, op. cit., p. 56.

38. Gow, op. cit.

39. Hunter, op. cit., p. 41.

40. Zoë Heller, 'Great Scot', *Vanity Fair*, June 1993.

41. Andrew Rissik, *The James Bond Man: The Films of Sean Connery* (Elm Tree, 1983), p. 5.

42. Mark Cousins, 'Kiss Kiss, Bang Bang', *Scotsman*, 3 May 1997.

43. Rissik, op. cit.

44. Callan, op. cit., p. 61.

45. Ibid.

46. Op. cit. Sellers, p. 28.

47. Since there has been so much confusion about the exact timings of Connery's *South Pacific* tour, here's an (I suspect incomplete) list of its various opening dates: *1953*: 5 October: Streatham Hill; 19 October: Golders Green Hippodrome; 3 November: Bristol Hippodrome; 24 November: Royal Court Liverpool (by which time he is playing Sergeant Kenneth Johnston); 15 December: Manchester Opera House; *1954*: 16 February: Aberdeen, Her Majesty's; 18 May: Coventry Hippodrome; 7 June: Leeds Grand; 2 August: Bristol, Theatre Royal; *1955*: 24 January: Stratford; 7 February: Streatham Hill; 21 February: Golders Green Hippodrome; 14 March: Coventry Theatre; 18 April: Blackpool Opera House; 16 May: Leeds Grand; 11 July: Birmingham; 8 August: Cardiff New Theatre; 29 August: Leicester Palace; 12 September: Plymouth Palace.

2 Treading the Boards

1. Quoted in Michael Feeney Callan, *Sean Connery*, revised edition (Virgin, 2002), p. 67.
2. Colin Dangaard, 'Connery', *Photoplay*, January 1984.
3. Julie Hamilton's own description of herself, in conversation with the author, 26 July 2007. Unless noted, all subsequent Hamilton quotes derive from this interview.
4. Alas, I can find no record of this show's broadcast.
5. Broadcast 21 August 1956.
6. Alvin Rakoff, private interview, 23 June 2007. Unless noted, all subsequent Rakoff quotes derive from this interview.
7. 'Tough and Taut', *News Chronicle*, 1 April 1957.
8. 'Mr Rakoff Knocks Out ITV', *Evening Standard*, 1 April 1957.
9. *Daily Echo*, 1 April 1957.
10. 'Sean Was a Knock-Out!', *Daily Mirror*, 1 April 1957.
11. 'Twilight of a Prize Fighter', *The Stage*, 4 April 1957.
12. Peter Black, 'Here Was a Summerskillian Sermon', *Daily Mail*, 1 April 1957.
13. Elizabeth Cowley, 'Slept in Coffins to Keep Fit', *Reveille*, 25 March 1957.
14. May 1957, p. 4.
15. See particularly Geoffrey Wansell, 'Connery the Monster', *Daily Mail*, 13 May 2000.
16. Included in the DVD *Hollywood Screen Tests Take 1* (Image Entertainment, 2002).
17. *Sean Connery: Profile*, BBC 1, 22 December 1981.
18. Kurt Loder, 'Great Scot', *Rolling Stone*, 27 October 1983.

Notes

3 Diane

1. Diane Cilento, *My Nine Lives* (Viking, 2006), p. 124.
2. Donald Seaman, 'I Throw a Tantrum', *Daily Express*, 5 April 1957.
3. Tony Richardson, *Long Distance Runner: A Memoir* (Faber, 1993), p. 102.
4. Ibid., pp. 102–3.
5. *Brits Go to Hollywood*, Channel 4, 22 November 2003.
6. 'Male Bonding', *Premiere*, August 1994.
7. Zoë Heller, 'Great Scot', *Vanity Fair*, June 1993.
8. Gordon Gow, 'A Secretive Person', *Films and Filming*, March 1974.
9. 'Cicely Floored 007 to Teach Him to Talk', *Daily Mail*, 1 June 1965.
10. Kenneth Passingham, *Sean Connery* (Sidgwick & Jackson, 1983), p. 54.
11. Richardson, op. cit., p. 103. John Osborne, incidentally, remembers that he and Penelope Gilliat would hear what he calls 'athletic agony' coming from the bedroom Richardson and Cilento shared during the 1960 Acapulco Film Festival. See Osborne, *Almost a Gentleman: An Autobiography: 1955–1966* (Faber, 1991), p. 183, and Cilento, op. cit., p. 236.
12. www.australianbiography.gov.au/cilento
13. Lana Turner, *Lana – the Lady, the Legend, the Truth* (New English Library, 1983), p. 117.
14. William McIlvanney, 'You Only Live Once', *Scotland on Sunday*, 17 August 2008.
15. Ibid.
16. Ibid.
17. *Sean Connery Talks to Gloria Hunniford*, ITV, 6 January 1984.
18. *Edinburgh Evening News*, 12 October 1959.
19. Geoffrey Macnab, 'Before Bond', *Sight and Sound*, June 1992.
20. Bill Hagerty, 'Carry On, Connery', *Daily Mirror*, 6 June 1974.
21. Oriana Fallaci, *Limelighters* (Michael Joseph, 1967), p. 223.
22. Cilento, op. cit., p. 137.
23. *The Times*, 2 November 1960.
24. Michael Feeney Callan, *Sean Connery*, revised edition (Virgin, 2002), p. 99.
25. *The Times*, 13 June 1961.
26. *The Times*, 4 November 1961.
27. Pete Hamill, 'Bottled in Bond', *Saturday Evening Post*, 6 June 1964.
28. The memo is shown in close-up in the documentary extra 'Inside *Dr No*' on the *Dr No* DVD (1999).

4 Bondage

1. Andrew Lycett, *Ian Fleming* (Weidenfeld & Nicolson, 1995), p. 393.
2. John Cork and Bruce Scivally, *James Bond: The Legacy* (Boxtree, 2002), p. 46.
3. The final charge-sheet came in at $950,000. See Alexander Walker, *Hollywood UK: The British Film Industry in the Sixties* (Stein and Day, 1974), pp. 186–9.
4. Cubby Broccoli (with Donald Zec), *When the Snow Melts: The Autobiography of Cubby Broccoli* (Boxtree, 1998), p. 164.
5. Ibid., p. 165.
6. Andrew Rissik, *The James Bond Man: The Films of Sean Connery* (Elm Tree, 1983), p. 29.
7. Ibid., p. 28.
8. 'Male Bonding', *Premiere*, August 1994.
9. *Brits Go to Hollywood*, Channel 4, 22 November 2003.
10. 'Male Bonding', *Premiere*, August 1994.
11. Henry Gris and Sheldon Lane, 'The Man Who's Got 007's Number', in Sheldon Lane (ed.), *For Bond Lovers Only* (Dell, 1965), p. 142.
12. Pete Hamill, 'Bottled in Bond', *Saturday Evening Post*, 6 June 1964.
13. Walker, op. cit., p. 187.
14. Leonard Mosley, 'Mr Kisskiss Bangbang', *New York Times*, 22 November 1964.
15. David Lewin, 'Sean Connery', in Peter Tipthorp (ed.), *James Bond in Thunderball* (Sackville, 1965), unpaginated.
16. Kurt Loder, 'Great Scot', *Rolling Stone*, 27 October 1983.
17. See the 'Inside *Dr No*' documentary on the *Dr No* DVD (1999).
18. Robert Sellers, *The Battle for Bond* (Tomahawk Press, 2007), p. 56.
19. Rakoff, in conversation with the author, 18 June 2007.
20. Hamill, op. cit.
21. Susan Barnes, 'Women and Me – by the Screen's James Bond', *Sunday Express*, 31 December 1961.
22. *Sunday Mail*, 18 May 1969.
23. Joan Collins, 'The Day I Said No to James Bond', *Sunday Telegraph*, 18 May 2008.
24. Michael Winner, *Winner Takes All: A Life of Sorts* (Robson, 2004), p. 84. The part eventually went to Alfred Lynch, to whom Connery had played second fiddle in *On the Fiddle*. Winner's producer, Daniel Angel, told Winner: 'Another B-picture actor! No one will ever be interested in Sean Connery.'

25. *The Times*, 4 May 1962.

26. *Illustrated London News*, 7 July 1962.

27. 'Brittle Essay on the Sex War', *The Times*, 21 June 1962.

28. Michael Feeney Callan, *Sean Connery*, revised edition (Virgin, 2002), p. 104.

29. Rissik, op. cit., p. 4.

30. *The Times*, 5 October 1962.

31. Walker, op. cit., p. 189.

32. Ibid.

33. Broccoli, op. cit., p. 177.

34. Shelley Winters, *The Middle of My Century* (Muller, 1990), pp. 454, 456.

5 Behind the Mask

1. Diane Cilento, *My Nine Lives* (Viking, 2006), p. 183, for quotes in this paragraph.

2. Tony Richardson, *Long Distance Runner: A Memoir* (Faber, 1993), p. 128.

3. *Daily Mail*, 2 December 1962.

4. *Daily Telegraph*, 1 December 1962.

5. Cilento, op. cit., p. 203.

6. Edwin Muir, *Scottish Journey* (Mainstream, 1979 (originally published in 1935)), p. 26.

7. Roderick Mann, 'There's not Much of Bond in Me, Says Mr. Connery', *Sunday Express*, 28 October 1962.

8. *Time*, 17 May 1963.

9. John Philp, 'Agent 007 Says Hello, Mum!', *Scottish Daily Mail*, 1 July 1963.

10. Interview with Tom Hutchinson, *Guardian*, 28 December 1971.

11. Andrew Rissik, *The James Bond Man: The Films of Sean Connery* (Elm Tree, 1983), p. 93.

12. Helen Mason, 'Mouth Cut as Connery Lets Fly in Film', *Sunday Express*, 25 August 1963.

13. *Woman of Straw* press book.

14. *Sunday Express*, 27 October 1963.

15. Ibid.

16. *Sunday Express*, 19 April 1964.

17. Pete Hamill, 'Bottled in Bond', *Saturday Evening Post*, 6 June 1964.

18. Patrick McGilligan, *Hitchcock: A Life in Darkness and Light* (Wiley, 2003), p. 642.

19. Robin Wood, *Hitchcock's Films Revisited*, revised edition (Columbia University Press, 2002), p. 188.

20. Ibid., p. 186.

21. Raymond Durgnat, *The Strange Case of Alfred Hitchcock* (Faber, 1974), p. 352.

22. François Truffaut, *Hitchcock* (Secker & Warburg, 1968), p. 252.

23. See 'The Trouble with Marnie' on the *Marnie* DVD extras.

24. Ibid.

25. Rissik, op. cit., p. 98.

26. Durgnat, op. cit., p. 353.

27. The loci classici of which are still the various sections on the film in Robin Wood's *Hitchcock's Films Revisited* (see n. 19 above).

28. Gordon Gow, 'A Secretive Person', *Films and Filming*, March 1974.

29. Truffaut, op. cit., p. 253.

30. Barry Norman, 'My Terms for Staying . . . by 007 James Bond', *Daily Mail*, 8 February 1964.

31. www.australianbiography.gov.au/cilento

32. I am indebted to my friend Sinclair McKay for the information that it was Guy Hamilton who invented the tetchy relations between Bond and Q. See his *The Man with the Golden Touch* (Aurum, 2008), p. 66.

33. Penelope Houston, '007', *Sight and Sound*, Winter 1964–5.

34. *Evening Standard*, 30 October 1964.

35. Brian McFarlane, *An Autobiography of British Cinema* (Methuen, 1997), p. 274.

36. Nina Hibbin, 'No, James Bond Is not "Fun" – He's Just Sick', *Daily Worker*, 12 October 1963.

37. J. Hoberman, 'Dr No not Dr Strangelove', *Sight and Sound*, December 1993.

38. Laura Mulvey, 'Visual Pleasure and Narrative Cinema', *Screen*, vol. 16, no. 3 (Autumn 1975).

39. 'Bondomania', *Time*, 11 June 1965.

40. Kenneth Passingham, *Sean Connery* (Sidgwick & Jackson, 1983), p. 76.

41. Rissik, op. cit., p. 92.

42. *Evening Standard*, 30 October 1964.

43. *Time*, 22 October 1965.

44. David Lewin, 'Sean Connery', in Peter Tipthorp (ed.), *James Bond in Thunderball* (Sackville, 1965), unpaginated.

6 A Not So Fine Madness

1. *Evening Standard*, 30 October 1964.
2. Unless noted, quotes in this and the next three paragraphs are from Diane Cilento, *My Nine Lives* (Viking, 2006), pp. 218, 228, 234, 238 and 239.
3. Victor Davis, 'The Dark Side of Sean Connery', *Mail on Sunday*, 17 April 1994.
4. Interview with David Lewin, *Playboy*, November 1965.
5. Zoë Heller, 'Great Scot', *Vanity Fair*, June 1993.
6. Kingsley Amis, *The James Bond Dossier* (Jonathan Cape, 1965), p. 14.
7. Ibid., p. 17.
8. Nigel Andrew, 'A Pin-Up Who Acts His Age', *Financial Times*, 6 April 1991.
9. Pete Hamill, 'Bottled in Bond', *Saturday Evening Post*, 6 June 1964.
10. Roderick Mann, '007 Hits the Trail for the Wild West', *Sunday Express*, 30 July 1967.
11. *Daily Express*, 17 March 1965; *Daily Sketch*, 7 April 1965.
12. Cilento, op. cit., p. 246.
13. *Daily Mail*, 15 April 1965.
14. Ken Adam, telephone interview with the author, February 2008.
15. Gill Pringle, 'Sean's Story', *Midweek*, 16 April 1999.
16. Lewin, *Playboy*, op. cit.
17. Ibid.
18. Quoted in the *New Yorker*, 20 March 1965.
19. In real-money terms.
20. Lewin, *Playboy*, op. cit.
21. David Lewin, 'Sean Connery', in Peter Tipthorp (ed.), *James Bond in Thunderball* (Sackville, 1965), unpaginated.
22. *Daily Mail*, 1 July 1965.
23. Lindsay Mackie, *Glasgow Herald*, 17 December 1983.
24. *Time*, 14 January 1966. By 1969, incidentally, he had dropped to sixteenth.
25. 'Now Bond Is Going Solo', *Daily Sketch*, 26 February 1966.
26. Andrew Rissik, *The James Bond Man: The Films of Sean Connery* (Elm Tree, 1983), pp. 104, 105.
27. *Daily Express*, 21 July 1966.
28. David Lewin, 'Power, Money, Freedom and the Change in Connery at 35', *Daily Mail*, 26 July 1966.
29. 'Oh, Oh, 7!: Thieves in the Night at Bond Home', *Evening News*, 2 April 1965.

30. 'Sean Connery's Home Raided', *Daily Telegraph*, 3 April 1965.

31. Harriet Lane Fox, '"Filthy Old House" For Sale', *Sunday Telegraph*, 18 November 2001.

32. Cilento, op. cit., p. 234.

33. crawleyscastingcalls.com/index.php?option=com_movies&Itemid=67&id=7&lettre=BOND

34. Lewin, 'Power, Money, Freedom and the Change in Connery at 35', *Daily Mail*, 26 July 1966.

35. 'James Bond's New Role – A Village Poet', *Evening News*, 13 October 1965.

36. Jack Bentley, 'Wanted: A New James Bond', *Sunday Mirror*, 18 June 1967.

37. *Daily Mail*, 25 July 1967.

38. Gordon Gow, 'A Secretive Person', *Films and Filming*, March 1974.

39. *Sean Connery Talks to Gloria Hunniford*, ITV, 6 January 1984.

40. Peter Evans, 'The Man Who Just Has to Escape from James Bond', *Daily Express*, 15 July 1966.

41. Roderick Mann, 'There's Not Much of Bond in Me, Says Mr Connery', *Sunday Express*, 28 October 1962.

42. Bentley, op. cit.

43. Simon Winder, *The Man Who Saved Britain: A Personal Journey into the Disturbing World of James Bond* (Picador, 2006).

44. Frank R. Cunningham, *Sidney Lumet* (University Press of Kentucky, 2001), p. 210.

45. Ben Fong-Torres, 'Connery, Sean Connery', *American Film*, May 1989.

46. Gow, op. cit.

7 Intermission

1. Cyril Aynsley, 'James Bond Steps In to Urge Home Rule for Scotland', *Daily Express*, 2 March 1967.

2. 'Seriously, Sean Could Become Mr Connery, MP', *Daily Sketch*, 30 December 1968.

3. 'Sean Connery in "Stop Egypt" Demand', *Daily Telegraph*, 27 May 1967. Among the other signatories were the directors Jack Clayton and Karel Reisz and the writers Chaim Bermant, Lionel Davidson, John Gross, Dan Jacobson, Jonathan Miller and Mordechai Richler.

4. Fidelma Cook, 'Home Is Where the Heart Is', *Mail on Sunday*, 28 March 1999.

5. Diane Cilento, *My Nine Lives* (Viking, 2006), p. 235.

6. Ibid. Connery himself says he has never taken anything stronger than the odd joint. See Cook, 'Home Is Where the Heart Is'.

7. Cary Grant, 'Archie Leach', *Ladies' Home Journal*, three issues: January/February, March and April 1963.

8. Cilento, op. cit.

9. Telephone conversation with the author, 10 January 2008.

10. Karin Goodwin, 'LSD Guru Foiled 1960s Drug Plot', *Sunday Times*, 8 October 2006.

11. Quoted in Charles Rycroft, *Reich* (Fontana, 1971), p. 102.

12. Michael Feeney Callan, *Sean Connery*, revised edition (Virgin, 2002), p. 177.

13. Lindsay Anderson, *The Diaries* (Methuen, 2004), p. 102.

14. On 18 July 1967.

15. Just as in Antonioni's *Blow-Up*, David Hemmings ended up playing the part.

16. '007 May Star as Bothwell in Film Epic', *Daily Mail*, 19 April 1967.

17. Oriana Fallaci, *Limelighters* (trans. Pamela Swinglehurst) (Michael Joseph, 1967), p. 214.

18. *Daily Express*, 9 May 1967.

19. Cilento, op. cit., p. 236.

20. 'The Dark Side of Sean Connery', *Mail on Sunday*, 17 April 1994.

21. *New Yorker*, 16 November 1968.

22. Quoted in John Hunter, *Great Scot* (Bloomsbury, 1993), p. 113.

23. *New Yorker*, 7 February 1970. Reprinted in Pauline Kael, *Deeper into Movies* (Caldar & Boyars, 1975), p. 103.

24. Gordon Gow, 'A Secretive Person', *Films and Filming*, March 1974.

25. Ibid.

26. *Daily Mail*, 27 September 1968.

27. See 'Inside *On Her Majesty's Secret Service*' on the special-edition DVD of *On Her Majesty's Secret Service*.

28. A month after its broadcast in America.

29. 'How 007 Connery Visited Russia and Made His "Worst Entrance and Best Exit" Ever', *Daily Express*, 19 April 1969.

30. Cilento, op. cit., p. 266. See also *Different Drummer: The Life of Kenneth Macmillan* (Faber and Faber, 2009), p. 223.

31. *Daily Mail*, 25 November 1969.

32. *Daily Telegraph*, 17 December 1969.

33. J. C. Trewin, *Illustrated London News*, 27 December 1969.

8 You've Had Your Six

1. Lindsay Anderson, *The Diaries* (Methuen, 2004), p. 202.
2. Tom Hutchinson, unheadlined interview with Connery, *Guardian*, 28 December 1971.
3. 'The Gilt Edged Bond', *Observer*, 16 January 1972.
4. David Picker talking on *Brits Go to Hollywood*, Channel 4, 22 November 2003. Earlier in the show he delivers himself of the opinion, 'I don't think they [Saltzman and Broccoli] took care of Sean.'
5. See 'Inside *Diamonds Are Forever*' on the special-edition DVD.
6. Roderick Mann, '007 Hits the Trail for the Wild West', *Sunday Express*, 30 July 1967.
7. Michael Cable, 'Look What Ten Years Have Done to 007', *Daily Mail*, 12 April 1971.
8. Cubby Broccoli (with Donald Zec), *When the Snow Melts: The Autobiography of Cubby Broccoli* (Boxtree, 1998), p. 221.
9. Jack Bentley, 'Wanted: A New James Bond', *Sunday Mirror*, 18 June 1967.
10. Robert Ottaway, unheadlined interview with Connery, *TV Times*, 10 August 1972.
11. Micheline Roquebrune talking in *Sean Connery: Close Up*, ITV, 1992.
12. Diane K. Shah, 'It's a Wonderful Life', *Empire*, October 1989.
13. *Sunday Telegraph*, 2 January 1972.
14. Michael Feeney Callan, *Sean Connery*, revised edition (Virgin, 2002), p. 181.
15. Connery interviewed by Sheridan Morley for the BBC. Transmission date not known. Interview available on the special-edition DVD of *Diamonds Are Forever*.
16. In Jay McInerney et al., *Dressed to Kill: James Bond – The Suited Hero* (Flammarion, 1996), p. 11.
17. *Sun*, 17 December 1971.
18. crawleyscastingcalls.com/index.php?option=com_movies&Itemid=67&id=10&lettre=BOND
19. *Sunday Telegraph*, 2 January 1972.
20. Hutchinson, op. cit.

9 Bergman in Bracknell

1. Robert Ottaway, unheadlined interview with Connery, *TV Times*, 10 August 1972.
2. Andrew Sarris, *The American Cinema: Directors and Directions 1929–1968*

(E. P. Dutton, 1968), p. 197.

3. Lindsay Mackie, 'The Battle Behind the Scenes Before the Comeback', *Glasgow Herald*, 7 December 1983.

4. Quoted in Andrew Rissik, *The James Bond Man: The Films of Sean Connery* (Elm Tree, 1983), p. 113.

5. Gordon Gow, 'A Secretive Person', *Films and Filming*, March 1974.

6. Tom Hutchinson, unheadlined interview with Connery, *Guardian*, 28 December 1971.

7. Sydney Edwards, 'Connery: Discovering the Truth . . .', *Evening Standard*, 24 March 1972.

8. Ibid.

9. Gow, op. cit.

10. Benedict Nightingale, 'Bottled in Bond, He's Vintage Connery', *New York Times*, 13 June 1987.

11. 'Licensed to Quack!', *Daily Mail*, 1 March 1973.

12. On page 209 of his memoir, *Adventures of a Suburban Boy* (Faber, 2003), Boorman remembers paying Connery only $100,000. He gives the higher figure on the commentary to the Region 1 DVD release of *Zardoz*, from which all subsequent quotes regarding *Zardoz* in this chapter are taken.

10 Other Times, Other Places

1. Quoted in Andrew Rissik, *The James Bond Man: The Films of Sean Connery* (Elm Tree, 1983), p. 139.

2. *Empire*, June 2004.

3. *Spectator*, 5 July 1975.

4. Russell Davies, 'The Sheikh from Scotland', *Observer*, 29 June 1975.

5. *Empire*, June 2004.

6. Benedict Nightingale, 'Bottled in Bond, He's Vintage Connery', *New York Times*, 13 June 1987.

7. John Boorman, *Adventures of a Suburban Boy* (Faber, 2003), p. 209.

8. Roderick Mann, 'What Sean Does in a Room Above the Bank', *Sunday Express*, 30 September 1973.

9. William Hall, 'Why I Had to Quit Britain', *Evening News*, 15 March 1975.

10. Mann, op. cit.

11. Rissik, op. cit., p. 143.

12. *Rolling Stone*, 19 February 1981; reprinted in Robert Emmet Long (ed.), *John Huston Interviews* (University of Mississippi Press, 2001), p. 104.

13. Lawrence Grobel, *The Hustons* (Bloomsbury, 1990), p. 705.

14. Mark Cousins, 'King of the Hill', *Sight and Sound*, May 1997.

15. Neil Sinyard, 'Heroic Irony', *Films Illustrated*, October 1981.

16. Oriana Fallaci, *Limelighters* (trans. Pamela Swinglehurst) (Michael Joseph, 1967), p. 216.

17. Ibid., p. 213.

18. *New Yorker*, 22 March 1976.

19. Hugh Herbert, 'The Canny Hero', *Guardian*, 5 December 1983.

11 Cast Adrift

1. Lindsay Mackie, 'The Battle Behind the Scenes Before the Comeback', *Glasgow Herald*, 7 December 1983.

2. Robert Ottaway, unheadlined interview with Connery, *TV Times*, 10 August 1972.

3. Ben Fong-Torres, 'Connery. Sean Connery', *American Film*, May 1989.

4. Andrew Yule, *Sean Connery: Neither Shaken Nor Stirred* (Little, Brown, 1993), p. 214.

5. Ibid., p. 218.

6. William Hall, 'Why I Had to Quit Britain', *Evening News*, 15 March 1975.

7. Ibid.

8. Quoted in Andrew Rissik, *The James Bond Man: The Films of Sean Connery* (Elm Tree, 1983), p. 178.

9. *New Yorker*, 31 December 1979.

10. 'Profile: Sean Connery', BBC1, 22 December 1981.

11. *Empire*, June 1992.

12 No Time for Heroics

1. Robert Slater, *Ovitz: The Inside Story of Hollywood's Most Controversial Power-Broker* (McGraw-Hill, 1997), p. 94.

2. *Empire*, June 1992.

3. Lynn Hirschbert, 'Michael Ovitz Is On the Line', *New York Times*, 9 May 1999.

4. Slater, op. cit., p. 94.

5. Ibid.

6. *Brits Go to Hollywood*, Channel 4, 22 November 2003.

7. crawleyscastingcalls.com/index.php?option=com_actors&Itemid=56&id=638&lettre=C

8. Paul Donovan, 'Monster butler set for screen', *Daily Mail*, 16 July 1980.

9. Lesley White, '"Sexiest Man Alive" Is Glad to Be Grey', *Sunday Times*, 17 October 1993.

10, Lee Pfeiffer and Philip Lisa, *The Films of Sean Connery* (third edition) (Citadel Press, 2001), p. 194.

11. Michael Feeney Callan, *Sean Connery*, revised edition (Virgin, 2002), pp. 231–2.

12. Edmund Wilson, 'Kay Boyle & the *Saturday Evening Post*', *Classics and Commercials*, reprinted in Edmund Wilson, *Literary Essays of the 1930s and 40s* (Library of America, 2007), p. 576.

13. Neil Sinyard, 'Sean Connery: Star and Actor', British Film Institute programme notes, December 1983.

13 Never Say *Never Say Never Again* Again

1. Andrew Yule, *Sean Connery: Neither Shaken Nor Stirred* (Little, Brown, 1993), p. 264.

2. Lindsay Mackie, 'The Battle Behind the Scenes Before the Comeback', *Glasgow Herald*, 17 December 1983.

3. Robert Sellers, *The Battle for Bond* (Tomahawk Press, 2007), p. 202.

4. Margaret Hinxman, 'Connery Back to Bondage', *You Magazine*, *Mail on Sunday*, 21 November 1982.

5. Ibid.

6. Sellers, op. cit., p. 191.

7. Mackie, op. cit.

8. George Perry, 'Why Connery Said Yes Again', *Sunday Times Magazine*, 6 November 1983.

9. *Sunday Express*, 5 June 1983.

10. *Wall Street Journal*, 14 October 1983.

11. Ibid.

12. Sellers, op. cit., pp. 203, 198.

13. *Chicago Sun Times*, 7 October 1983.

14. Connery in live conversation with Ian Johnstone, 13 December 1983, National Film Theatre.

15. Perry, op. cit.

16. Ibid.

14 Mentor Man

1. '. . . That's What He Gets for a Week's Work', Hilary Bonner, *Mail on Sunday*, 6 March 1983.
2. thehollywoodinterview.blogspot.com/2008/09/christian-slater-hollywood-interview.html.
3. Benedict Nightingale, 'Bottled in Bond, He's Vintage Connery', *New York Times*, 7 June 1987.
4. Cameron Docherty, 'Connery: The Superstar as Perfectionist', *Scotsman*, 16 June 1990.
5. *New Yorker*, 29 June 1987.
6. Ben Fong-Torres, 'Connery. Sean Connery', *American Film*, May 1989.
7. Nightingale, op. cit.
8. Diane K. Shah, 'It's a Wonderful Life', *Empire*, October 1989.
9. Ibid.
10. Fong-Torres, op. cit.
11. Robert Scheer, 'Back in the USSR', *Premiere*, April 1990.
12. Pete Hamill, 'Bottled in Bond', *Saturday Evening Post*, 6 June 1964.

15 From Russia with Love

1. Michael Feeney Callan, *Sean Connery*, revised edition (Virgin, 2002), p. 264.
2. Sally Ogle Davis, 'Master of the Hunt', *Daily Mail*, 17 April 1990.
3. Ibid.
4. Footage available on YouTube.
5. Andrew Yule, *Sean Connery: Neither Shaken Nor Stirred* (Little, Brown, 1993), p. 341.
6. *Premiere*, February 1992.
7. Brian Pendreigh, 'A Secret Weapon, Brought in from the Cold', *Scotsman*, 19 June 1992.
8. *New Yorker*, 26 July 1993.

16 Loose Ends

1. 'Mr Connery Explains Lure of 007', *The Times*, 12 April 1971.
2. *Observer*, 25 May 1958.
3. The entire speech can be seen on YouTube.
4. Quoted in Robert Sellers, *Sean Connery: A Celebration* (Robert Hale, 1999), p. 131.

5. 'Answers Please: Sean Connery', *You Magazine*, *Mail on Sunday*, 6 August 1995.

6. Quoted in the press book to *Woman of Straw*.

7. Michael Feeney Callan, *Sean Connery*, revised edition (Virgin, 2002), p. 304.

8. Sellers, op. cit., p. 134.

9. *Goldfinger* DVD extras: radio interviews.

10. Susan Barnes, 'Women and Me – by the Screen's James Bond', *Sunday Express*, 31 December 1961.

11. Marianne Gray, 'Double-oh 68', *Evening Standard Magazine*, 1 July 1999.

12. William McIlvanney, 'The Big Man', *Sunday Times*, 11 August 1996.

13. Chris Hughes, 'Sean Doesn't Speak Spanish and Men Give Him a Hard Time', *Daily Mirror*, 30 July 1998.

14. Auslan Cramb and George Jones, 'Knighthood Snub Was Political, Says Connery', *Daily Telegraph*, 25 February 1998.

15. Tom Nairn on *Brits Go to Hollywood*, Channel 4, 22 November 2003.

16. Cramb and Jones, op. cit.

17. Fidelma Cook, 'Knighthood Snub for Connery', *Mail on Sunday*, 22 February 1998.

18. Benjamin Svetkey, 'Gentlemen's Disagreement', *Entertainment Weekly*, 22 November 2002.

19. George Rush and Joanna Molloy, 'Ornery Connery's "Extraordinary" Feud', *New York Daily News*, 2 July 2003.

20. Sam Ashurst, 'Why Alan Moore Hates Comic-Book Movies', *Total Film*, February 2009.

21. Meg Henderson, 'Sean, You've Let Me Down', *Daily Mail*, 4 November 2004.

22. Richard Brooks, 'Double "No" from 007 on Book Deal', *Sunday Times*, 20 March 2005.

23. 'Connery Fed Up with Hollywood Idiots', *Daily Mail*, 1 August 2005.

24. Ibid.

25. Margaret Hinxman, 'Connery Back to Bondage', *You Magazine*, *Mail on Sunday*, 21 November 1982.

26. George Perry, 'The Man Who Is King', *The Times*, 6 October 1990.

27. Garth Pearce, 'The Seven Ages of Sean', *Evening Standard*, 8 February 1990.

28. George Feifer, 'Hard Man behind the Tough Image', *Sunday Telegraph*, 12 April 1981.

Bibliography

Books

Amis, Kingsley, *The James Bond Dossier*, Jonathan Cape, 1965

Anderson, Lindsay, *The Diaries* (ed. Paul Sutton), Methuen, 2004

Appleyard, Bryan, *The Pleasures of Peace: Art and Imagination in Post-War Britain*, Faber and Faber, 1989

Arley, Catherine, *Woman of Straw*, Fontana, 1958

Armes, Roy, *A Critical History of the British Cinema*, Secker & Warburg, 1978

Baker, Nicholson, *U and I*, Granta, 1991

Bennett, Tony and Janet Woollacott, *Bond and Beyond: The Political Career of a Popular Hero*, Macmillan, 1987

Bernstein, George L., *The Myth of Decline: The Rise of Britain Since 1945*, Pimlico, 2004

Booker, Christopher, *The Neophiliacs: A Study of the Revolution in English Life in the Fifties and Sixties*, Collins, 1969

Boorman, John, *Adventures of a Suburban Boy*, Faber and Faber, 2003

Boyd, William, *A Good Man in Africa*, Hamish Hamilton, 1981

Boyt, Susie, *My Judy Garland Life*, Virago, 2008

Broccoli, Cubby with Donald Zec, *When the Snow Melts: The Autobiography of Cubby Broccoli*, Boxtree, 1998

Callan, Michael Feeney, *Sean Connery*, Virgin, 2003

Cannadine, David, *Class in Britain*, Penguin, 2000

— *History in Our Time*, Penguin, 2000

— *In Churchill's Shadow: Confronting the Past in Modern Britain*, Allen Lane, 2002

Caughie, John (ed.), *Theories of Authorship*, Routledge & Kegan Paul, 1981

Chapman, James, *Licence to Thrill: A Cultural History of the James Bond Films* (revised edition), I. B. Tauris, 2007

Cilento, Diane, *The Manipulator*, Hodder & Stoughton, 1967

— *My Nine Lives*, Viking, 2006

Bibliography

Clarke, Nick, *The Shadow of a Nation: The Changing Face of Britain*, Weidenfeld & Nicolson, 2003

Clarke, Peter, *Hope and Glory: Britain 1900–1990*, Allen Lane, 1996

Comentale, Edward P., Stephen Watt and Skip Willman (eds), *Ian Fleming and James Bond: The Cultural Politics of 007*, Indiana University Press, 2005

Connery, Sean with Murray Grigor, *Being a Scot*, Weidenfeld & Nicolson, 2008

Connolly, Ray (ed.), *In the Sixties*, Pavilion, 1995

Cook, Pam and Claire Hines, ' "Sean Connery Is James Bond": Re-fashioning British masculinity', in Rachel Moseley (ed.), *Dress, Culture, Identity*, British Film Institute, 2005

Cork, John and Bruce Scivally, *James Bond: The Legacy*, Boxtree, 2002

Crichton, Michael, 'Sean Connery: A Propensity for Stylish Mayhem', in Danny Peary (ed.), *Close-Ups: The Movie Star Book*, Simon & Schuster, 1978

— *Rising Sun*, Arrow, 1992

Cunningham, Frank R., *Sidney Lumet*, University Press of Kentucky, 2001

Curran, James and Vincent Porter (eds), *British Cinema History*, Weidenfeld & Nicolson, 1983

Devine, T. M., *The Scottish Nation 1700–2007*, Penguin, 2006

Durgnat, Raymond, *A Mirror For England*, Faber and Faber, 1970

— *The Strange Case of Alfred Hitchcock*, Faber and Faber, 1974

Dyer, Richard, *Stars* (new edition), BFI, 1998

Eco, Umberto, *The Name of the Rose*, Picador, 1986

Fallaci, Oriana, *Limelighters* (trans. Pamela Swinglehurst), Michael Joseph, 1967

Finlay, Richard J., *Modern Scotland 1914–2000*, Profile, 2004

Fleming, Ian, *Casino Royale*, Jonathan Cape, 1953

— *Live and Let Die*, Jonathan Cape, 1954

— *Moonraker*, Jonathan Cape, 1955

— *Diamonds Are Forever*, Jonathan Cape, 1956

— *From Russia with Love*, Jonathan Cape, 1957

— *Dr No*, Jonathan Cape, 1958

— *Goldfinger*, Jonathan Cape, 1959

— *For Your Eyes Only*, Jonathan Cape, 1960

— *Thunderball*, Jonathan Cape, 1961

— *The Spy Who Loved Me*, Jonathan Cape, 1962

— *On Her Majesty's Secret Service*, Jonathan Cape, 1963

— *You Only Live Twice*, Jonathan Cape, 1964

— *The Man with the Golden Gun*, Jonathan Cape, 1965

— *Octopussy*, Jonathan Cape, 1966

Bibliography

Frayling, Christopher, *Ken Adam: The Art of Production Design*, Faber and Faber, 2005

Freedland, Michael, *Sean Connery: A Biography*, Weidenfeld & Nicolson, 1994

Gant, Richard, *Sean Connery: Gilt-Edged Bond*, Mayflower, 1967

Garnett, Mark and Richard Weight, *The A–Z Guide to Modern British History*, Jonathan Cape, 2003

Gillett, Philip, *The British Working Class in Postwar Film*, Manchester University Press, 2003

Green, Jonathon, *All Dressed Up: The Sixties and the Counterculture*, Jonathan Cape, 1998

Grobel, Lawrence, *The Hustons*, Bloomsbury, 1990

Gundle, Stephen, *Glamour: A History*, Oxford University Press, 2008

Hoberman, J., *The Dream Life: Movies, Media, and the Mythology of the Sixties*, The New Press, 2003

Honey, John, *Does Accent Matter?: The Pygmalion Factor*, Faber and Faber, 1989

Hunter, John, *Great Scot*, Bloomsbury, 1993

James, Clive, *Flying Visits*, Jonathan Cape, 1984

— *Cultural Amnesia*, Picador, 2007

Kael, Pauline, *I Lost It at the Movies*, Little, Brown, 1965

— *Kiss Kiss Bang Bang*, Calder & Boyars, 1970

— *Deeper into Movies*, Calder & Boyars, 1975

— *Reeling*, Marion Boyars, 1977

— *When the Lights Go Down*, Holt Rinehart Winston, 1980

— *Taking It All In*, Marion Boyars, 1986

— *State of the Art*, Arena, 1987

— *Hooked*, Marion Boyars, 1990

— *Movie Love*, Plume, 1991

Kurlansky, Mark, *1968: The Year that Rocked the World*, Jonathan Cape, 2004

Lane, Anthony, *Nobody's Perfect*, Knopf, 2002

Lane, Sheldon (ed.), *For Bond Lovers Only*, Dell, 1965

Le Carré, John, *The Russia House*, Hodder & Stoughton, 1989

Lee Moral, Tony, *Hitchcock and the Making of Marnie*, Scarecrow Press, 2005

Levin, Bernard, *The Pendulum Years: Britain and the Sixties*, Jonathan Cape, 1970

Lewin, David, 'Sean Connery', in Peter Tipthorp (ed.), *James Bond in Thunderball*, Sackville, 1965

Long, Robert Emmet (ed.), *John Huston Interviews*, University of Mississippi Press, 2001

Lycett, Andrew, *Ian Fleming*, Weidenfeld & Nicolson, 1995

McCabe, Bob, *Sean Connery*, Pavilion, 2001

MacDonald, Ian, *Revolution in the Head: The Beatles Records and the Sixties* (revised edition), Fourth Estate, 1997

McFarlane, Brian, *An Autobiography of British Cinema*, Methuen, 1997

— *The Encyclopedia of British Film*, Methuen, 2003

McGilligan, Patrick, *Hitchcock: A Life in Darkness and Light*, Wiley, 2003

McIlvanney, William, *Laidlaw*, Sceptre, 1992

McInerney, Jay et al., *Dressed to Kill: James Bond – The Suited Hero*, Flammarion, 1996

McKay, Sinclair, *The Man with the Golden Touch: How the Bond Films Conquered the World*, Aurum, 2008

Marwick, Arthur, *Class: Image and Reality in Britain, France and the USA since 1930*, Collins, 1980

— *The Sixties*, Oxford University Press, 1998

Masters, Brian, *The Swinging Sixties*, Constable, 1985

Melly, George, *Revolt Into Style: The Pop Arts in the 50s and 60s* (revised edition), Oxford University Press, 1989

Morden, Ethan, *Rodgers and Hammerstein*, Abrams, 1992

Morgan, Kenneth O., *Britain since 1945: The People's Peace* (third edition), Oxford University Press, 2001

Muir, Edwin, *Scottish Journey*, Mainstream, 1979 (originally published in 1935)

Müller, Jürgen (ed.), *Movies of the 60s*, Taschen, 2004

Murphy, Robert, *Sixties British Cinema*, British Film Institute, 1992

O'Brien, Geoffrey, *The Phantom Empire*, Norton, 1993

Osborne, John, *Almost a Gentleman: An Autobiography: 1955–1966*, Faber and Faber, 1991

Parker, John, *Arise Sir Sean Connery*, John Blake, 2005

Passingham, Kenneth, *Sean Connery*, Sidgwick & Jackson, 1983

Patrick, Vincent, *Family Business*, Futura, 1989

Pfeiffer, Lee and Philip Lisa, *The Films of Sean Connery* (third edition), Citadel Press, 2001

Rafferty, Terrence, *The Thing Happens*, Grove Press, 1993

Richardson, Tony, *Long Distance Runner: A Memoir*, Faber and Faber, 1993

Rigby, Ray, *The Hill*, Mayflower, 1965

Rissik, Andrew, *The James Bond Man: The Films of Sean Connery*, Elm Tree, 1983

Rollyson, Carl, *To Be a Woman: The Life of Jill Craigie*, Aurum, 2005

Roud, Richard (ed.), *Cinema: A Critical Dictionary*, Secker & Warburg, 1980

Rycroft, Charles, *Reich*, Fontana, 1971

Bibliography

Sanders, Lawrence, *The Anderson Tapes*, Dell, 1974

Sarris, Andrew, *The American Cinema: Directors and Directions 1929–1968*, E. P. Dutton, 1968

Schickel, Richard, *Clint Eastwood*, Jonathan Cape, 1996

Sellers, Robert, *Sean Connery: A Celebration*, Robert Hale, 1999

— *The Battle for Bond*, Tomahawk Press, 2007

Shipman, David, *The Great Movie Stars: The International Years*, Angus & Robertson, 1980

Slater, Robert, *Ovitz: The Inside Story of Hollywood's Most Controversial Power-Broker*, McGraw-Hill, 1997

Spicer, Andrew, 'Sean Connery: Loosening His Bonds', in Bruce Babington (ed.), *British Stars and Stardom: From Alma Taylor to Sean Connery*, Manchester University Press, 2001

Spinetti, Victor, *Up Front*, Robson, 2006

Stamp, Terence, *Coming Attraction*, Bloomsbury, 1988

— *Double Feature*, Bloomsbury, 1989

Stead, Peter, *Film and the Working Class*, Routledge, 1989

Tanitch, Robert, *Sean Connery*, Chapmans, 1992

Thomson, David, *The New Biographical Dictionary of Film*, Little, Brown, 2002

— *Nicole Kidman*, Bloomsbury, 2006

— *Have You Seen . . . ?* Allen Lane, 2008

Truffaut, François, *Hitchcock*, Secker & Warburg, 1968

Turner, Lana, *Lana – the Lady, the Legend, the Truth*, New English Library, 1983

Walker, Alexander, *Hollywood UK: The British Film Industry in the Sixties*, Stein and Day, 1974

— *National Heroes: British Cinema in the Seventies and Eighties*, Harrap, 1985

Wilson, Edmund, *Literary Essays of the 1930s and 40s*, Library of America, 2007

Winder, Simon, *The Man Who Saved Britain: A Personal Journey into the Disturbing World of James Bond*, Picador, 2006

Winner, Michael, *Winner Takes All: A Life of Sorts*, Robson, 2004

Winters, Shelley, *The Middle of My Century*, Muller, 1990

Wollen, Peter, *Signs and Meaning in the Cinema*, Secker & Warburg / British Film Institute, 1969

Wood, Robin, *Hitchcock's Films Revisited* (revised edition), Columbia University Press, 2002

Yule, Andrew, *Sean Connery: Neither Shaken Nor Stirred*, Little, Brown, 1993

Bibliography

Newspapers and magazines

American Film

Chicago Sun Times

Daily Echo

Daily Express

Daily Mail

Daily Mirror

Daily Sketch

Daily Telegraph

Daily Worker

Edinburgh Evening News

Empire

Entertainment Weekly

Evening News

Evening Standard

Film Comment

Films and Filming

Films Illustrated

Financial Times

Glasgow Herald

Guardian

Illustrated London News

Independent

Independent on Sunday

Ladies' Home Journal

Mail on Sunday

Midweek

Motion Picture

New York

New York Daily News

New York Times

New Yorker

News Chronicle

Night and Day

Observer

People Magazine

Photoplay

Playboy

Premiere

Radio Times

Reveille

Rolling Stone

Saturday Evening Post

Scotsman

Scottish Daily Mail

Screen

Sight and Sound

The Stage

Sun

Sunday Express

Sunday Mail

Sunday Mirror

Sunday Telegraph

Sunday Times

Time

Time Out

The Times

Times Educational Supplement

Total Film

TV Times

Vanity Fair

Wall Street Journal

Filmography

Murder on the Orient Express

1975   *Ransom*

The Wind and the Lion

The Man Who Would Be King

1976   *Robin and Marian*

The Next Man

1977   *A Bridge Too Far*

1978   *The First Great Train Robbery*

1979   *Meteor*

Cuba

1981   *Outland*

Time Bandits

1982   *Five Days One Summer*

Wrong Is Right

1983   *Never Say Never Again*

1984   *Sword of the Valiant*

1986   *Highlander*

The Name of the Rose

1987   *The Untouchables*

1988   *The Presidio*

1989   *Indiana Jones and the Last Crusade*

Family Business

1990   *The Hunt for Red October*

The Russia House

1991   *Highlander II: The Quickening*

Robin Hood: Prince of Thieves

1992   *Medicine Man*

1993   *Rising Sun*

1994   *A Good Man in Africa*

1995   *Just Cause*

First Knight

1996   *Dragonheart*

The Rock

1998   *The Avengers*

Playing by Heart

1999   *Entrapment*

2000   *Finding Forrester*

2003   *The League of Extraordinary Gentlemen*

Index

333

Index

337

Index